World Intellectual Property Report 2017

Intangible Capital in Global Value Chains

WIPO
WORLD
INTELLECTUAL PROPERTY
ORGANIZATION

© WIPO, 2017

World Intellectual Property Organization
34, chemin des Colombettes, P.O. Box 18
CH-1211 Geneva 20, Switzerland

ISBN: 978-92-805-2895-4

Attribution 3.0 IGO license
(CC BY 3.0 IGO)

Photo credits:
monsitj/Getty Images/iStockphoto
alexsl/Getty Images

Printed in Switzerland

Table of contents

Foreword

Technological innovations and openness of trade have profoundly changed the face of global production. Converting raw materials into parts and components, assembling final products and delivering them to the end consumer involves supply chains that span an increasing number of economies across the globe.

The emergence of these so-called global value chains has been a force for good: they have made a large range of consumer products more affordable, stimulated economic growth and promoted the integration of developing countries into the global economy – creating opportunities for economic development and the alleviation of poverty.

Intangible capital – notably in the form of technology, design and branding – permeates global value chains in important ways. It accounts for a good part of what consumers pay for in a product and determines which companies are successful in the marketplace. It also lies at the heart of the organization of global value chains: decisions on where to locate different production tasks and with whom to partner are closely tied to how companies manage their intangible capital.

A large number of research reports have been published on the causes and consequences of the rise of global value chains, and many of these reports have acknowledged the key role played by intangible capital. However, few insights are available on why, how and how much. With our *World Intellectual Property Report 2017*, we hope to help unpack the intangibles black box, in particular by shedding light on how intellectual property (IP) fits into this box.

The report begins by reviewing how global value chains have come about and how they are organized. Against this background, it reveals new estimates of the macro-economic contribution of intangible capital to global value chain production. These estimates show that intangibles account for around one-third of production value – or some 5.9 trillion United States dollars in 2014 – across 19 manufacturing industries.

Following the approach of our 2015 report, we complement these economy-wide perspectives with case studies of specific global value chains – namely, coffee, photovoltaics and smartphones. These three cases highlight the different mix of intangibles embedded in different consumer products and provide concrete insight into the role that different forms of IP play in generating returns to investments in innovation and branding.

In addition, they explore how developing economies – notably China – have succeeded in participating in global value chains by building their own intangibles, and what opportunities may exist to pursue similar strategies in the future.

The evolution of global value chains has been disruptive, with some companies thriving and others failing. It has accelerated the structural transformation of economies, with some workers losing their jobs and others seeing their skills richly rewarded. Technology continues to transform global patterns of production and is bound to lead to further disruption. For example, advances in 3D printing, robotics and automated manufacturing may well lead companies to relocate certain production tasks closer to the end consumer. In addition, the fast growth of emerging economies is set to prompt shifts in the geography of global value chains.

Policymakers need to respond to the disruptive forces unleashed by globalized production. Global value chains are a human creation and could be reversed, but this would risk even bigger disruption. Shaping them in such a way that they benefit societies as a whole is thus an important policy imperative.

As always, a report of this nature leaves important questions open. Most importantly, while we present – for the first time – concrete estimates of how much income accrues to intangibles in global value chain production, it remains to be established who ultimately gains this income. At the level of countries, cross-border ownership and sharing of intangible assets make it difficult to associate assets and earnings with a particular country location. At the level of individual earnings, little systematic evidence exists on how intangibles affect the compensation of workers at different skills levels. Future research that offers empirical guidance on these questions would be of great value.

We hope that this report will inform discussions on the evolving nature of global value chains taking place in different policy forums, and look forward to exploring the contribution of the IP system to global value chain production in our ongoing dialogue with Member States.

Francis GURRY
Director General

Acknowledgements

This report was developed under the general direction of Francis Gurry (Director General). It was prepared and coordinated by a team led by Carsten Fink (Chief Economist) and comprising Intan Hamdan-Livramento (Economist), Julio Raffo (Senior Economist) and Sacha Wunsch-Vincent (Senior Economist), all from WIPO's Economics and Statistics Division (ESD). Lorena Rivera León (Consultant) and Giulia Valacchi (Fellow) provided helpful research assistance.

The four report chapters draw on background research commissioned for this report. In particular, the estimates of the returns to intangible assets in global value chains presented in chapter 1 were prepared by Wen Chen, Reitze Gouma, Bart Los and Marcel P. Timmer (University of Groningen). Carol Corrado (The Conference Board) contributed written comments on their research. Additional substantive inputs on the measurement of intangible asset flows were provided by Tony Clayton (Imperial College London), Tom Neubig (Tax Sage Network) and Dylan Rassier (U.S. Bureau of Economic Analysis).

Luis F. Samper (4.0 Brands) and Daniele Giovannucci (Committee on Sustainability Assessment) contributed the background report for the case study on coffee in chapter 2. Written comments on this report were prepared by Luciana Marques Vieira (Universidade do Vale do Rio dos Sinos). Leontino Rezende Taveira (International Union for the Protection of New Varieties of Plants) offered valuable advice throughout the development of this case study. Premium Quality Consulting provided the coffee market data used in the chapter.

The case study on photovoltaics in chapter 3 relies on background research conducted by Maria Carvalho (London School of Economics), Antoine Dechezleprêtre (London School of Economics) and Matthieu Glachant (MINES ParisTech). Data were provided by ENF Solar.

Finally, the smartphone case study in chapter 4 draws on a background report prepared by Jason Dedrick (Syracuse University) and Ken Kraemer (University of California, Irvine). Robin Stitzing (Nokia) offered written comments on the report. Christian Helmers (Santa Clara University) provided research input for the trademark and industrial design mappings. Data were received from the Chief Economist Service of the European Union Intellectual Property Office, Clarivate Analytics, Deutsche Patent- und Markenamt (DPMA), IHS Markit, IPlytics and the U.K. Intellectual Property Office.

The report team benefited greatly from external reviews of the draft chapters by Patrick Low. Additional input, comments and data were provided by Janice Anderson, Mohsen Bonakdarpour, Roger Burt, Seong Joon Chen, Robert Cline, Alica Daly, Jenn Figueroa, Marina Foschi, Tim Frain, Kirti Gupta, Christopher Harrison, Vasheharan Kanesarajah, Michał Kazimiercza, Richard Lambert, Cecilia Jona-Lasinio, Moshe Leimberg, Robert Lemperle, Lutz Mailänder, Keith Maskus, Raymond Mataloni Jr., Yann Ménière, Sébastien Miroudot, David Muls, Amanda Myers, Giovanni Napolitano, Tim Pohlmann, Marie Paule Rizo, Pekka Sääskilahti, Thomas Verbeet, Nathan Wajsman, Pamela Wille, Irene Wong and Brian York.

Samiah Do Carmo Figueiredo and Caterina Valles Galmès provided valuable administrative support.

Finally, gratitude is due to editorial and design colleagues in the Communications Division for leading the production of the report, especially to Toby Boyd for his editing work. The WIPO Library provided helpful research support throughout the report's development and the Printing Plant provided high-quality printing services. All worked hard to meet tight deadlines.

Disclaimer

This report and any opinions reflected therein are the sole responsibility of the WIPO Secretariat. They do not purport to reflect the opinions or views of WIPO Member States. The main authors of this report also wish to exonerate everyone who has contributed to or commented on the report from responsibility for any errors or omissions.

Executive summary

A consumer buys a new smartphone. What exactly is she paying for?

The phone consists of many parts and components manufactured all over the world, and the price needs to cover the cost of those. She is also paying for the labor of the people who made the components and assembled the final product, and for services such as transportation and the retailing of the product in a physical store or online. And, very importantly, she is paying for intangible capital – the technology that runs the smartphone, its design and its brand name.

Today, production is global. Companies perform different production stages in different locations around the world. At each stage of the supply chain or global value chain for each product, value is generated by workers, by production machinery and, increasingly, by intangible capital – things one cannot touch, but which are crucial to the look, feel, functionality and general appeal of a product. Intangible capital is crucial in determining success in the marketplace – which companies succeed and which fail.

Is it possible to quantify the importance of intangible capital? What types of intangibles are most valuable at different production stages and for different consumer products? How do companies manage their intangible assets in global value chains, and what role does intellectual property (IP) play in generating a return on these assets?

Although there have been numerous studies on the rise of global value chains, little evidence is available to answer these questions. This report endeavors to help fill that gap. It does so at the macroeconomic level, by presenting original estimates of the income accruing to intangible assets in 19 global manufacturing value chains, and it also explores the role of intangibles in greater detail through case studies of specific value chains for smartphones, coffee and solar cells.

Insight into the role of intangible assets in global value chains matters from a policy perspective. Investments in intangible capital are a key source of economic growth, and better understanding how those assets are generated and exploited in a globalized marketplace may help policymakers refine the enabling environment for such investments.

Similarly, acquiring intangible assets is a key imperative for policymakers in developing economies seeking to support local firms that strive to upgrade their production capabilities in global value chains.

The rise of global value chains

Production processes have been unbundled and spread around the world...

The growth of global value chains is a key distinguishing feature of the so-called second wave of globalization that set in some time in the second half of the 20th century. The invention of the steam engine in the 18th century unleashed the first globalization wave, which peaked early in the 20th century. International commerce during the first wave mostly consisted of trade in commodities and fully assembled manufactured goods. What stands out about international commerce in the second globalization wave is the unbundling of the production process and the spreading of different production stages across different locations around the world. As a result, trade patterns have shifted toward multidirectional trade in intermediate goods within particular industries.

Several forces supported this shift in the organization of global production:

- Falling costs of international trade made it cost-effective to disperse production across a number of locations. Cheaper and faster transportation had already propelled international trade during the first globalization phase. The advent of air transport, the spread of containerization and other innovations lowered transport costs even further.

- Progressively more liberal trade policies after the Second World War – following the proliferation of protectionist policies in the interwar period – also helped to lower the costs of shipping goods from one country to another.

- Modern information and communication technologies (ICTs) were critical in enabling dispersed production. In particular, rapidly falling communication costs and ever more powerful computing technology allowed companies to coordinate complex production processes involving many locations around the world.

... unleashing rapid growth in world trade, outpacing global output growth

As a result, international commerce boomed. As parts and components cross borders several times before the resulting products are finally assembled – and often exported again – growth in world trade has outpaced global output. The ratio of trade to gross domestic product (GDP) has more than doubled over the last half-century (figure 1).

Figure 1

Growth in world trade outpaces growth in world output

Trade as a percentage share of GDP

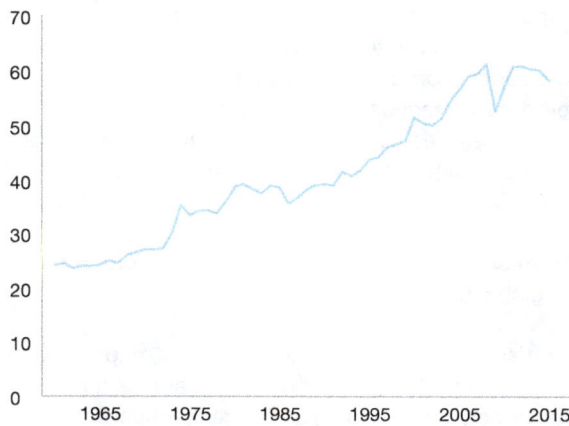

See figure 1.2.

Intangible capital has become more important in global value chain production

Global value chain production in the 21st century is popularly characterized by the so-called smile curve – first proposed in the early 1990s by the chief executive officer of the company Acer, Inc. As illustrated in figure 2, the smile curve recognizes the increased importance of pre- and post-manufacturing stages and posits that those stages account for ever-higher shares of overall production value. The growing smile shown in figure 2 reflects that intangible capital – in the form of technology, design and brand value as well as workers' skills and managerial know-how – has become critically important in dynamically competitive markets. Firms continuously invest in intangible capital to stay ahead of their rivals.

As economies have grown richer, consumers' preferences have shifted toward goods that respond to differentiated tastes and offer a broader "brand experience."

Figure 2

Production in the 21st century – a growing smile

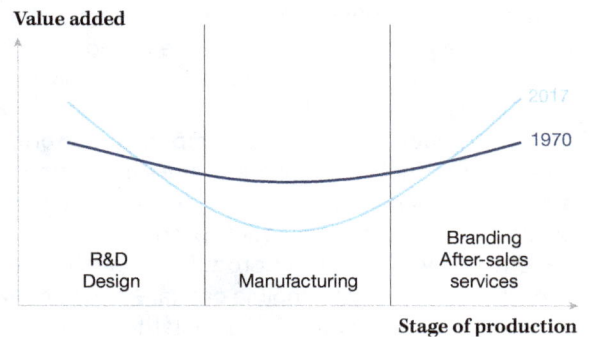

See figure 1.4.

What return accrues to intangible assets?

While appealing and intuitive, the concept of the smile curve has its limitations. It may reasonably portray the distribution of value added for firms performing all production stages. But it is more difficult to apply at the economy-wide level, where firms' value chains intersect and overlap. In addition, it does not provide any insight into what precisely generates value added at different production stages. For example, "higher value added" does not necessarily coincide with underlying activities being more profitable, associated with better paying jobs, or generally "more desirable."

One can gain a better understanding of what generates value in global value chains by quantifying how much income accrues to labor, tangible capital and intangible capital used in global value chain production. In research for this report, economists Wen Chen, Reitze Gouma, Bart Los and Marcel Timmer performed precisely such an analysis (see chapter 1). Their approach consisted of two steps. First, they assembled macroeconomic data on shares of value added in 19 manufacturing product groups spanning 43 economies plus one rest-of-the-world region which together captured around one-quarter of global output. Then they decomposed value added at each stage into the incomes accruing to labor, tangible capital and intangible capital – as illustrated in figure 3.

Figure 3

Decomposing global value chains

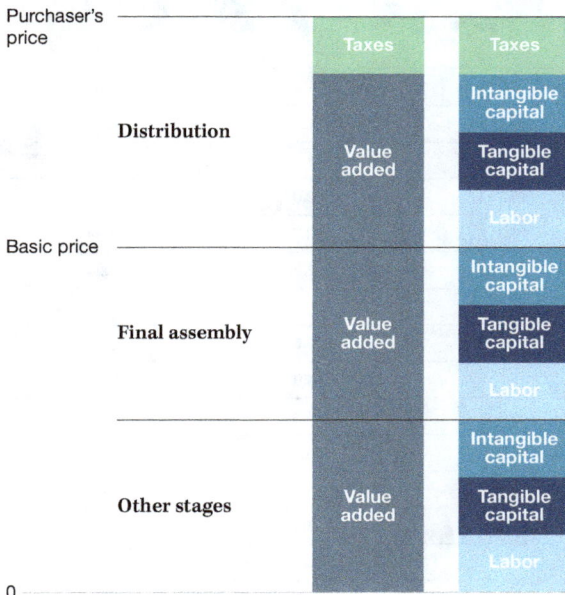

See figure 1.6.

Intangible capital accounts for around one-third of production value...

Figure 4 presents the resulting income shares accruing to the three production factors for all products manufactured and sold worldwide from 2000 to 2014. The intangibles share averaged 30.4 percent throughout this period, almost double the share for tangibles. Interestingly, it rose from 27.8 percent in 2000 to 31.9 percent in 2007, but has stagnated since then. Overall income from intangibles in the 19 manufacturing industries increased by 75 percent from 2000 to 2014 in real terms. It amounted to 5.9 trillion United States dollars (USD) in 2014.

... with food products, motor vehicles and textiles accounting for around one-half of income to intangibles

Which product global value chains use intangibles most intensively? Table 1 presents the factor income shares in 2014 for the 19 manufacturing product groups in descending order of their global output size. For all product groups, intangible capital accounts for a higher share of value added than tangible capital.

The intangibles share is especially high – and more than double the tangibles share – for pharmaceutical, chemical and petroleum products. It is also relatively high for food products as well as computer, electronic and optical products. In terms of absolute returns, the three largest product groups – food products, motor vehicles and textiles – account for close to 50 percent of the total income generated by intangible capital in the 19 manufacturing global value chains.

Figure 4

Intangible capital captures more value than tangible capital

Value added as a percentage of the total value of all products manufactured and sold worldwide

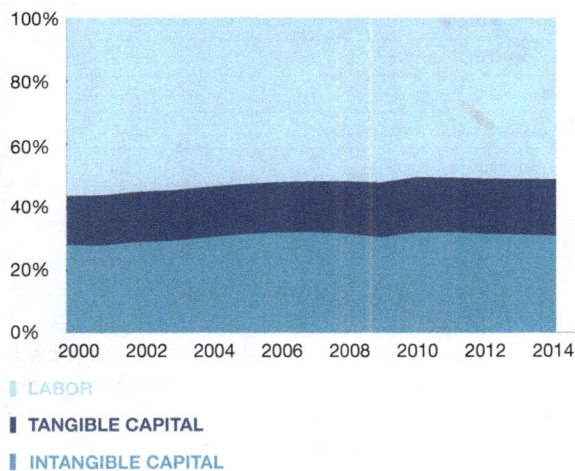

LABOR
TANGIBLE CAPITAL
INTANGIBLE CAPITAL

See figure 1.7.

These and other figures presented in this report offer for the first time an estimate of the return to intangible asset investments in global value chain production, which has so far largely escaped measurement. Nonetheless, they also leave a number of questions open and come with methodological caveats. For example, which economies harvest the returns from intangible capital? The question is obvious, but the answer is elusive. For one thing, through transfer pricing and related practices, companies can easily shift profits from one location to another. Thus, an intangible asset may originate in one economy, but most of its returns may show up in another. More fundamentally, increasing cross-border ownership and sharing of intangibles is undermining the very notion of location-bound assets and earnings.

Table 1

Income shares by manufacturing product group, 2014

Product group name	Intangible income share (%)	Tangible income share (%)	Labor share (%)	Global output (USD bn)
Food, beverages, and tobacco products	31.0	16.4	52.6	4,926
Motor vehicles and trailers	29.7	19.0	51.3	2,559
Textiles, apparel and leather products	29.9	17.7	52.4	1,974
Other machinery and equipment	27.2	18.8	53.9	1,834
Computer, electronic and optical products	31.3	18.6	50.0	1,452
Furniture and other manufacturing	30.1	16.3	53.7	1,094
Petroleum products	42.1	20.0	37.9	1,024
Other transport equipment	26.3	18.5	55.2	852
Electrical equipment	29.5	20.0	50.6	838
Chemical products	37.5	17.5	44.9	745
Pharmaceutical products	34.7	16.5	48.8	520
Fabricated metal products	24.0	20.8	55.2	435
Rubber and plastics products	29.2	19.7	51.1	244
Basic metals	31.4	25.6	43.0	179
Repair and installation of machinery	23.6	13.2	63.2	150
Paper products	28.0	20.9	51.1	140
Other non-metallic mineral products	29.7	21.5	48.9	136
Wood products	27.5	20.0	52.5	90
Printing products	27.1	21.2	51.7	64

Source: Chen et al. (2017).

The precise nature of intangible capital and how it affects the business models of global value chain participants differs widely across industries. The case studies on coffee, photovoltaics and smartphones in this report offer more concrete perspectives on the nature of intangible capital and prevailing business strategies.

The case of coffee

Coffee is one of the most important traded agricultural commodities. It is the source of income for nearly 26 million farmers in over 50 developing economies, but 70 percent of coffee demand comes from high-income countries. Most of the value added of coffee sold also accrues to high-income countries. This partly reflects the short shelf life of roasted coffee, which implies that most of the roasting is done close to where the coffee is consumed. More importantly, it reflects the economic importance of downstream activities in the global value chain.

Intangible capital in the coffee supply chain mainly consists of downstream technological innovations and branding

The case study on coffee highlights two key forms of intangible capital in the global value chain (see chapter 2):

- Technology associated with coffee farming and with turning coffee into a high-quality and appealing consumer product. Patent data suggest that the most innovative value chain stages are those closer to the consumer, including the processing of beans and especially the final distribution of coffee products (figure 5). The latter stage includes the modern espresso machines and coffee capsules found in many homes and offices.

- Brand reputation and image, which allow consumer product firms to differentiate their offering from those of their rivals. Branding plays an important role in all coffee market segments, including soluble and roasted coffee sold in grocery stores, espresso-based coffee products and retail coffeehouses.

Figure 5

Most coffee-related innovation occurs in activities close to the consumer

Share of firms and patent applications related to coffee at each stage of the value chain

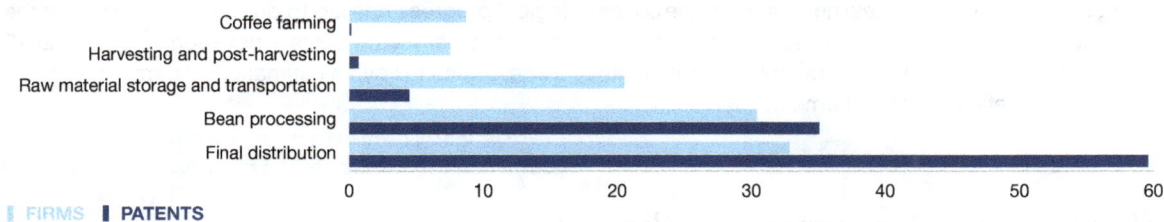

FIRMS **PATENTS**

See figure 2.5.

In addition to technology and branding assets, the lead firms in the global coffee value chain benefit from long-term relationships with distributors downstream. As a result, the global coffee value chain is largely buyer-driven and dominated by a relatively small number of multinational companies headquartered in the large coffee-consuming countries.

Different waves of coffee consumption...

Shifting consumer preferences have prompted three waves of coffee consumption that have progressively transformed the global value chain:

- The first wave centered on consumers who largely consume their coffee at home. The products – in the form of packaged roasted coffee beans, soluble coffee and, more recently, single-serving capsules – are standardized, with price differences reflecting variation in the quality of coffee blends.

- The second wave emerged with consumers who prefer to consume coffee in a social setting. Products in this market segment range from the typical Italian espresso to more elaborate concoctions of coffee plus foamed milk. In addition to coffee itself, most of the coffee shops in this market segment offer a distinct ambiance to attract their consumers. The quality of the coffee beans used in the second wave tends to be higher than those in the first wave. In addition, the second wave introduced voluntary sustainability standards (VSSs), informing consumers of the coffee's origin and whether farmers receive fair wages.

- The third wave market segment targets consumers with discerning coffee tastes, willing to pay premium prices for their coffee. They

are interested in knowing where their coffee beans are sourced, how they have been farmed and how best to brew the beans in order to fully appreciate the flavor, body, aroma, fragrance and mouthfeel of the coffee. The coffee beans tend to be of superior quality to those used in the other two market segments.

... are reshaping the global coffee value chain...

The first wave still accounts for 65 to 80 percent of the total quantity of coffee consumed, but only 45 percent of the global market value. This reflects higher unit prices commanded in the second and third waves (see figure 6). The second and – more recently – third waves are reshaping the governance of the global coffee value chain. In particular, sourcing of coffee in the first wave has traditionally been market-based, with buyers blending different types of coffee from different parts of the world. The introduction of VSSs in the second wave established more direct ties between coffee growers and downstream value chain participants. These ties are of even greater importance in the third wave and have, in fact, shortened the value chain by cutting out intermediaries in the coffee trade.

... with the third wave opening opportunities for upgraded participation by coffee farmers

The shift in consumer preferences associated with the second and especially the third wave has opened up opportunities for upgraded participation by coffee farmers in exporting countries. The emphasis in this market segment is akin to the wine industry's flavor profile, which valorizes the *terroir*, grape variety and craftsmanship involved in producing the wine.

Information on the origin and variety of the coffee beans, how they were farmed and processed, and if the farmers are adequately compensated has become an integral part of selling coffee. For coffee farmers, direct communication with buyers can sometimes lead to the sharing of technology and know-how, helping to upgrade the coffee farm and its processing. Figure 6 shows how the higher prices commanded in the third wave are associated with better remuneration of coffee farmers.

Figure 6

Third-wave coffee commands the highest price, and farmers gain better remuneration

Distribution of income by market segments (USD/lb)

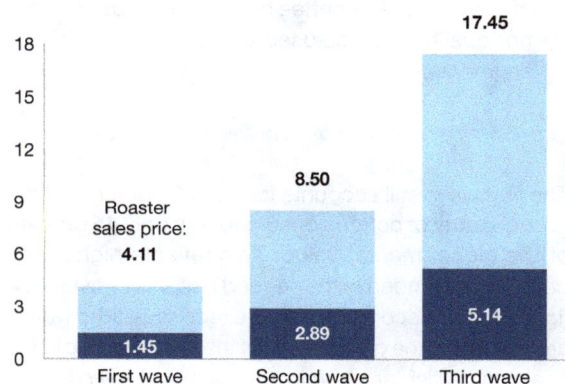

See figure 2.3.

Responding to coffee demand in the third wave, more and more coffee growers are investing in efforts to differentiate their offering from generic coffee, adopting their own branding strategies. In addition, some coffee-producing countries are actively pursuing the branding of coffees originating from their countries in overseas markets, while associations of coffee growers and other entities have been seeking IP rights to protect their brand assets in key consumer markets – such as the Juan Valdez brand from Colombia and the Jamaican Blue Mountain Coffee label.

The case of photovoltaics

Thanks in part to supportive public policies, demand for photovoltaic (PV) systems has grown exponentially since the early 2000s. At the same time, rapid technological progress has led to dramatic reductions in the price of solar PV modules – between 2008 and 2015 alone, prices fell by an estimated 80 percent.

Cost-reducing innovations have shaped competitive dynamics in the PV value chain

The case study on the PV value chain describes how crystalline PV systems emerged as the dominant PV technology (see chapter 3). Their production entails five main stages: purification of silicon, the manufacturing of ingots and wafers, production of PV cells, assembly of modules and their integration into PV systems. The intangible assets of value chain participants largely consist of advanced technology, especially in the more upstream stages. This technology often requires specific know-how which companies keep secret, though patenting has grown rapidly, especially since 2005 (figure 7).

Companies in the United States, Germany, Japan and Australia traditionally accounted for the bulk of product innovation in the industry. However, over time PV panels and systems have essentially turned into commodities – the key competitive factor is how much electricity they can produce per dollar invested. As a result, the dynamics of the industry have been profoundly driven by strategies to reduce production costs. Successful market participants were able to lower their cost structures by investing in more powerful production equipment, realizing efficiencies through complementary process innovations and achieving large-scale production.

Innovation remains geographically concentrated

Innovation in PV technology remains geographically concentrated. The vast majority of PV patents are filed in China, Germany, Japan, the Republic of Korea and the United States, with Chinese innovators emerging as the largest source of patent filings from 2010 onward (figure 7). Interestingly, the distribution of patenting activity across origins varies markedly by PV-related technology, with Chinese entities, for example, focusing more on solar module technology and less on cell technology than other origins (figure 8).

Figure 7

A few country origins account for most PV patenting activity

First filings of PV-related patents by origin, 2000-2015

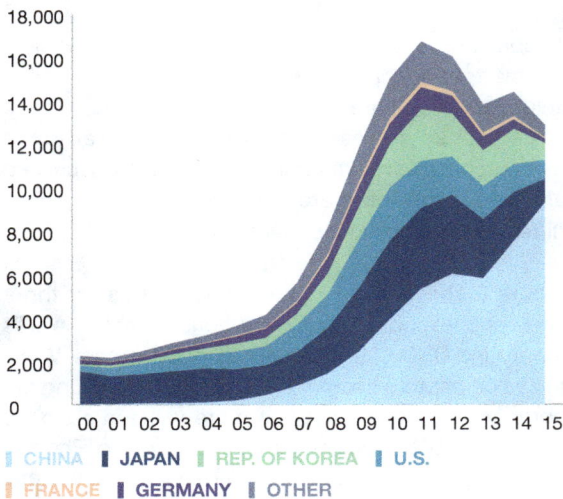

CHINA ▮ JAPAN ▮ REP. OF KOREA ▮ U.S.
FRANCE ▮ GERMANY ▮ OTHER

See figure 3.8.

Figure 8

The focus of patenting activity varies by country origin

Percentage distribution of first patent filings by origin and value chain segment, 2011-2015

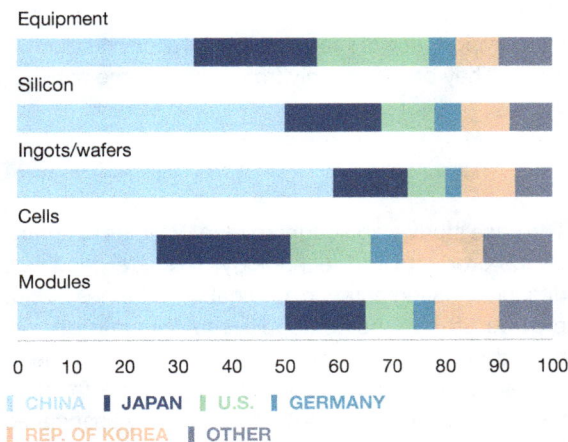

CHINA ▮ JAPAN ▮ U.S. ▮ GERMANY
REP. OF KOREA ▮ OTHER

See figure 3.10.

China has emerged as the dominant force in the PV global value chain...

Participation in the PV global value chain has shifted markedly over the last decade, in particular with the relocation of upstream and midstream production activities to China. PV products initially invented in high-income countries decades ago were no longer protected by patents, and Chinese firms successfully acquired the knowledge to manufacture PV components efficiently along the PV value chain. They did so through two main channels:

- Chinese companies acquired PV technologies by purchasing state-of-the-art production equipment from international suppliers.

- When entering the industry in the 2000s, Chinese PV companies benefited from the arrival of skilled engineers and executives from abroad, bringing technological knowledge, capital and professional networks to China.

... realigning the global PV innovation landscape

The shift in global value chain production – combined with the steep fall in prices – put many traditional PV manufacturers in the United States, Europe and elsewhere under competitive pressure, resulting in bankruptcies and acquisitions. This partly explains the decline in PV patent filings worldwide after 2011, which was driven by the traditional origins of PV innovation (see figure 7). China is the only major patenting origin to have seen continued patenting growth after 2011.

However, the picture is more nuanced. With a saturated solar PV market and low prices that result in tight profit margins, surviving firms have stepped up their investments in research and development (R&D) to develop new cost-competitive PV technology. A closer look at the patent data reveals that patent applications per applicant have continued to grow in the traditional origins since 2011, suggesting an increase in patenting among surviving firms. Indeed, among those firms patent filings have been growing faster than R&D outlays, suggesting that patent rights may well become more important in securing future returns to R&D.

15

A second response to market saturation and tight profit margins is for PV manufacturers to move downstream by getting involved in project development and building up reputational assets through branding activities. Such a strategy can help companies generate demand for their upstream products and increase profit margins, especially in local and less competitive service markets.

The case of smartphones

Relatively few lead firms dominate the smartphone value chain

Smartphone value chains are dominated by a relatively small number of lead firms that operate under strong brands and invest heavily in technology and product design. The case study looks at three such lead firms – Apple, Samsung and Huawei – and specific smartphone models they offer (see chapter 4). Key features of the smartphone value chain are the following:

- In addition to their own technology, lead firms source components and technology from third parties which can also be innovative. Certain components – such as phone chipsets and batteries – are highly complex and have their own global supply chains behind them.

- Lead firms require access to technology employed in interoperability and connectivity standards, such as the fourth-generation (4G) Long-Term Evolution (LTE) cellular standard. Companies such as Nokia, Ericsson, Qualcomm, InterDigital, Huawei, Samsung, NTT DoCoMo and ZTE contribute patented technologies to the development of such standards, which are defined by standard-setting organizations. Access to these technologies typically entails the payment of licensing fees.

- Smartphones require a mobile operating system and other dedicated mobile software applications, often from third parties. Samsung, Huawei and others use Android developed by Google, whereas Apple produces its own iOS system.

- In the case of Apple, assembly of the final product is performed by large original design or contract manufacturers. Samsung mostly internalizes the assembly in its own factories, while Huawei uses both internal and external assembly.

- Lead firms have their own stores as well as using third-party retailers to distribute their products to consumers, with Apple relying the most on its own stores.

Estimates of value capture show that lead firms generate substantial returns from their intangible capital – especially Apple...

To obtain insight into the return to intangibles in the case of smartphones, the case study estimates so-called value capture shares of the three lead firms. These value capture shares are conceptually similar to the macroeconomic returns to intangible capital discussed above, though there are important methodological differences reflecting the availability of underlying data.

Figure 9 shows the value capture shares for three smartphone models. For every iPhone 7 that Apple sells for around USD 809, it gets to keep 42 percent. While the value capture shares of Huawei and Samsung are comparable, Apple captures more value in absolute terms than its two competitors, reflecting the iPhone's premium price and its substantially higher sales volume. These figures underscore the high returns accruing to intangible capital in this industry, especially for Apple.

... though other firms benefit as well

It would be too simplistic to conclude, however, that only the lead firms generate returns to intangible capital. Certain component suppliers offering proprietary technology in the United States and Asia achieve significant margins, and so do technology providers such as Qualcomm, but contract manufacturers performing final assembly realize relatively low margins, reflecting the minor importance of intangible capital at this production stage. They benefit mainly from high-volume activity.

Smartphone value chain participants rely heavily on IP to generate a return on their intangible capital

The case study also sought to map IP filings to smartphone products and technology. This is exceedingly difficult. Existing patent classification schemes do not provide off-the-shelf categories for all smartphone-related inventions. Indeed, many inventions at the heart of a smartphone's functionality may not be found in the classification categories most directly associated with smartphones such as "portable communication terminals" and "telephone sets."

Figure 9

Smartphone lead firms take a large chunk of value

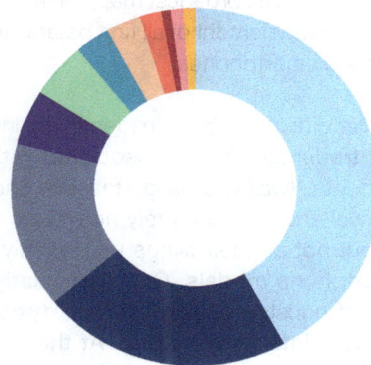

42%
Apple

22%
Cost of materials

15%
Distribution and retail

5%
IP licenses

5%
Unidentified material

3%
Other U.S.

3%
Taiwan (Province of China)

2%
Unidentified labor

1%
Labor (China)

1%
Rep. of Korea

1%
Japan

Apple iPhone 7

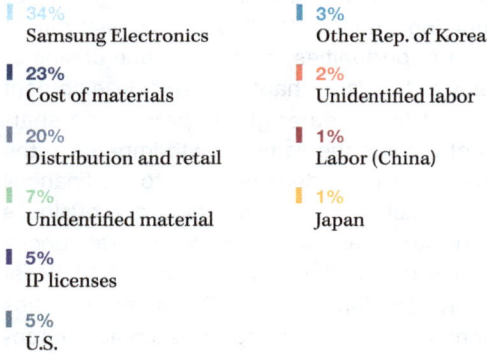

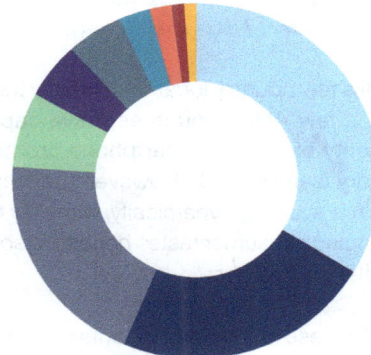

34%
Samsung Electronics

23%
Cost of materials

20%
Distribution and retail

7%
Unidentified material

5%
IP licenses

5%
U.S.

3%
Other Rep. of Korea

2%
Unidentified labor

1%
Labor (China)

1%
Japan

Samsung Galaxy S7

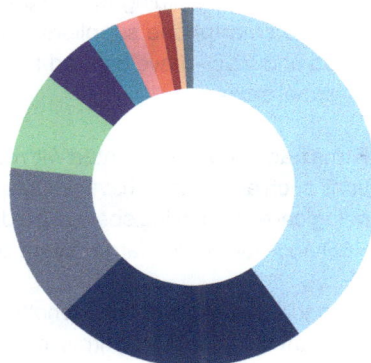

42%
Huawei

20%
Cost of materials

15%
Distribution and retail

9%
Unidentified material

5%
IP licenses

3%
Other China

2%
Rep. of Korea

2%
Unidentified labor

1%
Labor (China)

1%
Taiwan (Province of China)

1%
U.S.

Huawei P9

See figure 4.4.

In addition, many inventions may not be unique to smartphones or may not even have been thought of as being relevant to smartphones when the patents were filed, for example global positioning system (GPS) technology. The broadest mapping approach suggests that up to 35 percent of all first patent filings worldwide relate to smartphones.

Similar difficulties arise in identifying industrial design and trademark filings associated with smartphone products. Available filing statistics show that Apple, Huawei and Samsung rely heavily on these forms of IP, but not all their filings necessarily relate to their smartphone models. One particularly fast-growing area of industrial design filing activity concerns graphical user interfaces (GUIs). At the European Union Intellectual Property Office, Apple filed 222 industrial design applications on GUIs between 2009 and 2014, while Samsung filed 379.

Value capture is geographically concentrated, but is shifting over time

Only a few country locations, mostly the United States and a few Asian countries, have captured the vast majority of value in smartphone production in recent history (see figure 9). However, the smartphone value chain is evolving dynamically, with new technology and changing consumer tastes benefiting some players and challenging others:

- Chinese market participants have rapidly upgraded their technological capabilities. Huawei, for example, has evolved from a supplier of telecommunications equipment and low-end mobile phones to a lead supplier of high-end smartphones, investing heavily in R&D and building up a global brand. Other Chinese smartphone suppliers – such as Xiaomi, Oppo and Vivo – have entered the top 10 in terms of global sales.

- Firms traditionally associated with assembly operations such as Foxconn have created their own technological edge, having spent considerable sums on R&D and building up large patent portfolios.

- Even the assembly of smartphones is undergoing constant shifts, with lead firms at times struggling to meet high demand, leading to experiments with new manufacturers or assembly locations such as India in the case of Apple and Viet Nam for Samsung.

- Participation in patent pools for newer technological standards such as LTE see relatively strong participation by Internet firms such as Google and companies from China and the Republic of Korea, notably Huawei, ZTE and Samsung.

The future of global value chains

Global value chains have emerged as the 21st-century face of international commerce. They have tied together national economies as never before and have helped integrate numerous developing countries into the global economy. How will they evolve further, and what role is there for policy to ensure that they support economic growth and rising living standards around the world?

As shown in figure 1, the world's trade-to-GDP ratio has more than doubled over the past 50 years, but it has not seen any increase since the global financial crisis unfolded in 2008. Research suggests that the stagnating trade-to-GDP ratio may well reflect diminished opportunities for global value chains to spread any further (see chapter 1). This development may suggest that greater global production sharing will not provide the same growth impetus in the future that it did in the decades prior to the financial crisis. At the same time, technological and business innovations as well as shifting consumer preferences will continue to transform global production. Most prominently, developments in 3D printing, robotics and automated manufacturing have already reconfigured supply chains in a number of industries, and further progress in these areas may well unleash more profound change. These developments may lead to the "re-shoring" of certain production tasks, implying less trade. But the deployment of such technologies could still help spur economic growth.

Whatever their causes, shifts in global value chains disrupt prevailing patterns of production – and this should be the chief concern for policymakers. Production tasks offshored abroad may lead affected workers to lose their jobs or experience declining wages. Trade protection is not the answer to such disruption. Reversing open markets could be highly disruptive in and of itself. Instead, policymakers should aim to provide a social safety net that cushions the adverse effects of unemployment and to institute measures to facilitate the retraining of affected workers.

Indeed, policies aimed at addressing disruption arising from global value chain shifts are, in principle, no different from policies that seek to address disruption naturally arising in any economy that undergoes structural transformation as part of the economic growth process.

For policymakers in low- and middle-income economies, a key question is how they can support the upgrading of global value chain production capabilities by local firms. Experience from successful upgrading in East Asia suggests that establishing a mix of policies conducive for investments in intangible assets – including through balanced IP policies – should be a key priority. In addition, governments can play a constructive role in identifying pre-existing industrial capabilities – often at the level of sub-regions – and leveraging them by removing constraints on entrepreneurial activity. In doing so, it is important to adopt a global value chain perspective as the opportunities and challenges of local entrepreneurs evolve with global market trends.

Successful global value chain upgrading in all likelihood does not entail a zero-sum game among national economies. While it may lead to the displacement of some global value chain participants, it is an inherently dynamic phenomenon. Technological change and new product cycles invariably prompt continuous reconfigurations of global value chains that create entry opportunities for some firms and may force the exit of others. In addition, successful global value chain upgrading generates economic growth that enlarges the market for global value chain outputs as a whole.

IP and other intangibles add twice as much value to products as tangible capital

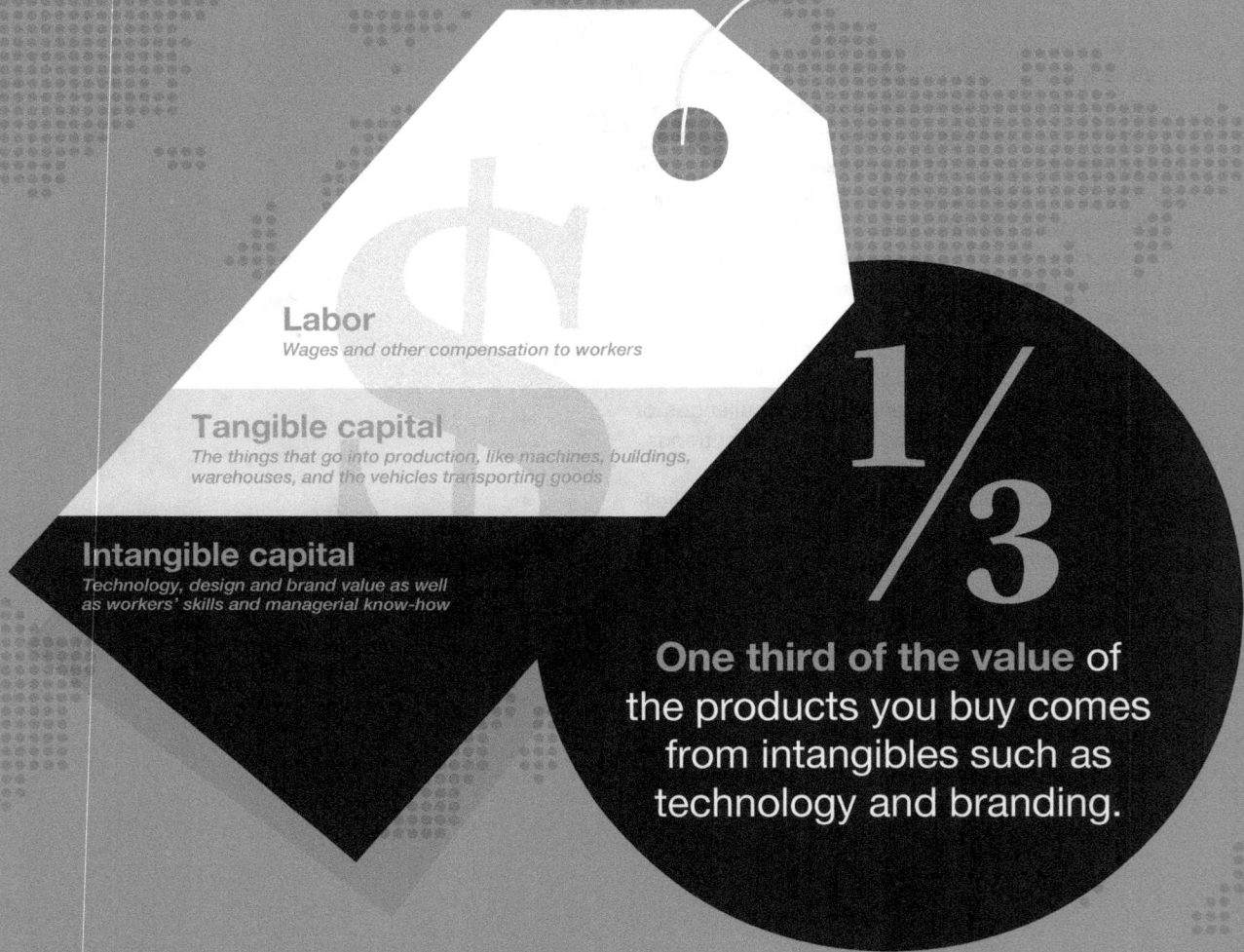

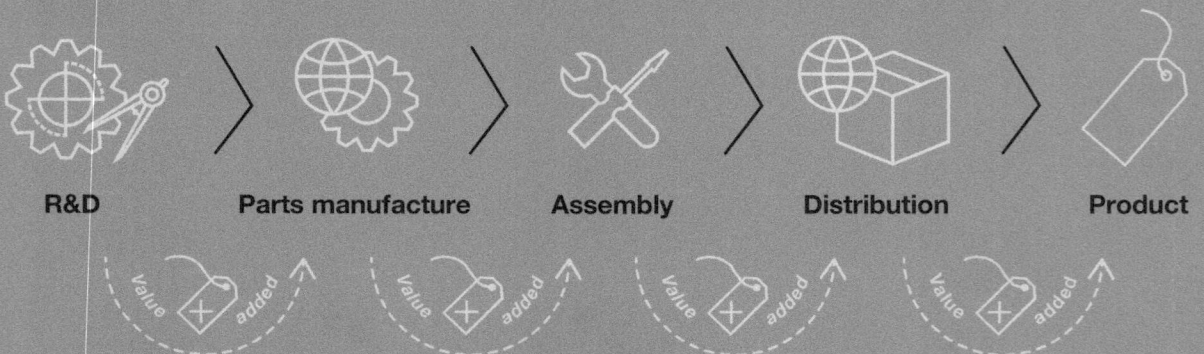

Labor
Wages and other compensation to workers

Tangible capital
The things that go into production, like machines, buildings, warehouses, and the vehicles transporting goods

Intangible capital
Technology, design and brand value as well as workers' skills and managerial know-how

1/3

One third of the value of the products you buy comes from intangibles such as technology and branding.

R&D > Parts manufacture > Assembly > Distribution > Product

Value added *Value added* *Value added* *Value added*

Value added = The difference between outputs and inputs at each stage of the global production chain.

Source: World Intellectual Property Report 2017

Chapter 1
Global value chains: the face of 21st-century international commerce

Technology, business innovations and falling trade costs have profoundly transformed the organization of global production. The production process has been unbundled, and different production stages spread across different locations. Complex international supply chains – also referred to as global value chains – have emerged, whereby firms ship intermediate goods across the world for further processing and, eventually, final assembly. Among the most far-reaching changes unleashed by the growth of global value chains has been the integration of selected developing economies into the global economy, coinciding with rapid economic growth in those economies. One prominent scholar has characterized this development as "perhaps the most momentous global economic change in the last 100 years."[1]

The rise of global value chains has gone hand in hand with the growing importance of intangible assets in economic activity. Previous editions of the *World Intellectual Property Report* have documented the rapid growth of investments in technology, design and branding – outpacing the growth of traditional bricks-and-mortar investments.[2] In fact, the two trends are directly connected. Intangible assets shape global value chains in two important ways. First, the organization of international supply chains – and especially the offshoring of labor-intensive manufacturing tasks to lower-wage economies – entails the transfer of technological and business knowledge from one location to another. Such knowledge is often subject to various forms of intellectual property (IP), including registered IP such as patents and industrial designs, and unregistered IP such as copyright and trade secrets. Second, technology, design and branding determine success in the marketplace and thus affect how value is distributed within global value chains.

Despite a large number of studies on global value chain trade, relatively little is known about how companies manage their intangible assets when offshoring production abroad, and how much production value derives from those assets. This report seeks to help fill that knowledge gap. It does so in two parts. First, it distills the insights from existing global value chain studies and reveals original research on the macroeconomic contribution of intangible assets to value added. Second, it explores the role of intangible assets at the microeconomic level in the case of three industries – coffee, photovoltaics and smartphones. These case studies will be presented in chapters 2, 3 and 4, respectively.

This opening chapter seeks to set the scene by reviewing how global value chains have come about, exploring economic research on their organization and providing new evidence on the contribution of intangible assets. In particular, section 1.1 provides a brief summary of the growth of global value chains over recent decades and section 1.2 introduces key concepts surrounding the organization and governance of global value chains. Against this background, section 1.3 presents original estimates of the returns accruing to intangible assets in global value chain production. Section 1.4 then takes a closer look at how firms participating in global value chains manage their intangible assets, and how firms in economies at early stages of industrial development may acquire them. This discussion provides the context for the case studies in chapters 2, 3 and 4. Finally, section 1.5 offers some policy-oriented reflections on the evolution of global value chains.

1.1 – Characterizing the growth of global value chains

The growth of global value chains is a key distinguishing feature of the so-called second wave of globalization that set in some time in the second half of the 20th century. The invention of the steam engine in the 18th century unleashed the first globalization wave, which peaked early in the 20th century. International commerce during the first wave mostly consisted of trade in commodities and fully assembled manufactured goods. Countries' export and import patterns at that time largely reflected their sectoral comparative advantages and disadvantages.[3] What stands out about international commerce in the second globalization wave is increased *vertical specialization* – countries concentrating on particular stages of production. As a result, trade patterns have shifted toward multidirectional trade in intermediate goods and services within particular industries.[4]

Several forces supported greater vertical specialization. Falling costs of international trade made it cost-effective to disperse production across a number of locations. Cheaper and faster transportation already propelled international trade during the first globalization phase. The advent of air transport, the spread of containerization and other innovations lowered transport costs even further. Progressively more liberal trade policies after the Second World War – following the proliferation of protectionist policies in the interwar period – also helped to lower the costs of shipping goods from one country to another. It is worth noting that even small declines in trade costs – whether due to cheaper transportation or less import protection – can have a strong effect on global value chain formation, because such costs occur every time different parts and components cross national borders before final assembly.[5]

Equally important, modern information and communication technologies (ICTs) were critical in enabling dispersed production across several locations. As will be further explained below, deciding whether or not to geographically separate production involves a trade-off between lower production costs offered by dispersed production and higher coordination costs associated with geographical separation. Rapidly falling communication costs and ever more powerful computing technology shifted this trade-off in favor of dispersed production.[6]

Figure 1.1

More gross exports for every dollar of export value added

Share of export value added in gross exports, world total

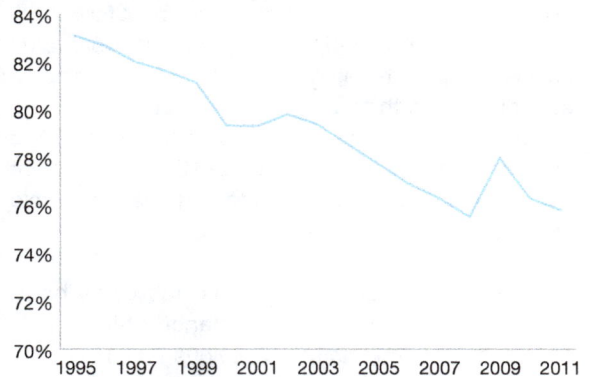

Note: Export value added refers to the domestic value added in countries' gross exports.

Source: Trade in Value Added Database, OECD.

One way of illustrating the rise of global value chains is to calculate the share of export value added in overall gross exports. If products' parts and components cross national borders several times before they reach consumers, gross export values associated with these products will exceed the export value added in each of the production locations. Growing global value chain trade should thus prompt a decreasing share of export value added in gross exports; and figure 1.1 shows that this has indeed happened – globally, the share fell by 7 percentage points between 1995 and 2011.

Unfortunately, given the complexity of capturing value added in trade statistics, export value added data are not available before 1995 and after 2011. For both a longer-term and more recent perspective, figure 1.2 depicts the evolution of the world's trade-to-gross domestic product (GDP) ratio. Trade as a proportion of GDP rose nearly 240 percent between 1960 and 2015. Note that trade and GDP values are not directly comparable: trade captures traded output on a revenue basis whereas GDP measures total output on a value-added basis. Nonetheless, the sharp increase over the last half-century likely reflects the rise of global value chains – again, more gross trade for every dollar of output.

Figure 1.2

Growth in world trade outpaces growth in world output

Trade as a percentage share of GDP

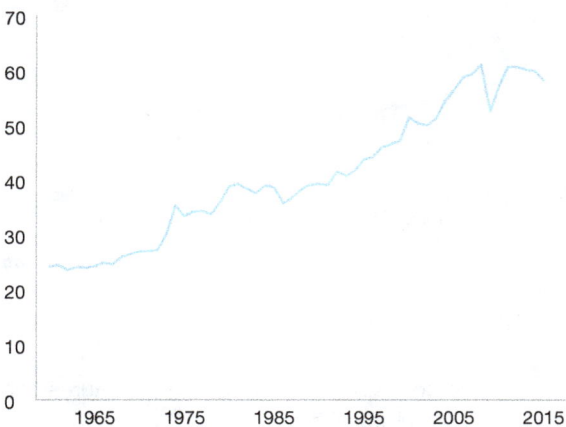

Note: Trade is defined as exports plus imports.

Source: World Bank World Development Indicators.

Figure 1.2 also shows that the trade-to-GDP ratio reached its peak in 2008, saw a sharp fall in the course of the global financial crisis, and has stagnated since. It is still too early to tell whether this is a cyclical phenomenon associated with the weak economic recovery from the financial crisis or a structural and lasting phenomenon. However, some evidence suggests that vertical specialization may indeed have reached its limits and global value chains may not further proliferate as they have over the past few decades.[7]

Notwithstanding the profound imprint of global value chains on world trade, it is worth asking whether global value chains have a truly global reach. Figure 1.3 offers a perspective on this question by showing the share of domestic and foreign value added in overall exports for selected middle-income economies. Foreign value added reflects the imports of intermediate goods and services used in the production of exported goods. The figure also offers a breakdown of foreign value added by source country.

Figure 1.3

Global value chains have a regional face

Value added share of exports, in percent

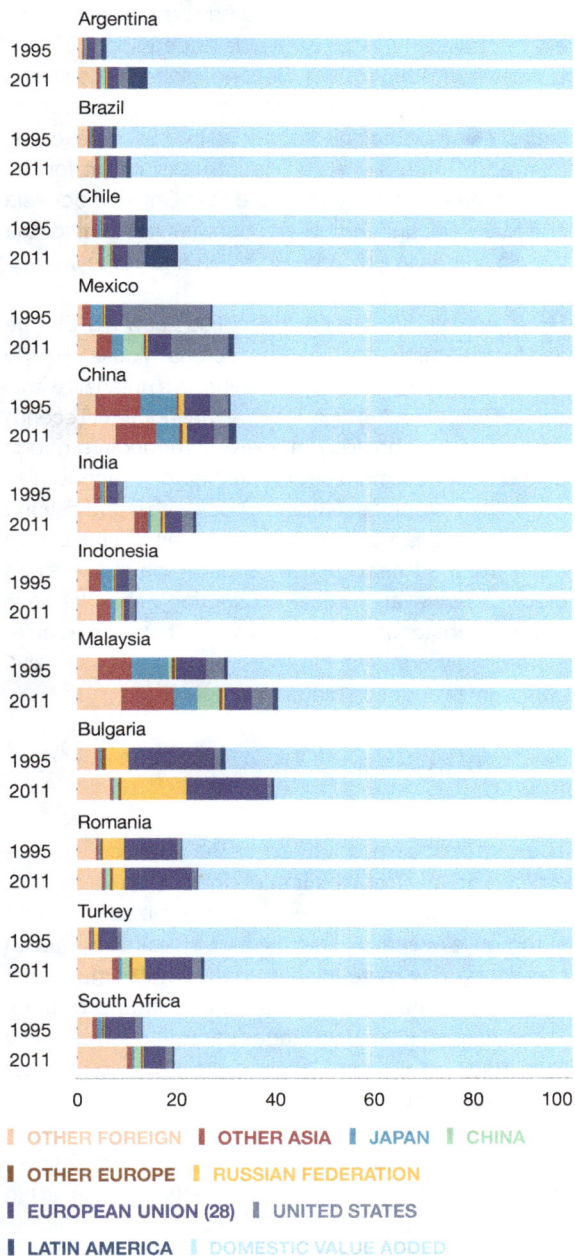

Note: The (foreign) shares shown are what are known as global value chain backward participation shares, defined as the ratio between the value-added content of imports from the source country and the gross exports of the exporting country.

Source: Trade in Value Added Database, OECD.

At least two insights emerge from figure 1.3. First, while virtually all economies have seen an increase in the share of foreign value added, some are more closely integrated into vertical production networks than others. For example, the foreign value added shares in Argentina, Brazil and Indonesia are substantially lower than those of Bulgaria, China, Malaysia and Mexico. India and Turkey stand out as having seen the largest increases in the foreign value added share of their exports from 1995 to 2011. Second, global value chains have a regional face: the United States accounts for the largest share of foreign value added in Mexico's exports; East and Southeast Asian countries account for the largest foreign value added shares in China, Indonesia and Malaysia; and European countries account for the largest shares in Bulgaria, Romania and Turkey.

More generally, studies have identified East Asia, Europe and North America as the three regional blocks with the strongest supply chain relationships. In a nutshell, within each of these blocks, high-income "headquarter" economies export technology-intensive intermediate goods and services to middle-income "factory" economies which then export assembled goods within and beyond the region. Japan, Germany and the United States have been the lead headquarter economies in the three blocks.[8] However, vertical production networks have evolved substantially over time, with China in particular increasingly entering the more technology-intensive upstream production stages.

1.2 – How global value chains are organized and governed

The concept of production in the 21st century has evolved greatly from the first notions of mass production in the early 20th century. As epitomized by Ford's automotive assembly line, the focus back then was on converting raw materials into parts and components which were then manufactured into final products. There were relatively few stages of production and they took place within close geographical proximity, if not under the roof of the same factory.

Production in the 21st century is popularly characterized by the so-called smile curve – first proposed in the early 1990s by the chief executive officer of the company Acer, Inc. As illustrated in figure 1.4, the smile curve recognizes the increased importance of pre- and post-manufacturing stages and, in fact, submits that those stages account for ever-higher shares of overall production value.

Figure 1.4

Production in the 21st century – a growing smile

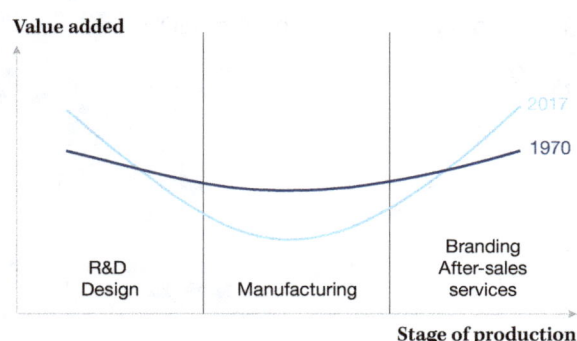

Note: Branding is shown as a post-manufacturing production stage, although certain branding activities may already occur at early pre-manufacturing stages.

The simple concept of the smile curve captures two important structural shifts:

- First, technological progress has been considerably faster in manufacturing than in services. As discussed in WIPO (2015), this trend has implied a shift of labor and capital from manufacturing to services and consequently a rising share of services in economic output. In terms of figure 1.4, the share of manufacturing in firms' overall cost structure has progressively fallen.

- Second, intangible assets – in the form of technology, design and brand value as well as workers' skills and managerial know-how – have become critically important in dynamically competitive markets. Firms continuously invest in intangible capital to stay ahead of their rivals. As economies have grown richer, consumers' preferences have shifted toward goods that respond to differentiated tastes and offer a broader "brand experience."[9]

Faced with 21st-century smile curves, how have firms organized production along the value chain? The answer depends in part on the nature of the final product and the technology underlying manufacturing. In this regard, one can broadly distinguish two basic supply chain configurations, as shown in figure 1.5. On the one hand, there are "snake-like" configurations, in which production proceeds sequentially from upstream to downstream, with value being added at each stage – not unlike in the classic Ford example.

On the other hand, there are "spider-like" configurations in which a variety of parts and components come together for assembly of the final product.[10] For example, as will be further discussed in chapters 2, 3 and 4, the coffee and photovoltaic supply chains tend to resemble a snake configuration, whereas the smartphone supply chain looks more like a spider. But most supply chains are a complex mixture of these two polar configurations.

In either configuration, firms face two overarching questions. Should they perform different production tasks themselves or outsource those tasks to other firms? And where should those tasks be located?

As to the first question, one important insight from economy theory is that firms outsource certain production tasks whenever the transaction cost of providing specific goods or services through the market is lower than the costs of coordination within a single organization.[11] In practice, firms are more likely to integrate different tasks whenever there are strong synergies from doing so – say, from combining product development and manufacturing. In addition, concerns about technology and business know-how leaking to competitors may also favor vertical integration (see section 1.4). Nonetheless, greater production complexity, the increased importance of pre- and post-manufacturing stages, the standardization of certain manufacturing processes, and improved information and communication technologies have, over time, favored greater firm specialization.

As to the question of where different production tasks should be located, some tasks – notably in agriculture and mining – depend closely on the location of natural resources. Where this is not the case, various trade-offs apply. On the one hand, combining different tasks in one location reduces coordination and trade costs. On the other hand, spreading those tasks to different locations – whether within the same country or abroad – allows firms to benefit from the advantages different locations can offer. These advantages may take the form of access to specialized skills, lower cost structures, or proximity to end-consumer markets.[12] The combination of technological advances, business innovations and falling trade costs has, over time, prompted the progressive unbundling and geographical dispersion of the production process.[13]

Figure 1.5

Supply chain configuration: snakes versus spiders

(a) Snake configuration

| Raw material | > | Processed intermediate good 1 | > | Processed intermediate good 2 | > | Final consumer good |

(b) Spider configuration

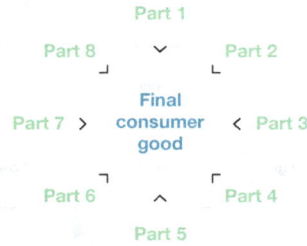

The most dramatic consequence has been the offshoring of labor-intensive manufacturing stages to developing economies with a relatively abundant supply of workers and thus lower wage costs. Greater vertical specialization across economies, in turn, has pushed the trough of the smile curve downwards – as illustrated in figure 1.4.[14]

Note that vertical specialization may occur within and across firms. In some cases, firms have offshored manufacturing by setting up a subsidiary in a foreign country. In other cases, they have outsourced and offshored manufacturing to independent firms. The precise shape of global value chains – the number of firms involved and their relationship to one another – differs substantially across industries. Nonetheless, it is possible to distinguish between different governance models of global value chains. In particular, academic research has juxtaposed buyer-driven chains with producer-driven chains.[15] In buyer-driven chains, large retailers and branded merchandisers lead value chains and set production and quality standards that independent suppliers need to meet. In supplier-driven chains, the lead firms possess advanced technological capabilities and are more vertically integrated, but draw on independent suppliers for specialized inputs.

Table 1.1

Different types of global value chain governance

Governance type	Complexity of transactions	Ability to codify transactions	Capabilities of supplying firms	Description
Market	Low	High	High	Buyers respond to specifications and prices set by suppliers; transactions require little explicit coordination; it is easy to switch suppliers.
Modular value chains	High	High	High	Buyers transmit complex but codified information, for example design files, to suppliers which the latter can flexibly accommodate; coordination remains low and switching partners remains possible.
Relational value chains	High	Low	High	Tacit knowledge must be exchanged between buyers and suppliers for transactions to occur; the buyer–seller relationship may rely on reputations, social and spatial proximity and the like; high levels of coordination make it costly to switch partners.
Captive value chains	High	High	Low	Low supplier capability requires significant intervention and control on the part of the lead firm, encouraging the latter to "lock in" suppliers to appropriate the benefits of growing capability.
Hierarchy	High	Low	Low	High complexity, low ability to codify and low supplier capability imply that the lead firm has to perform supply chain tasks in-house.

Source: Gereffi et al. (2005).

Gereffi et al. (2005) develop a more elaborate theory of global value chain governance based on how lead firms interact with other firms in the value chain. They consider three dimensions of such interactions: the *complexity* of information and knowledge transfer required for transactions in the value chain; the extent to which this information and knowledge can be *codified* and hence efficiently transmitted; and the *capabilities* of the firms in relation to the value chain transaction. On the basis of these three dimensions, they identify five types of value chain governance, as presented in table 1.1.

At one end of the spectrum, market-based governance models require little coordination between suppliers and buyers connected at a particular stage in the value chain, and both sides can switch partners relatively easily. As the complexity of transactions increases, the ability to codify relevant information and knowledge decreases and the capability of supplying firms diminishes, high levels of coordination are required and partner switching becomes progressively more difficult. At the limit, arm's-length relationships between firms connected at a value chain stage become impossible and lead firms have to perform supply chain tasks in-house.

1.3 – What return accrues to intangible assets?

While appealing and intuitive, the concept of the smile curve has its limitations. It may reasonably portray the distribution of value added for some global value chain lead firms, but it is more difficult to apply at the economy-wide level where firms' value chains intersect and overlap.[16] More importantly, it does not provide any insight into what generates value added at different production stages. In particular, higher value added does not necessarily coincide with underlying activities being more profitable, associated with better-paying jobs, or generally "more desirable." For example, higher value-added activities may be highly capital-intensive, in which case it is not clear that workers involved in them receive higher wages compared to lower value-added activities.[17] Similarly, value-added figures alone do not reveal how much intangible capital contributes to global value chain production – the focus of this report – as value added reflects the return of all the inputs into production.

Indeed, understanding what precisely generates value in global value chains requires analysis of how much income accrues to labor, tangible capital and intangible capital used in global value chain production. In research performed for this report, economists Wen Chen, Reitze Gouma, Bart Los and Marcel Timmer performed precisely such an analysis. Their approach consisted of two steps.

Box 1.1

Assembling and slicing up global value chains

There are no readily available macroeconomic data on global value chain production. Some information is available in national accounts and in trade statistics, but neither offer a full picture. National accounts statistics provide information on production value added, but are classified by industrial activity. For example, value added in the motor vehicle industry captures the manufacture of auto parts and components as well as the final assembly of cars. But it does not capture the upstream production of materials, the business services supporting production or the downstream distribution of cars to the end consumer. To complicate matters further, many parts and components come from abroad – which is precisely what makes value chains global. Trade statistics offer information on imported intermediate goods, but are classified by product and not industrial activity.

To assemble metrics of value added in global value chains, Chen et al. (2017) built on previous research that has sought to track the flow of products across industries and countries. Relying on concordances between industry and trade statistics, they combined national input-output tables with international trade data to construct a world input-output table (WIOT). This contains data on 55 industries – of which 19 are manufacturing – in 43 economies plus one rest-of-the-world region, which together represent more than 85 percent of world GDP. One can think of the WIOT as a large matrix which breaks down the value added of each industry in each country into either intermediate inputs flowing to other industries (either at home or in another country) or finished products for final consumption (again, either at home or in another country).

One complicating factor concerns the measurement of value added in the distribution stage. Input-output tables represent the distribution sector as a so-called margin industry, which means that the final products that wholesalers and retailers buy are not treated as intermediate inputs. To arrive at a measure of distribution value added, Chen et al. calculated a distribution margin as the ratio of the price paid by final consumers (less product taxes) to the price received by producers, then applied the resulting margin to a product's total sales.

The next step was to slice up the assembled value-added statistics according to the incomes accruing to the underlying production factors. First, labor income was calculated for each industry in each country, drawing on national labor force surveys and additional data sources. Second, Chen et al. estimated tangible capital income by applying a rental price for such capital to national accounts data on capital stock, again in each industry and each country. The rental price consisted of an industry-specific depreciation rate plus an assumed real rate of return of 4 percent. Importantly, Chen et al. removed selected intangible capital assets – notably R&D, computer software and databases, and artistic originals – from capital stocks wherever those assets were covered in national account statistics. Intangible capital income was then calculated by subtracting labor income and tangible capital income from value added.

Finally, using the industry-product flow relationships contained in the WIOT and the factor decomposition of value added in each industry and each country, it was possible to calculate the contribution of labor, tangible capital and intangible capital at the level of product global value chains.

First, they assembled macroeconomic data on value-added shares in 19 manufacturing product groups spanning 43 economies plus one rest-of-the-world region which together captured around one-quarter of global output. Their data allowed them to divide global value chain production into three stages: distribution, final assembly and all other stages. As an example, the resulting database showed the value added of the distribution stage in the sales price of cars for which the final assembly took place in Germany.

As a second step, Chen et al. (2017) decomposed value added at each stage and in each country into the incomes accruing to labor, tangible capital and intangible capital – as illustrated in figure 1.6. They did so by first subtracting labor income and imputed tangible capital income from value added – relying on available data on wages, employment, tangible capital asset stocks and an assumed rate of return on tangible capital of 4 percent. The remaining residual then represents the income accruing to intangible capital.

The logic behind this approach is to recognize that intangible capital is firm-specific and different from other factor inputs, because companies cannot freely order or hire it. In other words, intangible capital is the "yeast" that creates value from labor and market-mediated investment in assets.[18] Box 1.1 provides a fuller overview of the analytical steps performed by Chen et al.; their research paper offers more detailed technical explanations.

The research by Chen et al. (2017) breaks new ground in at least two respects. First, it offers for the first time an estimate of the return to intangible asset investments in global value chain production. Notwithstanding promising efforts to quantify such investments, their macroeconomic value has so far largely eluded measurement.[19] Second, it includes the distribution stage in the analysis, which is important as global value chains with major retailers – for example, Nike – will likely realize returns to their intangibles at this stage.[20]

Figure 1.6

Decomposing global value chains

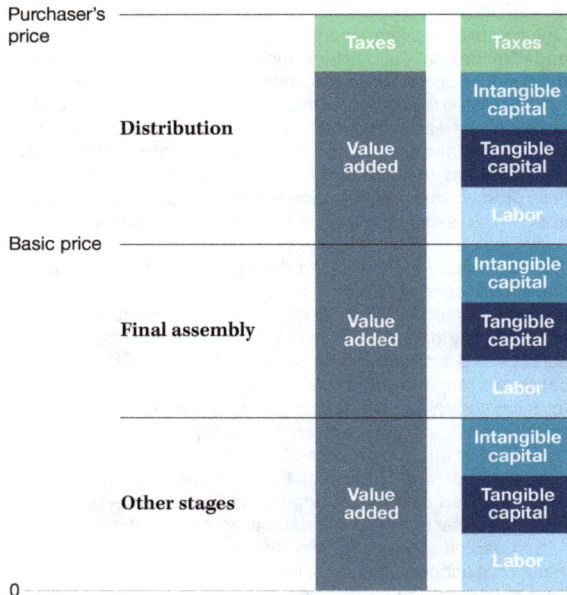

Source: Chen et al. (2017).

Turning to the research findings, figure 1.7 presents the income shares accruing to the three production factors for all manufacturing products from 2000 to 2014. The intangibles share averaged 30.4 percent throughout this period, almost double the share for tangibles. Interestingly, it rose from 27.8 percent in 2000 to 31.9 percent in 2007, but has stagnated since then. Overall income from intangibles in the 19 manufacturing industries increased by 75 percent from 2000 to 2014 in real terms. It amounted to 5.9 trillion United States dollars (USD) in 2014.[21]

One interpretation of the rising share for intangibles is that global manufacturing firms benefited from increased opportunities for offshoring labor-intensive activities to lower wage economies. Intuitively, in competitive markets, wage cost savings will lower final output prices; if capital costs remain the same, the intangibles share must go up by virtue of its definition as a residual – intangibles will constitute a larger share of a smaller whole. However, this trend appears to have peaked in 2007 – just before the global financial crisis. This finding seems consistent with the stagnating trade-to-GDP ratio shown in figure 1.2 and empirical studies suggesting that vertical specialization may have reached its limits.[22]

Which product global value chains use intangibles most intensively? Table 1.2 presents the factor income shares in 2014 for the 19 manufacturing product groups in descending order of their global output size. For all product groups, intangible capital accounts for a higher share of value added than tangible capital. The intangibles share is especially high – and more than double the tangibles share – for pharmaceutical, chemical and petroleum products. It is also relatively high for food products as well as computer, electronic and optical products. In terms of absolute returns, the three largest product groups – food products, motor vehicles and textiles – account for close to 50 percent of the total income generated by intangible capital in the 19 manufacturing global value chains.

While the intangibles share increased for almost all of the 19 product groups during the period 2000-2014, it did so more sharply for some than for others. Figure 1.8 depicts the trend for four of the largest product groups. As it shows, the intangibles share increased only slightly for food and textile products, but more substantially for motor vehicles and electronic products.

Figure 1.7

Intangible capital captures more value than tangible capital

Value added as a percentage of the total value of all products manufactured and sold worldwide

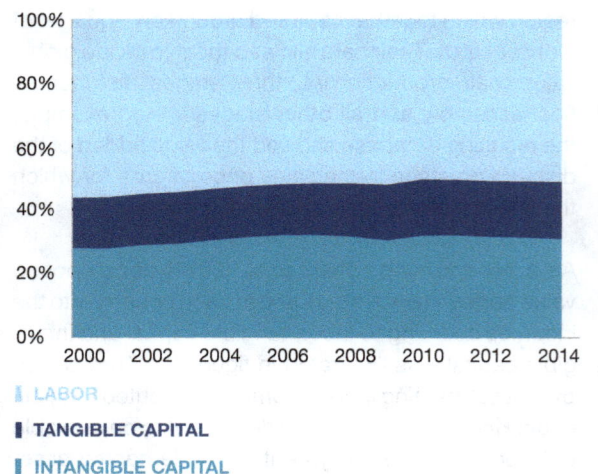

▮ LABOR
▮ TANGIBLE CAPITAL
▮ INTANGIBLE CAPITAL

Source: Chen et al. (2017).

Table 1.2

Income shares by manufacturing product group, 2014

Product group name	Intangible income share (%)	Tangible income share (%)	Labor share (%)	Global output (USD bn)
Food, beverages, and tobacco products	31.0	16.4	52.6	4,926
Motor vehicles and trailers	29.7	19.0	51.3	2,559
Textiles, apparel and leather products	29.9	17.7	52.4	1,974
Other machinery and equipment	27.2	18.8	53.9	1,834
Computer, electronic and optical products	31.3	18.6	50.0	1,452
Furniture and other manufacturing	30.1	16.3	53.7	1,094
Petroleum products	42.1	20.0	37.9	1,024
Other transport equipment	26.3	18.5	55.2	852
Electrical equipment	29.5	20.0	50.6	838
Chemical products	37.5	17.5	44.9	745
Pharmaceutical products	34.7	16.5	48.8	520
Fabricated metal products	24.0	20.8	55.2	435
Rubber and plastics products	29.2	19.7	51.1	244
Basic metals	31.4	25.6	43.0	179
Repair and installation of machinery	23.6	13.2	63.2	150
Paper products	28.0	20.9	51.1	140
Other non-metallic mineral products	29.7	21.5	48.9	136
Wood products	27.5	20.0	52.5	90
Printing products	27.1	21.2	51.7	64

Source: Chen et al. (2017).

This may suggest that opportunities to offshore production of food and textiles were already largely realized, whereas the latter industries could still take advantage of such opportunities between 2000 and 2007.

At what stage of production does income accrue to intangible capital? The global value chain decomposition suggests that distribution and the final production stage each account for around a quarter of the intangibles income, and the other stages for the remaining half.[23] This division signifies the importance of intangibles in upstream activities – not only the production of parts, components and materials, but also a wide variety of business services as well as agriculture and mining activities.

The contribution of different production stages to intangibles income varies greatly across product groups, as shown in figure 1.9. Intuitively, the pattern that emerges seems to correspond broadly to the distinction between buyer-driven and producer-driven global value chains introduced in section 1.2.

Buyer-driven global value chains such as textile, furniture and food products realize larger returns to intangibles at the distribution stage whereas producer-driven global value chains such as motor vehicles, electronics and machinery realize those returns before final production.

The findings by Chen et al. (2017) underscore the importance of intangible assets in generating value in global value chain production. However, they also leave a number of questions open and come with several methodological caveats. One unresolved question is what precisely accounts for the income attributed to intangibles. Under Chen et al.'s methodology, this income captures all the firm-specific returns that go beyond market-mediated returns to tangible capital and labor. That clearly includes brand reputation and image, technological edge and design appeal that sets apart the products of one firm from those of another – intangible assets for which firms seek different forms of IP rights. It also includes organizational and managerial know-how that may be protected by trade secrets.

Figure 1.8

Different product groups see different trends

Intangible income as a percentage of the value of all products manufactured and sold worldwide

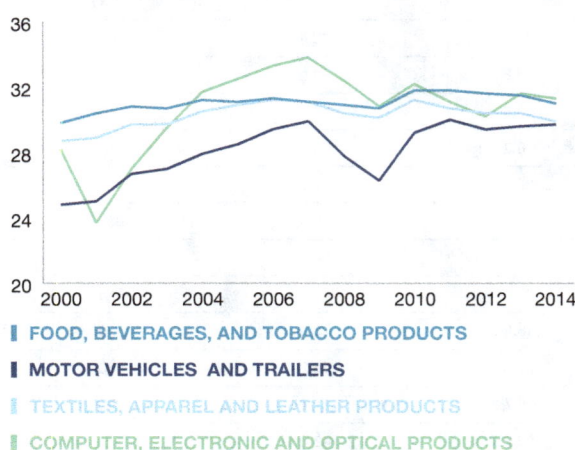

■ FOOD, BEVERAGES, AND TOBACCO PRODUCTS

■ MOTOR VEHICLES AND TRAILERS

■ TEXTILES, APPAREL AND LEATHER PRODUCTS

■ COMPUTER, ELECTRONIC AND OPTICAL PRODUCTS

Source: Chen et al. (2017).

However, it may also include other factors – beyond reputational and knowledge assets – that generate large economic returns. For example, the high intangibles share for petroleum products (see table 1.2) is likely to reflect the resource rents accruing to oil producers.[24] Supply-side and demand-side economies of scale may be other sources of market power that may not relate directly to intangible assets.

A second unresolved question is which economies harvest the returns from intangible capital. The question is obvious, but the answer is elusive. For one thing, through transfer pricing and related practices, companies can easily shift profits from one location to another (see box 1.2). Thus, an intangible asset may originate in one economy, but most of its returns may show up in another. More importantly, increasing cross-border ownership and sharing of intangibles is undermining the very notion of location-bound assets and earnings.

Finally, several caveats apply to the research by Chen et al. (2017) that should be kept in mind in interpreting their findings:[25]

- The validity of the findings relies heavily on the quality of the underlying data. While there has been important statistical progress in measuring global production networks, important measurement gaps remain.

For example, it is hard to capture international trade in services adequately, and there are also challenges in measuring value added in the distribution stage. In addition, the use of international input-output tables relies on relatively strong assumptions, such as firms in a given industry and country exhibiting similar production structures.

- As already mentioned, transfer mispricing and related practices – in particular between related parties – may distort the distribution of value added along the global value chain (see box 1.2). This could lead to biases in the income share estimates by production stage, as shown in figure 1.9. However, to the extent that such practices merely shift profits from one production stage to another, they should not affect the estimates of income shares involving all production stages, as presented in figures 1.7 and 1.8 and table 1.2.

- The allocation of intangible capital to different production stages – as shown in figure 1.9 – may also be affected by how global value chain lead firms are classified statistically. For example, if "factory-free" goods producers are classified as retailers or wholesalers, returns to intangible assets will be recorded at the distribution stage; if they are classified as manufacturers, these returns will be recorded at one of the other production stages.

1.4 – How intangible assets permeate global value chains

In light of the substantial value generated by intangible assets, a key question is how firms holding such assets manage them within their global production networks. A related and equally important question is how firms not holding intangible assets can acquire them. To address these questions, it is helpful to distinguish between two types of intangible assets:

- *Knowledge assets* cover technology and design as well as organizational, logistical, managerial and related know-how. A common characteristic of knowledge assets is that they are non-rival in nature and – in contrast to tangible assets – not necessarily tied to any particular location. For example, the R&D for a new car may occur in one location, but once the car is developed its production can be spread across a large number of locations.

Figure 1.9

Buyer-driven versus producer-driven global value chains

Intangible income by production stage, percentage shares in 2014

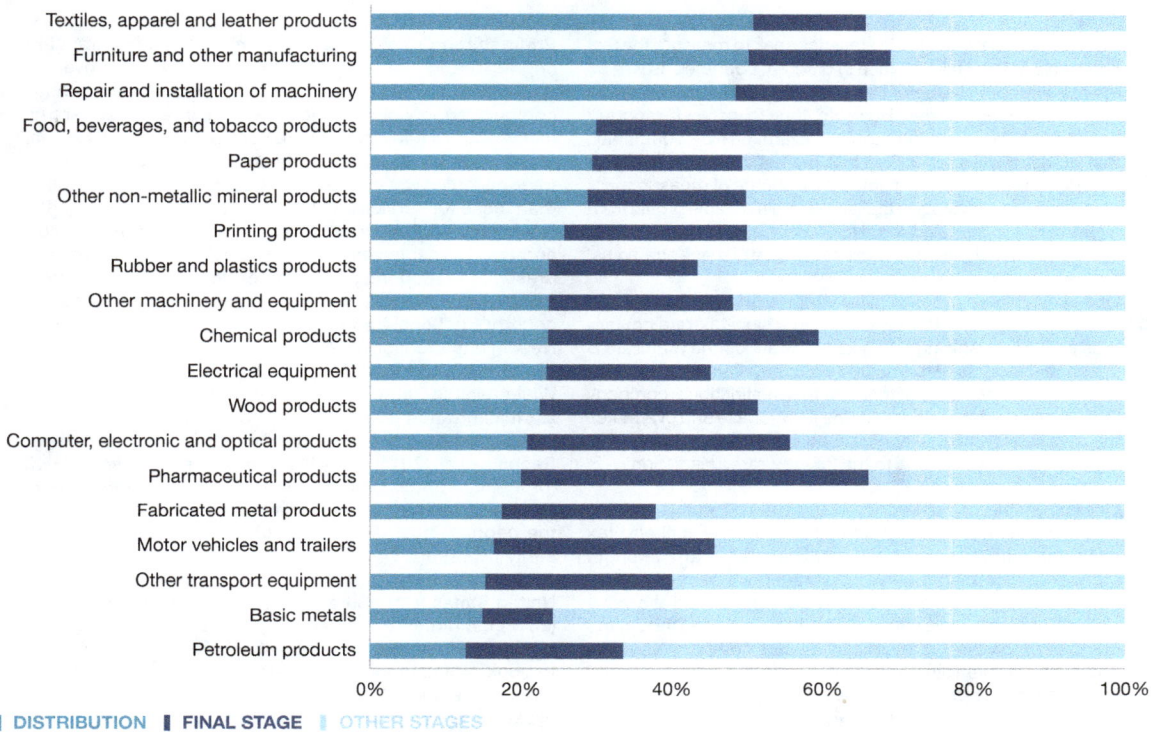

DISTRIBUTION   FINAL STAGE   OTHER STAGES

Source: Chen et al. (2017).

- *Reputational assets* consist of the goodwill that consumers extend to a company's brand – partly because of satisfaction derived from previous brand purchases and partly because of the image associated with different brands. Reputational assets are rival in nature: brands only have reputational value if used in relation to a single product or firm. In addition, while brands can sometimes gain an international reputation, they generally do not seamlessly flow across borders; companies may possess strong reputational assets in some markets, but not in others.[26]

Managing knowledge assets

In order to reap returns from investments in innovation, firms must be able to appropriate their knowledge assets. Ideally, they would want to capture the full rewards from those assets without any knowledge leaking to competitors.[27]

In practice, such "perfect appropriation" is typically not possible. How high a return a firm will reap will depend, among other things, on how it controls the flow of its knowledge.

At the outset, when generating new knowledge, firms face a well-known trade-off. On the one hand, they have incentives to keep their innovations secret to maintain their edge over competitors. Trade secrecy laws protect confidential information from unauthorized disclosure, though competitors may still be able to reverse-engineer products placed in the market. On the other hand, firms may be able to take out IP rights for their innovations, in which case they need to disclose them but benefit from exclusivity – at least for a limited time. Several factors will influence the preferred knowledge management strategy. Certain knowledge assets – such as process technology and organizational know-how – can easily be kept secret, whereas others – such as product design – cannot.

Box 1.2

How transfer mispricing and related practices distort global value chain measurement

National accounts and trade statistics seek to measure the real economic activity taking place in different countries as well as the real economic value of trade in goods and services taking place between countries. However, they rely on self-reported financial accounts and customs declarations by companies that do not always reflect the true market value of underlying economic transactions. An important source of measurement bias stems from strategies that seek to shift taxable profits from high-tax-rate to low-tax-rate jurisdictions. Intangibles – frequently in the form of IP rights – are often at the core of these strategies.

One widely noted practice is transfer mispricing. An example is shown in figure 1.10. Company A in a high-tax-rate country sells its IP to its affiliate B in a low-tax-rate country; affiliate B in turn licenses this IP to a related company, C, in another high-tax-rate country. To the extent that this multinational company (MNC) understates the price for the IP purchase and overstates the royalties for the use of IP, it is able to shift profits from the high-tax-rate jurisdictions to the low-tax-rate jurisdiction.

One key enabler of transfer mispricing is the difficulty of valuing intangible assets. Transfer pricing rules in financial and tax accounting frameworks have established the arm's-length standard, according to which transactions between related companies under common control are to be priced at a value similar to a comparable transaction with an unrelated third-party company. However, intangible assets are company-specific, and comparable third-party transactions typically do not exist, so transfer prices can only be imputed or estimated. In addition, the value of intangible assets can be highly uncertain, especially at an early stage when the resulting goods or services have not yet been commercialized. This uncertainty offers companies substantial leeway in setting IP sales prices and royalty rates between affiliated entities.

From a statistical perspective, transfer mispricing as outlined in figure 1.10 leads to an understatement of value added in the high-tax-rate jurisdictions and its overstatement in the low-tax-rate jurisdiction. In addition, it distorts trade statistics – the low-tax-rate country's imports of IP services would be understated and its exports of such services would be overstated.[28]

Profit-shifting may take other forms. Instead of transferring IP to a foreign affiliate, companies may also over- or under-invoice IP-intensive intermediate inputs traded within company supply chains and for which, again, there are no market-based reference prices. Such practices imply similar shifts in value added from one country to another, but the trade distortion would show up in goods trade statistics rather than those for services. Other related practices include the "merchanting of services" through Special Purpose Entities, and arrangements whereby MNCs establish a commercial presence in a country but are not considered permanent establishments for tax purposes and thus not included in a country's national trade statistics – as further discussed in Neubig and Wunsch-Vincent (2017).

While reliable figures are hard to come by, it is clear that tax minimization practices of MNCs lead to sizeable shifts in reported profits across jurisdictions. At the micro level, Seppälä et al. (2014) study the value chain of a Finnish MNC for a single precision machinery product. On the basis of invoice-level internal company data, they conclude that the geographical distribution of profits does not necessarily represent where the MNC's most valuable assets are located. At the macro level, using survey data from the United States (U.S.) Bureau of Economic Analysis, Rassier (2017) estimates the extent of profit shifting among U.S. MNCs; he finds that R&D-intensive firms are more inclined to book profits to foreign affiliates than non-R&D-intensive firms, underlining the important role played by intangible assets in tax minimization practices. Drawing on a variety of sources and making several assumptions, Neubig and Wunsch-Vincent (2017) conservatively estimate that global profit shifting associated with cross-border IP transactions alone could amount to USD 120 billion annually, or 35 percent of the reported total cross-border trade in IP services. Most prominently, Ireland's GDP registered a 26 percent increase in 2015 which largely reflected the inflow of intangible and other internationally mobile assets from MNCs locating their headquarters in Ireland.[29]

Figure 1.10

Shifting profits to an IP-owning intermediary

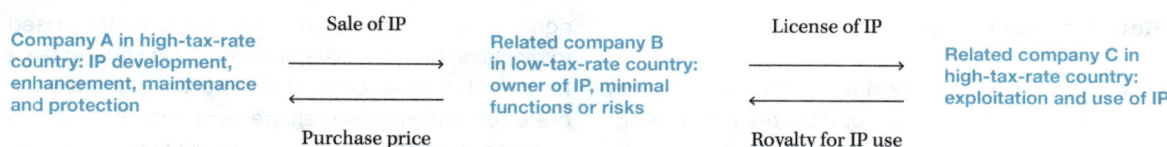

	Sale of IP		License of IP	
Company A in high-tax-rate country: IP development, enhancement, maintenance and protection	⟶	**Related company B in low-tax-rate country: owner of IP, minimal functions or risks**	⟶	**Related company C in high-tax-rate country: exploitation and use of IP**
	⟵		⟵	
	Purchase price		Royalty for IP use	

Source: Neubig and Wunsch-Vincent (2017).

Similarly, IP rights extend to certain knowledge assets – technological inventions in the case of patents – but not to others, for example many types of service innovations.

Knowledge assets can sometimes also take the form of specialized workers' skills. Retaining those skills is often an important part of a company's knowledge management strategy. Yet it is also constrained by law; there are limits, for example, on how far non-compete clauses in employment contracts can prevent workers from starting their own business or leaving to competitors.[30]

As mentioned in section 1.2, knowledge management considerations determine the organization of global value chains – in particular, whether firms vertically integrate different production tasks or whether they outsource those tasks to independent suppliers.[31] Outsourcing may generate substantial cost savings, but it may also risk key knowledge assets leaking to future competitors. Much depends on the relationships governing global value chains, as outlined in table 1.1. Knowledge leakage is bound to be a concern in relational and captive value chains, especially when global value chain lead firms transfer tacit knowledge to partner firms that might emerge as future competitors. For this reason, MNCs sometimes limit knowledge transfers to older technologies, leakage of which would not pose an immediate competitive threat.[32] At the same time, secure IP rights can help companies in transferring proprietary technologies within the supply chain and actually facilitate the outsourcing of different production tasks.

In yet other circumstances, firms may openly share or license some of their knowledge assets, partly to encourage adoption of new technologies and partly to obtain access to technology owned by other firms. The latter consideration has been important for so-called complex technologies – defined as technologies that consist of numerous separately patentable inventions with possibly widespread patent ownership. Complex technologies include most ICTs, which have seen the fastest growth in patenting over the past three decades. Through cross-licensing arrangements, companies negotiate access to technologies they require to commercialize their own innovations.[33]

In most circumstances, IP protection is a crucial element of a firm's knowledge management strategy. One study for the UK economy, for example, found that slightly more than one-half of investments in intangible assets were in assets protected by different IP rights.[34]

Figure 1.11

International patent filings focus on fewer offices than international trademark filings

Share of the top five offices in world total non-resident patent and trademark filings, 2015

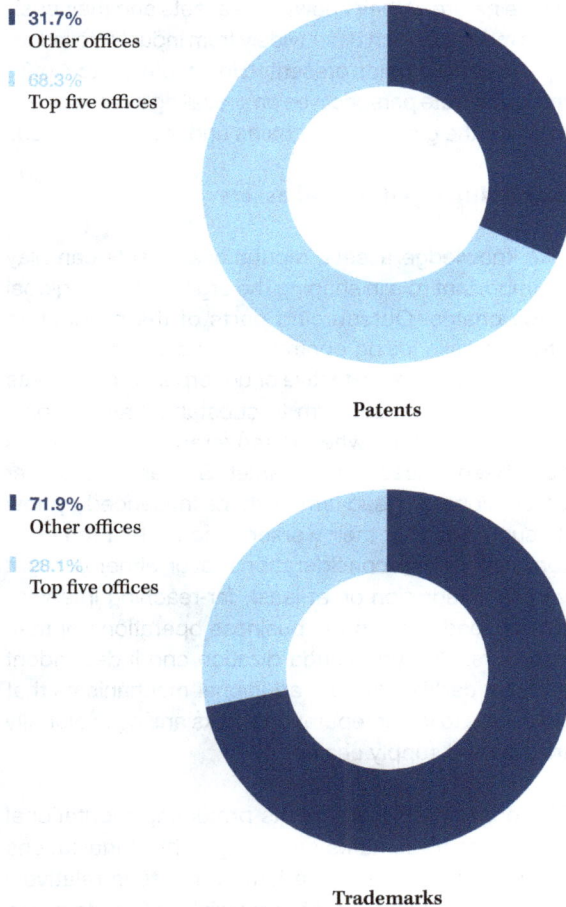

31.7%
Other offices

68.3%
Top five offices

Patents

71.9%
Other offices

28.1%
Top five offices

Trademarks

Note: To account for different trademark filing systems around the world, trademark statistics refer to the number of classes specified in trademark applications.

Source: WIPO IP Statistics Database, July 2017.

However, deciding for which knowledge asset to seek IP rights, and in which countries, requires careful planning. Obtaining patent rights in particular is costly, especially when pursued in many countries. For this reason, companies often limit their patent coverage to countries hosting the largest economies and countries in which global value chain production takes place.

This explains why the world's five largest recipients of patent filings from abroad – the national patent offices of China, Japan, the Republic of Korea, and the United States as well as the European Patent Office – account for close to 70 percent of the world total in non-resident patent filings (see figure 1.11).[35] Other than China, relatively few patents flow to low- and middle-income economies.

Notwithstanding these general observations, the knowledge management strategies of firms depend crucially on the nature of their knowledge assets and their business models, which differ widely from industry to industry. The case studies presented in chapters 2 to 4 offer more concrete perspectives on prevailing strategies – at least for the global value chains under consideration.

Managing reputational assets

Like knowledge assets, reputational assets can play an important role in shaping the organization of global value chains. Outsourcing parts of the production process risks losing control over the quality of parts and components. Defective or underperforming inputs might expose a lead firm to substantial reputational risks – especially when discovered after products have been placed in the market. Similarly, consumer perceptions of a lead firm might be influenced by how its suppliers treat their workers and protect the environment. These considerations favor either outright vertical integration or, at least, far-reaching intervention by lead firms in the business operations of their suppliers. Product standardization and independent supplier certification are additional mechanisms that help firms to lower reputational risks arising in globally fragmented supply chains.

The principal IP instruments protecting reputational assets are trademarks and geographical indications (GIs). While acquiring trademark rights is relatively cheap, managing a global portfolio of trademarks also requires careful planning and strategic decision-making. To begin with, trademarks may not only cover product names, but also two- and three-dimensional shapes, sounds, colors and other features associated with them. In contrast to patents, which companies mostly protect in countries where global value chain production takes place, companies have strong reasons to protect at least their main trademarks in all the markets in which they are or plan to be active. Uncertain trademark ownership can prove costly, especially once new products have been commercialized.

For this reason, the global trademark portfolios of large multinational enterprises often consist of tens of thousands of trademarks. In addition, the distribution of non-resident trademark filings is less concentrated compared to patents: the five largest offices – the national trademark offices of Canada, China, the Russian Federation and the U.S. as well as the European Union Intellectual Property Office – account for less than 30 percent of the world total (see figure 1.11).

Catch-up and industrial development

As pointed out in the introduction to this chapter, the growth of global value chains has coincided with both rapid industrial development in certain low- and middle-income economies and the integration of these economies into the global economy. Above all, China has been at the forefront of this transformation, with its economy often referred to as "the world's factory," but a number of other economies in Asia, Eastern Europe and other parts of the world have also seen far-reaching industrial development through participation in global value chains. The causal relationship between these developments is not clear-cut, however. Has global value chain participation spurred industrial development in a way that would not have been possible otherwise, or did the successful economies just happen to have the right preconditions for industrial development which prompted their participation in global value chains?

Most likely, the answer lies somewhere in the middle. Global value chains arguably embraced those economies offering the most conducive environments – including competitive access to capital and labor, needed skills, reliable infrastructure and fast-growing markets. At the same time, the transfer of production capacity to those economies likely offered opportunities for industrial upgrading that otherwise might not have come about. One critical question in this context is how firms in successfully industrializing economies were able to "catch up" and acquire the knowledge and reputational assets that enabled their global value chain participation.

Economic research has long analyzed how knowledge assets diffuse to catch-up economies. In particular, it has distinguished among four main diffusion channels:[36]

- Firms in catch-up economies acquire knowledge through *reverse engineering* products and technologies available in the marketplace.

This form of knowledge diffusion may be seen as the reverse side of the imperfect appropriability of knowledge assets by lead firms, as discussed above. IP rights may limit the use of reverse-engineered technologies by catch-up firms – at least insofar as they are protected in a given jurisdiction. At the same time, publicly available patent records offer a rich source of technological knowledge that catch-up firms can and do employ in their own R&D activities.[37]

- Partnerships between global value chain lead firms and catch-up firms can entail the transfer of knowledge from the former to the latter. Such partnership may take the form of *technology licensing* contracts, which – in addition to licensing patented knowledge – often entail the transfer of relevant non-codified knowledge. Instead of licensing their technology to independent firms, global value chain lead firms may insist on taking an equity stake in the knowledge-acquiring firm, leading to *joint venture arrangements*. At the limit, they may only be willing to transfer knowledge to a catch-up economy by establishing a *wholly-owned subsidiary*. A key question involving this diffusion channel is whether acquisition of the knowledge asset is limited to the local partner firm or whether it diffuses beyond that firm, for example through customer and supplier linkages or skilled worker movements (see below).

- Firms in catch-up economies can gain access to knowledge assets by *importing capital goods* which embed technological knowledge. In particular, the import of production equipment can allow catch-up firms to upgrade their manufacturing capabilities to the state-of-the-art. Foreign sellers of such equipment may also train local workers to use and maintain it – building up an important complementary knowledge base.

- Finally, to the extent that knowledge assets take the form of human skills, the *movement of skilled workers* represents an important channel through which knowledge diffuses from one firm to another. Skilled workers may move from foreign global value chain lead firms to catch-up firms, or they may start their own firm. Equally important, they may move from locally established foreign subsidiaries to local firms, thereby helping to diffuse knowledge throughout the catch-up economy.

Public policies in relation to trade, investment, migration and IP have a bearing on diffusion outcomes, although the effects are not always clear-cut. For example, restricting trade may inhibit diffusion through importing technology-intensive capital goods, but could also promote diffusion by encouraging foreign investment.

Whatever the diffusion channel, successful technology diffusion relies critically on the *absorptive capacity* of catch-up economies to understand and apply foreign-grown knowledge. Effective absorptive capacity relies on human capital able to understand and apply technology, organizational and managerial know-how, and institutions that coordinate and mobilize resources for technology adoption. In many cases, absorptive capacity also entails the ability to undertake incremental technological and organizational innovation in order to adapt technology to local needs. Some countries have been more successful at creating absorptive capacity than others. In particular, economists have argued that at least part of the success of the fast-growing East Asian countries lay in their ability to ignite a process of technological learning and absorption that provided the basis for economic catch-up.[38]

Economists have paid less attention to how firms in catch-up economies can acquire reputational assets. In addition to building product portfolios of high and consistent quality, it is clear that strong brand reputation and image require substantial and often market-specific investments in advertising. Inducing consumers to switch brands may be especially challenging in mature industries with long-established competing brands. Firms' branding strategies often evolve in line with their growing manufacturing capabilities. For example, companies in Japan, the Republic of Korea and more recently China at one time pursued a low-cost and low-price strategy; over time, they were able to raise prices and quality, thus moving from largely generic products into premium brands. Other companies, including companies in the ICT industry, have made a name as providers of certain components, or as assembly and contract manufacturers – for example, Asus, Acer and Foxconn; alternatively, they may have focused on business customers before entering the end-consumer markets with a more established brand, such as in the case of Huawei. Yet other companies have bought established brands from companies in high-income economies.[39]

Again, the opportunities and challenges for industrial catch-up vary markedly from industry to industry and the case studies presented in chapters 2 to 4 offer at least selective perspectives on what has contributed to catch-up in the global value chains under consideration.

1.5 – Concluding reflections

Global value chains have emerged as the 21st-century face of international commerce. They have tied together national economies as never before and have helped integrate numerous developing countries into the global economy. How will they further evolve, and what role is there for policy to ensure that they support economic growth and rising living standards around the world? Drawing on this chapter's discussion, this final section seeks to offer some policy-oriented reflections on these two questions.

The future of global value chains

As described in section 1.1, the world's trade-to-GDP ratio has more than doubled over the past 50 years, but it has not seen any growth since the global financial crisis unfolded in 2008. This may well reflect the persistent shortfall in aggregate demand to which many economists attribute the weak recovery from the crisis.[40] Indeed, preliminary data for 2017 suggest trade growth is again outpacing global output growth.[41] At the same time, several studies suggest that the stagnating trade-to-GDP ratio may well have structural foundations and that vertical specialization may have reached a natural limit (see sections 1.1 and 1.3). There is also some evidence that the scope for further improvements in transport technology to increase trade may be exhausted.[42]

Should policymakers worry about the trade "slowdown" having structural foundations? At one level, yes. Greater vertical specialization in the world economy may not provide the same growth impetus in the future as it has throughout the second globalization wave. At the same time, technological and business innovations as well as shifting consumer preferences will continue to transform global production. Most prominently, developments in 3D printing, robotics and automated manufacturing have already reconfigured supply chains in a number of industries, and further progress in these areas may well unleash more profound change. These developments may well lead to the "re-shoring" of certain production tasks. Such an outcome would imply less cross-border trade in intermediate goods. However, the deployment of such technologies could help spur economic growth.

A declining trade-to-output ratio in this case would be a sign of progress, rather than a source of concern.

Another key factor shaping global value chains is the upgrading of production capabilities in catch-up economies. Chiefly, evidence suggests that Chinese firms increasingly source parts and components domestically, rather than importing them from abroad.[43] This development similarly reduces reliance on cross-border trade and may well have contributed to the world's stagnating trade-to-GDP ratio. However, upgraded production capabilities should again ultimately enhance growth.[44]

Whatever their causes, shifts in global value chains disrupt prevailing patterns of production – and this should arguably be the chief concern of policymakers. Production tasks offshored abroad may lead affected workers to lose their jobs. More generally, evidence suggests that greater vertical specialization has put pressure on unskilled labor in high-income economies and contributed to rising income inequality. One prominent study, for example, estimates that import competition explains one-quarter of the decline in U.S. manufacturing employment between 1990 and 2007.[45] One important question in this context is how the growing role of intangible capital in global value chain production affects the compensation of workers at different skills levels. One hypothesis is that the growing role of intangibles has been especially beneficial for the most talented workers – so-called superstars.[46] However, there is no systematic evidence supporting this hypothesis.

How should policymakers respond to the disruption brought about by shifting global value chains? Trade protection is not the answer. As discussed in section 1.1, progressive trade liberalization has been one of the factors enabling the growth of global value chains. As global value chain formation is highly sensitive to underlying trade cost, reversing open markets could be highly disruptive in and of itself. In addition, it would not re-establish old production patterns, as today's production technology has evolved greatly. Instead, economists generally advocate providing a social safety net that cushions the adverse effects of unemployment and instituting measures that facilitate the retraining of affected workers. Indeed, policies aimed at addressing disruption arising from global value chain shifts are, in principle, no different from policies that seek to address disruption naturally arising in any economy that undergoes structural transformation as part of the economic growth process.

Upgrading global value chain capabilities

For policymakers in low- and middle-income economies, a key question is how they can support the upgrading of global value chain production capabilities by local firms. This question is sometimes phrased in terms of "moving up the value chain" or "capturing more value from global value chain participation." However, such value-oriented perspectives can be misleading. As pointed out in section 1.3, value added may not be the right metric to evaluate the profitability or rewards accruing to capital and labor from global value chain participation. In addition, the notion of "value capture" may suggest that global value chain participation is "zero sum", generating large profits for some participants – presumably lead firms – at the expense of others. However, while differences in bargaining power may well affect the vertical distribution of profits, global value chain income largely accrues to the capital and labor employed in global value chain production. The returns to capital and labor, in turn, depend on economies' endowment with these production factors and how productively they are employed.

Indeed, the question of how to upgrade global value chain capability is in principle no different from the more general question of how to spur industrial development. Thus, policy prescriptions that economists have formulated to promote industrial growth also apply to global value chain upgrading. These include, notably, building up institutions that promote technological learning and a growing absorptive capacity, as described in section 1.4. Nonetheless, the growth of global value chains raises some special considerations for both industrial and trade policy.

As to the former, industrial policy strategies have seen much evolution over the past decades – both in practice and in academic thinking.[47] Yet, if there is one evolving consensus, it is that governments have an important role to play in identifying pre-existing industrial capabilities – often at the level of sub-regions – and leveraging them by removing constraints on entrepreneurial activity and appropriately targeting complementary public investments.[48] Depending on the industry in question, it may be important to adopt a global value chain perspective when analyzing the opportunities and challenges faced by local entrepreneurs. Such a perspective may be relevant, for example, in identifying niche capabilities that could be further developed for new or upgraded global value chain participation, or in monitoring trends in end-consumer markets around the world that create opportunities for local firms.

At this analytical stage, it is also useful to ask what role different forms of IP can play in supporting opportunities for global value chain upgrading.

As for trade policy, opportunities for successful global value chain participation rely, of course, on open markets that allow companies to seamlessly import intermediate inputs and export processed goods. Equally important, they rely on deeper integration measures that facilitate the conduct of business along the supply chain. Such deeper integration measures include promoting the compatibility of regulatory measures, harmonizing product and technology standards and opening markets for business services supporting global value chain production. In the area of IP, for example, businesses face considerable costs in protecting their different IP rights across a large number of jurisdictions. Cooperation initiatives – such as the WIPO filing systems for patents, trademarks and industrial designs – help IP users lower these costs, while leaving the final decision on whether to grant an IP right to participating member states.

As a final note, successful global value chain upgrading in all likelihood does not entail a zero-sum game among national economies. While it may lead to the displacement of some global value chain participants – and can thus create disruption, as pointed out above – it is inherently a dynamic phenomenon. Technological change and new product cycles invariably prompt continuous reconfigurations of global value chains that create entry opportunities for some firms and may force the exit of others. In addition, successful global value chain upgrading generates economic growth that enlarges the market for global value chain outputs as a whole.

Notes

1. See Baldwin (2012).

2. See WIPO (2011, 2013, and 2015).

3. See, for example, Krugman (1995) for a more in-depth discussion of the two globalization waves.

4. Hummels et al. (2001) estimate the contribution of vertical specialization to the growth of international trade in selected countries.

5. See Yi (2003) for a formal exposition of this point.

6. See Baldwin (2012) for further discussion.

7. Constantinescu et al. (2016) document a decline in long-run trade-GDP elasticity.

8. See Baldwin (2012).

9. See WIPO (2011, 2013, and 2015) for further discussion of how competitive market forces incentivize investments in intangible assets and the growing role of branding.

10. Baldwin and Venables (2013) first introduced the distinction between snake- and spider-type supply chain configurations.

11. See Coase (1937) and Alchian and Demsetz (1972).

12. Baldwin and Venables (2013) show that the type of supply chain configuration – whether snake or spider – has complex implications for the balance between centrifugal forces favoring dispersed production and centripetal forces favoring the co-location of different production tasks.

13. Fort (2016) provides evidence of how improved ICTs have favored production fragmentation in the case of U.S. firms. Interestingly, the effect seems even stronger for domestic outsourcing than for foreign outsourcing.

14. Differences in wage costs are not the only reason for firms to source goods from foreign economies. The economic literature has long recognized that economies of scale and product differentiation are an important force behind specialization and trade, especially between high-income economies with comparable wage costs. See Helpman and Krugman (1985).

15. See Gereffi and Fernandez-Stark (2016) for a recent overview.

16. See Baldwin et al. (2014).

17. Krugman (1994) pointed this out long ago.

18. This approach follows Prescott and Visscher (1980) and Cummins (2005).

19. For estimates of intangible asset investments in selected economies, see Corrado et al. (2013).

20. In this respect, Chen et al. (2017) extend the earlier global value chain accounting exercise presented in Timmer et al. (2014).

21. Final output values of manufacturing goods were deflated using the U.S. Consumer Price Index.

22. See, in particular, Constantinescu et al. (2016) and Timmer et al. (2016).

23. The precise shares in 2014 were 27.0 percent for distribution, 26.6 percent for final production and 46.4 percent for other stages. The distribution share declined slightly from 2000. The share of final production fell by 4.2 percentage points whereas the share of other stages rose by 5.5 percentage points.

24. In fact, the intangibles share for petroleum products seems to correlate closely with the global oil price. See Chen et al. (2017).

25. See Chen et al. (2017) for an elaboration of these and additional caveats.

26. See chapter 2 in WIPO (2013) for further discussion on the special characteristics of reputational assets.

27. See Teece (1986) for an elaboration of the appropriation concept.

28. In balance-of-payment statistics, IP-related services appear as "charges for the use of intellectual property not included elsewhere" and "sale of proprietary rights arising from research and development," as further detailed in the *Manual on Statistics of International Trade in Services 2010* produced by the Interagency Taskforce on Statistics of International Trade in Services (2011).

29. See "Ireland's 'de-globalised' data calculate a smaller economy," *Financial Times*, July 18, 2017.

30. See chapter 1 in WIPO (2015) for further discussion.

31. In fact, knowledge management is at the heart of modern theories of the multinational enterprise. See Teece (2014) for a recent review of the literature.

32. See Maskus et al. (2005) for survey-based evidence to this effect.

33. See chapter 2 in WIPO (2011) and chapter 4 in this report for further discussion.

34. See Goodridge et al. (2016).

35. This share refers to 2015 patent filings, as reported in the WIPO IP Statistics Database: www3.wipo.int/ipstats.

36. For more comprehensive literature reviews, see Hoekman et al. (2005) and Arora (2009).

37. See WIPO (2011).

38. See chapter 1 in WIPO (2015) and Nelson and Pack (1999) for further discussion.

39. See chapter 1 in WIPO (2013) for further discussion.

40. See chapter 1 in WIPO (2015).

41. The International Monetary Fund's July 2017 update of its World Economic Outlook predicts trade growth of 4 percent and output growth of 3.5 percent.

42. Cosar and Demir (2017) find that containerization has prompted significant cost savings in maritime shipping, which in turn explains a significant amount of the global trade increase. However, most of the trade-increasing effect of containerization has already been realized.

43. Constantinescu et al. (2016) report a falling share of Chinese imports of parts and components in merchandise exports.

44. Samuelson (2004) shows in a theoretical model that a low-income economy upgrading production capabilities activities in which a high-income economy previously held a comparative advantage can, under certain circumstances, lower per capita income in the latter. However, world per capita income would always rise.

45. See Autor et al. (2013).

46. See Rosen (1981) for the seminal discussion on the economics of superstars. Haskel et al. (2012) offer a theoretical framework that explains how economic integration can boost the real earnings of superstars.

47. See Rodrik (2004).

48. See the approaches to industrial and innovation policy formulation advocated by Foray (2014) and Rodrik (2008).

References

Alchian, A.A. and H. Demsetz (1972). Production, information costs, and economic organization. *American Economic Review*, 62(5), 777-795.

Arora, A. (2009). Intellectual property rights and the international transfer of technology. In WIPO (ed.), *The Economics of Intellectual Property*. Geneva: WIPO, 41-64.

Autor, D.H., D. Dorn and G.H. Hanson (2013). The China syndrome: local labor market effects of import competition in the United States. *American Economic Review*, 103(6), 2121-2168.

Baldwin, R. (2012). Global Supply Chains: Why They Emerged, Why They Matter, and Where They Are Going. *CEPR Working Paper No. 9103*.

Baldwin, R. and A. Venables (2013). Spiders and snakes: offshoring and agglomeration in the global economy. *Journal of International Economics*, 90(2), 245-254.

Baldwin, R., T. Ito and H. Sato (2014). The Smile Curve: Evolving Sources of Value Added in Manufacturing. Mimeo available at: www.uniba.it/ricerca/dipartimenti/dse/e.g.i/egi2014-papers/ito.

Chen, W., R. Gouma, B. Los and M. Timmer (2017). Measuring the Income to Intangibles in Goods Production: A Global Value Chain Approach. *WIPO Economic Research Working Paper No. 36*. Geneva: WIPO.

Coase, R.H. (1937). The nature of the firm. *Economica*, 4(16), 386-405.

Constantinescu, C., A. Mattoo and M. Ruta (2016). The global trade slowdown: cyclical or structural? *Journal of Policy Modeling*, 38(4), 711–722.

Corrado, C., J. Haskel, C. Jona-Lasino and M. Iommi (2013). Innovation and intangible investment in Europe, Japan, and the United States. *Oxford Review of Economic Policy*, 29(2), 261-286.

Cosar, K. and B. Demir (2017). Shipping Inside the Box: Containerization and Trade. *CEPR Discussion Paper No. 11750*.

Cummins, J.G. (2005). A new approach to the valuation of intangible capital. In Corrado, C., J. Haltiwanger and D. Sichel (eds), *Measuring Capital in the New Economy*, NBER Book Series Studies in Income and Wealth, 47-72.

Foray, D. (2014). *Smart Specialisation: Opportunities and Challenges for Regional Innovation Policy*. London: Routledge.

Fort, T.C. (2016). Technology and Production Fragmentation: Domestic *versus* Foreign Sourcing. *NBER Working Paper 22550*.

Gereffi, G., J. Humphrey and T. Sturgeon (2005). The governance of global value chains. *Review of International Political Economy*, 12(1), 78-104.

Gereffi, G. and K. Fernandez-Stark (2016). *Global Value Chain Analysis: A Primer* (2nd edition). Durham, NC: Duke University Center on Globalization Governance & Competitiveness.

Goodridge, P., J. Haskel and G. Wallis (2016). UK Intangible Investment and Growth: New Measures of UK Investment in Knowledge Assets and Intellectual Property Rights. Research commissioned by the UK Intellectual Property Office.

Haskel, J., R.Z. Lawrence, E.E. Leamer and M.J. Slaughter. (2012). Globalization and U.S. wages: modifying classic theory to explain recent facts. *Journal of Economic Perspectives*, 26(2), 119-140.

Helpman, E. and P. Krugman (1985). *Market Structure and Foreign Trade*. Cambridge, MA: MIT Press.

Hoekman, B.M., K.E. Maskus and K. Saggi (2005). Transfer of technology to developing countries: unilateral and multilateral policy options. *World Development*, 33(10), 1587-1602.

Hummels, D., J. Ishii and K.-M. Yi (2001). The nature and growth of vertical specialization in world trade. *Journal of International Economics*, 54(1), 75-96.

Interagency Taskforce on Statistics of International Trade in Services (2011). *Manual on Statistics of International Trade in Services 2010 (MSITS 2010)*. Geneva, Luxembourg, Madrid, New York, Paris and Washington D.C.: United Nations/International Monetary Fund/Organisation for Economic Co-operation and Development/Statistical Office of the European Union/United Nations Conference on Trade and Development/World Tourism Organization/World Trade Organization.

Krugman, P. (1994). Competitiveness: a dangerous obsession. *Foreign Affairs*, 73(2), 28-44.

Krugman, P. (1995). Growing world trade: causes and consequences. *Brooking Papers on Economic Activity*, (1), 327-377.

Maskus, K.E., S.M. Dougherty and A. Mertha (2005). Intellectual property rights and economic development in China. In Fink, C. and K.E. Maskus (eds), *Intellectual Property and Development: Lessons from Recent Economic Research*. New York: Oxford University Press and World Bank, 295-331.

Nelson, R.R. and H. Pack (1999). The Asian miracle and modern growth theory. *The Economic Journal*, 109(457), 416-436.

Neubig, T.S. and S. Wunsch-Vincent (2017). A Missing Link in the Analysis of Global Value Chains: Cross-Border Flows of Intangible Assets, Taxation and Related Measurement Implications. *WIPO Economic Research Working Paper No. 37*. Geneva: WIPO.

Prescott, E.C. and M. Visscher (1980). Organization capital. *Journal of Political Economy*, 88, 446-461.

Rassier, D. (2017). Intangible Assets and Transactions within Multinational Enterprises: Implications for National Economic Accounts. *WIPO Economic Research Working Paper No. 38*. Geneva: WIPO.

Rodrik, D. (2004). Industrial Policy for the Twenty-First Century. *CEPR Discussion Paper No. 4767*.

Rodrik, D. (2008). Normalizing Industrial Policy. *Commission on Growth and Development, Working Paper No. 3*. Washington, DC: World Bank.

Rosen, S. (1981). The economics of superstars. *American Economic Review*, 71(5), 845-858.

Samuelson, P.A. (2004). Where Ricardo and Mill rebut and confirm arguments of mainstream economists supporting globalization. *Journal of Economic Perspectives*, 18(3), 135-146.

Seppälä, T., M. Kenny and J. Ali-Yrkkö (2014). Global supply chains and transfer pricing: insights from a case study. *Supply Chain Management*, 19(4), 445-454.

Teece, D.J. (1986). Profiting from technological innovation: implications for integration, collaboration, licensing and public policy. *Research Policy*, 15, 285-305.

Teece, D.J. (2014). A dynamic capabilities-based entrepreneurial theory of the multinational enterprise. *Journal of International Business Studies*, 45, 8-37.

Timmer, M., A.A. Erumban, B. Los, R. Stehrer and G.J. de Vries (2014). Slicing up global value chains. *Journal of Economic Perspectives*, 28(2), 99-118.

Timmer, M., B. Los, R. Stehrer and G.J. de Vries (2016). An Anatomy of the Global Trade Slowdown Based on the WIOD 2016 Release. *Groningen Growth and Development Centre Research Memorandum No. 162*, University of Groningen.

WIPO (2011). *World Intellectual Property Report 2011: The Changing Face of Innovation*. Geneva: World Intellectual Property Organization.

WIPO (2013). *World Intellectual Property Report 2013: Brands – Reputation and Image in the Global Marketplace*. Geneva: World Intellectual Property Organization.

WIPO (2015). *World Intellectual Property Report 2015: Breakthrough Innovation and Economic Growth*. Geneva: World Intellectual Property Organization.

Yi, K.-M. (2003). Can vertical specialization explain the growth of world trade? *Journal of Political Economy*, 111(1), 52-102.

Intangibles are key to seizing new opportunities in the coffee market

Farmers can boost their earnings by selling premium coffees. That means upgrading their farms and investing in branding.

Coffee sales prices
(in USD/lb)

Roaster sales price
$4.11

Roaster sales price
$8.50

Roaster sales price
$17.45

Conventional coffee

Coffee shops

Independent baristas

Export price
$1.45

Export price
$2.89

Export price
$5.14

Chapter 2
Coffee: how consumer choices are reshaping the global value chain

Coffee is one of the most widely consumed beverages in the world; nearly 35,000 cups are drunk every second on any given day.[1] In the United States – the biggest market in terms of size and value – three-quarters of the population drinks coffee.[2]

As a commodity, coffee is produced in the Global South but mainly consumed in the Global North. Around 70 percent of the demand for it comes from high-income countries. These countries tend to be located in the northern hemisphere and are referred to as the coffee-importing countries. The coffee-producing countries, on the other hand, lie in the southern hemisphere and fall within the low- to middle-income brackets.

Coffee is one of the most important traded agricultural commodities, especially for producing countries. It is the income source for nearly 26 million farmers in over 50 developing economies.[3] For seven countries in particular, coffee exports account for more than 10 percent of total export earnings over the past three decades.[4] While the importance of coffee exports for countries' incomes has been decreasing over time, upgrading their participation in the global coffee value chain can contribute to their economic development, especially in combating poverty.

The popularity of coffee is growing. More and more countries outside the traditional coffee-importing countries such as Japan and those in Europe are increasing their coffee consumption levels. The Food and Agriculture Organization (FAO) and the International Coffee Organization (ICO) separately estimate that the growth in consumption is faster in less developed economies.[5] In addition, new coffee products and services are attracting more consumers to drink coffee by varying how, what, when and where coffee products are consumed.

Studying the global value chain for coffee offers important insights into how poorer economies that rely on agricultural commodities may upgrade their value chain activities to benefit from international trade. Traditionally, the coffee global value chain has been dominated by market/buyer-driven governance, with most value generated by downstream participants. However, recent developments in a newer coffee market segment offer opportunities for upstream coffee producers to enhance their value chain participation.

One way for coffee participants to capture higher value added along the coffee global value chain is investing and owning intangible assets.

This chapter looks at the role of intangible assets in the coffee global value chain. It starts by describing how the chain has evolved over the decades, underlining the importance of coffee consumers in driving today's global value chain. Section 2.2 then focuses on the role of intangible assets in the global value chain, paying particular attention to how the distribution of value added is influenced by these assets. Section 2.3 takes a closer look at how intangible assets have been used in upgrading activities along the value chain, and discusses how technology flows between different participants in the chain.

2.1 – The changing nature of the coffee value chain

2.1.1 – From coffee cherries on a tree to the coffee in a mug – an international value chain

As for most traded commodities, the coffee supply chain resembles a snake. It begins with the farmer who chooses the coffee tree variety, and farms and harvests the coffee cherries. The mature coffee cherries then undergo different post-harvesting processes to yield green coffee. Depending on the market structures in place in the different coffee-producing countries, post-harvesting processes may take place at the farm site, in a cooperative, at a wet or dry mill owned by local traders, or even at a mill owned by exporters.

The exporters or cooperatives then select the green coffees by their density, size and color, and pack them according to specific definitions and standards set by coffee importers or industrial users such as roasters and soluble coffee producers.

Green coffees arriving in bulk in coffee-importing countries are stored in warehouses. The importers may mix and blend different green coffees from various countries in response to requests from buyers. They then sell these blends or the green coffee shipments to roasters or soluble coffee manufacturers.

The roasters or soluble coffee manufacturers may also blend the green coffee according to their needs. They then roast the green coffee using their own roasting recipes and protocols to obtain particular flavor profiles adapted to the regional taste preferences of their customers.

Box 2.1

Trading coffee is risky

Coffee prices are highly volatile because coffee yield is sensitive to weather conditions and outbreaks of disease.[6] This wide price fluctuation makes coffee transactions risky for both buyers and sellers. In order to mitigate this risk, the futures market is used as a reference for most green coffee transactions.

The buyers – importers, roasters and soluble coffee producers – enter into a standard commercial contract with the sellers – coffee farmers, exporters or importers – using price benchmarks set by the international exchange platforms in New York for Arabica coffee and London for Robusta coffee.[7] These prices are usually defined in the contract on a price-to-be-fixed basis, with a given quality of coffee specified, to be delivered at a specific delivery location within a specified time frame. An agreed differential is established and is later combined with the price of green coffee as fixed at different intervals by the buyer and seller at the stipulated futures delivery month.[8]

The absolute price received by the seller can be significantly different from the price paid by the buyers because final future prices are usually decided at separate times.

Certain key participants help to reduce the risk in coffee trading. In particular, importers and trading houses play an important role in facilitating coffee trade by taking on some of the transaction risk. For example, the buyer-seller contract will specify that acceptance of the coffee products on arrival is "subject to approval of sample." If the buyer rejects the coffee shipment because the product fails to meet the quality standard or a specific technical standard, the seller will need to take possession of the coffee at the destination.

Coffee farmers and/or exporters based in coffee-producing countries are usually unable to address or absorb this extra cost and additional risk. Instead, intermediaries will be in a better position to find a different buyer for the shipment, while also finding an alternative solution for the original buyer who has rejected it.

Source: ICO and World Bank (2015) and Samper et al. (2017).

Figure 2.1

How coffee flows across the global value chain

Overview of the coffee global value chain showing modifications for newer market segments

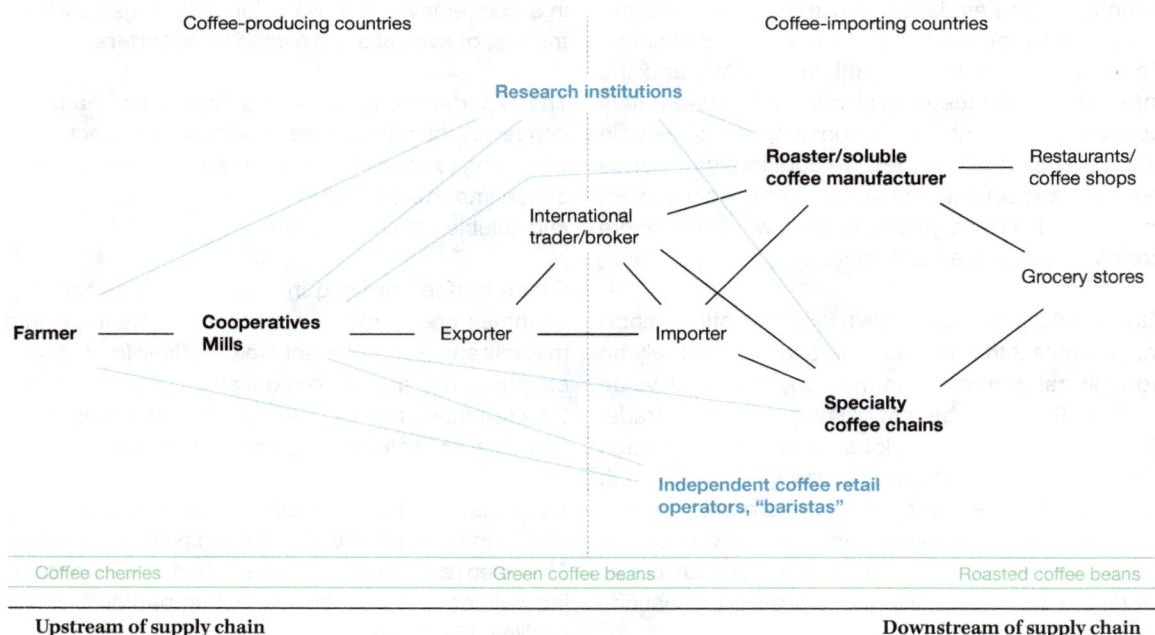

Source: WIPO based on Ponte (2002) and Samper et al. (2017).

Note: Black lines indicate traditional links between participants; blue lines indicate relatively new links influenced by the growing importance of the second and third wave market segments.

Figure 2.1 shows the coffee supply chain. It is international in two main respects. First, as noted above, most coffee is consumed in rich importing countries such as the United States, Germany, Japan, France and Italy. While coffee-producing countries have also increasingly consumed coffee in recent decades, their levels of consumption are still significantly below those of their richer counterparts.[9]

Second, the short shelf life of roasted coffee beans necessitates that most of the roasting is done close to where it is consumed. Packaging and distribution technologies were not adequate to preserve the quality and taste of roasted coffee beans until recently. This slow technological development made it difficult for roasters in coffee-producing countries to export their roasted coffees worldwide. Therefore, coffee-producing countries tend to export green coffee – as an intermediate good in the value chain – and blending and roasting tends to take place in importing countries.

2.1.2 – Putting consumers first – how new forms of demand are changing the global value chain

The coffee global value chain is traditionally characterized as being buyer-driven, with roasters, large retailers and branded merchandisers capturing most of the value. These downstream participants are also the ones who set the production and quality standards for the rest of the industry.

However, this market-based governance is slowly changing. Two new market segments of coffee consumption are shifting the perception of coffee consumption from coffee-as-a-product to a coffee-plus-social-content product and service. Drinking coffee has become more social, and coffee consumers have become more discerning.

These new market segments provide opportunities for different participants to upgrade their role along the chain.

Demand for coffee is segmented into three market categories: conventional, differentiated and experiential. These segments are also referred to as the first, second and third waves, respectively. They differ according to target consumers, product offerings and prices.

The first wave – a "conventional" market segment

The first wave market segment accounts for the largest share of coffee consumption in terms of both volume and market value. Samper et al. (2017) estimate that it constitutes 65 to 80 percent of total coffee consumption, and USD 90 billion or 45 percent of the total value of the global coffee market.[10]

The target consumers for this segment mainly drink their coffee at home. Consumption is typified by daily need-for-energy coffee drinking and reasonably priced products which consumers can purchase easily at any large retail chain or small grocery store.

The products – in the form of packaged roasted coffee beans, soluble coffee and, more recently, single-serving capsules – are standardized, but there may be significant differences with regard to taste to reflect regional preferences. The differences between competing products can be reduced to the quality of the coffee blend in relation to its price.

Until a few decades ago, the quality of most coffee beans used in these products ranged from low to mediocre, but that emphasis on lower-grade coffee beans is shifting as large roasters such as JAB and Nestlé have introduced new products to cater to more sophisticated consumers. These products include single-serving capsules from single-sourced origins or blends of higher-grade coffee beans.

Governance of the coffee global value chain in this market segment is market driven. The coffee buyers – importers, roasters and soluble coffee manufacturers – purchase their green coffee based on cost considerations. If prices of Arabica beans are higher than those of Robusta beans, buyers may decide to purchase more Robusta beans and process them to attain specific standards. In addition, the origin of the green coffee has not been a significant selling factor in this segment. Importers, roasters and soluble coffee manufacturers will source coffee beans from many different places as long as their quality standard is met.

Participants in the coffee value chain take on risks when trading green coffee on the open market. Coffee prices tend to fluctuate significantly over time, and so contracts in the futures market are used (see box 2.1).

The second wave – a "differentiated" market segment

The second wave market segment targets consumers who prefer to consume coffee in a social setting. In this segment, consumers are able to appreciate a wide range of espresso-based beverages in a comfortable and convenient location.

Coffee products in the second wave range from the typical Italian espresso to more elaborate concoctions of coffee plus foamed milk. These beverages are prepared according to specific standard techniques by experienced servers, or baristas. In addition, importance is attached to the social element of consuming coffee; most coffee shops in this market segment offer a distinct ambiance to attract their customers.

The quality of the coffee beans used tends to be higher than those in the first wave. Over the last couple of decades, specialty coffee shops have been appealing to ethically aware consumers by offering drinks made from sustainably farmed beans whose farmers have been appropriately rewarded.

As with the first wave, governance of the global value chain for the second wave is market-based. However, the increased consumer interest in where the coffee beans are sourced, how they are farmed and whether the farmers receive fair wages offers differentiation opportunities to participants, enabling them to upgrade their activities along the value chain. Voluntary sustainability standards (VSSs) contribute to the image of specialty coffee shops, reinforcing the impression of social responsibility and perceived value, and distinguishing coffee in the second wave from first wave brands.

The third wave – an "experiential" market segment

The third wave market segment targets consumers with discerning coffee tastes, and is priced accordingly. Consumers in this market are willing to pay premium prices for their coffee. In exchange, they want to know where their coffee beans are sourced, how they have been farmed and how best to brew the beans in order to fully appreciate the flavor, body, aroma, fragrance and mouthfeel of the coffee.

The coffee products in this segment include the story behind the farming of the coffee beans as well as their roasting recipes and beverage preparation techniques. The emphasis is akin to the wine industry's flavor profile, which valorizes the *terroir*, grape variety and craftsmanship involved in producing a wine.

The quality of the coffee beans tends to be superior to the other two market segments. Producers in this market focus on premium-grade coffee portfolios, with different blending and roasting techniques tailored to the beans. Baristas have deep product knowledge of the coffee beans, and may even have played a role in cultivating the coffee plants.

Governance of the third wave global value chain is known to be relational. The emphasis on direct connection to the coffee farmers has led to a shortened value chain (compare the traditional chains in black with the newer chains in blue in figure 2.1). In this segment, cooperation between farmers and baristas has often led to product innovation, including new ways of preparing coffee beverages.

In comparison to the first two waves, consumption in this segment is still low relative to the market as a whole, but it is growing fast.

2.2 – Intangible assets and value added

Ownership of intangible assets plays an important role in the coffee global value chain and helps explain how income is distributed along the coffee global value chain.

Formal intangible assets such as technology, designs and brands are important in helping participants in the chain appropriate returns to their innovation investments. These intangible assets are usually protected by formal intellectual property (IP) rights such as patents, utility models, industrial designs, trademarks, copyrights and trade secrets.

Informal intangible assets are also crucial in helping participants gain a higher share of income. For example, the baristas' craftsmanship and know-how in blending and roasting particular coffee beans account for significant value added in the third wave market segment.

Moreover, access to distribution channels in coffee-importing countries is crucial in ensuring that coffee products are seen by potential consumers.

Table 2.1

The three coffee market segments

	First wave – conventional	Second wave – differentiated	Third wave – experiential
Target consumers	Daily consumption, mostly consumed at home but could be elsewhere	Wide coffee beverage selection, usually consumed in a social setting	Socially aware coffee consumers – aficionados, who are willing to pay a premium for high-quality coffees which meet ethical standards
Consumer needs	• Energy	• Energy • Social experience • Ethical awareness and/or social consciousness	• Energy • Social experience • Ethical awareness and/or social consciousness
Products and services	• Packaged roasted coffee blend • Soluble (or instant) coffee • Single-serving pods	• Espresso beverages such as caffè latte, latte macchiato and the like • Know-how regarding different brewing techniques for the coffee beverages – usually standardized • Some knowledge of the origin of the coffee beans as well as farming methods • Ambiance of the coffee shop	• Single-origin coffee beans • Blending and roasting usually done in-house • Extensive know-how regarding different brewing techniques to enhance the flavor and aroma of each coffee • Deep knowledge of the origin of coffee beans and farming methods • Ambiance of the coffee shop
Production types	• Standardized mass production • Standardized quality	• Different types of espresso-based coffee • Relatively standardized coffee-brewing techniques and service • Caters to the social experience of drinking coffee, similar to a coffee house	• Tailored coffee origin-roast-technique service • Baristas tend to have vast knowledge of the coffee beans as well as the proper technique for brewing and preparing the beverage
Distribution channels	• Grocery stores • Food service outlets	• Grocery stores • Online • Specialty coffee chains	• Independent coffee retail operations • Online
Price point	Low	Mid to high	High to very high
Global value chain governance	Mostly market-driven	Mostly market-driven	Mostly relational

Source: WIPO based on Humphrey (2006), Garcia-Cardona (2016) and Samper et al. (2017).

2.2.1 – Drinking versus growing coffee: an uneven income distribution

A significant share of the value added to coffee along its production chain is added close to where the coffee is consumed. Five factors account for this pattern.

First, roasted coffee beans lose their flavor and aroma quickly, so most beans are exported as green beans in order to preserve their quality.

Coffee is also exported as soluble coffee. However, soluble coffee production is capital-intensive, which may pose a barrier to entry in some coffee-producing countries. And while these countries are increasingly exporting coffee in soluble form, the unit value they get is less than that of coffee-importing countries.[11]

One reason for this discrepancy in trade value is likely due to branding capabilities and access to distribution channels.[12]

Second, different continents and regions show distinctive preferences for the types of coffee beans used – blends of Arabica and Robusta coffee beans, or single origin – and even the degree of coffee bean roast. For example, Northern European countries prefer their coffee blends to consist of lighter roasted Arabica beans, while their Southern counterparts prefer darker roasts of coffee blends that include Robusta beans.[13] Roasters and soluble coffee manufacturers located close to consumers tend to be better placed than their competitors in coffee-producing countries to tailor the blend and roast to regional preferences.

In addition to tailoring blends and roasting degrees to specific regional preferences, large roasters locate their roasting facilities so as to benefit from economies of scale. For example, a roasting facility in Germany may roast and blend coffee for several European brands, reducing its costs and increasing its production levels.

Third, industrial policies implemented in coffee-importing countries tend to favor the importation of unprocessed, mainly green, coffee beans over roasted and processed (soluble) coffee. This trade restriction in the form of tariff escalation inflates the cost of any roasted or even processed coffee exported by coffee-producing countries.

However, it is worth noting that for many coffee-importing countries – particularly the more developed economies – tariffs on coffee have been steadily reduced through various bilateral, regional and multilateral trade agreements. And today, while tariff escalation remains an issue, tariffs on roast and processed coffee tend to be low in the European Union and the United States; by contrast, India and Ghana have duties on soluble coffee of 35 and 20 percent respectively.[14]

Moreover, a study conducted by ICO (2011) shows that this tariff escalation is likely to have a higher impact on coffee consumers residing in less developed countries than their developed counterparts. In particular, consumers in developed countries will continue to purchase coffee even when the price of coffee beverage increases. This implies that coffee consumers in these countries will continue to consume their favorite imported coffee even if there is an increase in tariff-equivalent tax imposed on those imports.

There are also regulatory measures affecting the import of roasted and processed coffee from coffee-producing countries, such as sanitary and phytosanitary measures, which are not trade restrictions per se but may entail higher compliance costs for firms in coffee-producing countries.

Fourth, most product and process innovations related to processing coffee were developed in coffee-importing countries. Many apparatuses were invented and introduced on both sides of the Atlantic Ocean to maximize the taste and flavor of coffee by roasting, grinding and even percolating the coffee beans.[15]

Soluble coffee manufacturing, which involves more processing than coffee roasting, was arguably invented during the U.S. Civil War so that soldiers could easily drink caffeinated beverages.[16] However, Nestlé, with its patented technology for producing powdered soluble milk, was able to improve on the taste of soluble coffee, and so dominate the soluble coffee market.[17]

Ownership of coffee-related patented technologies has been useful in helping launch new coffee products and services. The patents and industrial designs owned by Nespresso on its coffee machines and capsules helped cement Nestlé's strong presence in catering to coffee consumers in the first wave market segment. Most of these patents have now expired, but both Nestlé and Nespresso continue to be strong brand names in the coffee market.

And lastly, branding is an important investment to build consumers' trust and gain market share in the relatively saturated coffee market. Research has shown that branded products can command higher prices than their generic counterparts.[18] Many roasters and soluble coffee producers and retailers invest heavily in this intangible asset, to differentiate themselves from their competitors and gain goodwill. Both Nescafé and Starbucks are well-recognized trademarked names, popular with coffee consumers worldwide.

Coffee-producing countries are slowly adopting IP protection to capitalize on their intangible assets. While many of the latest advances in coffee-related patentable technologies still take place in coffee-importing countries (see part 2.2.3 below), some coffee-producing countries are also developing their own coffee-processing capacities. Brazil, for example, has been producing roasted and soluble coffee to rival roasters and soluble manufacturers in more developed economies.

These countries are also pursuing branding more actively as a way to differentiate their coffees from others. For example, a few countries have been investing in protecting their coffee beans through geographical indications (GIs) and trademarks. Coffee beans originating from Jamaica (Blue Mountain) and Colombia (Milds) have fetched premium prices.[19]

However, ownership of these formal intangible assets is not enough to achieve the same level of access to consumers in more developed economies. The buyer-driven nature of the value chain, in addition to the difficulty of accessing distribution channels in the importing countries, makes it challenging for upstream coffee producers to compete in the downstream coffee market. But this rigid governance structure is slowly changing with the rise of the third wave market segment.

2.2.2 – How coffee participants' income varies according to the activity performed

Participants' income is distributed according to the activity they perform in the coffee value chain. As mentioned in chapter 1, this value added by different activities is a function of the capital and labor costs at the different steps of the chain. In particular, intangible capital plays a crucial role in explaining the value added along the chain.

The consumption traits characterized by the three coffee market segments affect the contribution of each participant. In some cases, the emphasis of the market segment creates new opportunities for participants, giving them a way to increase the value added of their activity. For example, their role as intermediaries between coffee farmers and buyers means importers and exporters can play an additional role as agents promoting the supply and certification of VSS coffees in the second wave.

In the third wave, by contrast, the direct link between farmers and independent coffee retailers eliminates the need for intermediaries and shortens the supply chain.

Participation in the different market segments also affects participants' ability to upgrade their activities and gain higher remuneration, especially those in the second and third waves. Table 2.2 provides a simplified overview of participants' roles and the related intangible assets. It relates back to figure 2.1 in showing how roles and links between participants have changed in the newer market segments. For example, direct trade between the farmers and independent retailers (in blue in figure 2.1), emphasizes the new intangible assets that farmers are now able to use to their advantage (marked with an asterisk in table 2.2).

Intense competition in the first wave

As noted above, the first wave market segment accounts for the largest share of the world's coffee consumption in terms of both volume and value. The sheer volume of coffee products sold in this market segment gives the downstream value chain participants – roasters, soluble coffee producers and retailers – significant power over the other participants in the supply chain. Cost-saving measures obtained along the chain are usually absorbed by these producers.

This market segment is a prime example of a buyer-driven global value chain.

However, competition between coffee producers in this market segment is high. This has led to significant consolidation of brands in the last few decades. Seven companies account for nearly 40 percent of coffee sold by retail grocers. They include international brands such as Jacobs Kronung (Germany), Maxwell House (United States), and Nescafé (Switzerland). These brands compete side-by-side with grocery store private brands for market share.

Due to the intense competition, the main consideration for downstream participants is to keep costs low while maintaining standards that consumers have come to know. Any slight change in price may induce consumers to switch to a different brand.

Figure 2.2 illustrates the distribution of income between coffee-importing and coffee-exporting countries in the grocery retail market for the period 1965-2013.[20] Since 1986, roasters and soluble coffee manufacturers in coffee-importing countries (in light blue in the figure) have gained a higher share of the total income in the market than participants in coffee-producing countries (in dark blue). In addition, the figure shows how coffee-producing countries' income moves in tandem with global coffee prices, as captured by the ICO composite price index. There has been a particularly close link between the two since 1989, when the International Coffee Agreement (ICA) quota restriction was abandoned (see box 2.2).

Table 2.2

Coffee participants, their value added activities and their intangible assets

Participant	Main value added activities	Main actors	Risks	Intangible assets	Geographical location
Farmers	• Grow and harvest coffee crops. • Many are connected to cooperatives or farmers associations. Coffee cherries are processed (in wet or dry processes) at the farm or by the next participant in the chain.	• Farmers and/or coffee growers; most of the farmers grow their coffee crop on less than five hectares of land.	• Crops and harvest are affected by changes in climate. • The high volatility of coffee prices and domestic exchange rates are a threat to farmers' incomes.	• Farming methods (whether traditional or not).* • Trademarks and/or geographical indications.*	• In over 50 less developed countries.
Cooperatives, Mills	• Cooperatives build on economies of scale to reduce the cost of cleaning, sorting and/or grading green coffee. • May sometimes export or roast the coffee. Most sell to exporters according to exporters' needs. • Mills treat cherries and /or perform hulling (removing remaining fruit from beans). They operate like cooperatives in some areas.	• Cooperatives are usually located in other regions and do not directly compete with one another.	• Price volatility, credit risks and inability to control hulling or dry-milling operations.	• Some cooperatives are owned by or supported by the state. • The link between cooperatives and farmers helps in disseminating new farming methods or even new coffee varieties to plant.*	• In coffee-producing countries.
Coffee exporters and importers	• Coffee beans from farmers, cooperatives, etc. are purchased and prepared for exportation. • Some coffee exporters also perform post-harvesting processes such as cleaning. • Coffee beans are mechanically grouped by their density, size and color to comply with definitions and standards set by clients. Milling may be outsourced. • Importers store the green coffee and may blend it. • Provide logistical arrangements to handle large inventories and deliver product to roasters in timely manner. • As of more recently, they also perform traceability and certification services due to their connection to both upstream and downstream coffee actors.	• Many coffee exporters are connected to international importers or trading houses. • Three firms arguably control 50 percent of the world's coffee imports: Volcafe and ECOM of Switzerland, and Neumann Coffee Gruppe of Germany. • Large coffee farmers and cooperatives may also be coffee exporters.	• Highly leveraged business with exposure to price and exchange rate fluctuations.	• Trade secrets. • Strong network/link to both upstream and downstream coffee supply chain providers. • Know-how regarding blending, grading and some processing. • Patents. • Can attest to farming methods and support eco-labelling or any other types of certifications as demanded by their clients.*	• Exporters have procurement agencies located close to the farms in coffee-producing countries. • Importers tend to be located in coffee-consuming countries.
Roasters and soluble manufacturers	• Process green coffee beans based on regional preferences as well as to standard specifications using both proprietary technologies and firm-specific know-how. • Distribute roasted and soluble coffee to various coffee retail outlets, depending on the standard specification of that market segment. • Invest in packaging and branding to differentiate products from those of competitors.	• Nestlé, JAB-Jacobs Douwe Egberts, Strauss, J.M. Smucker Co. Folgers Coffee, Luigi Lavazza SpA, Tchibo GmbH and Kraft Heinz Co. represent nearly 40 percent of the major roasting companies in the retail grocery market. • Nescafe (owned by Nestlé of Switzerland) and DEK and Dr. Otto Suwelak of Germany are the top soluble coffee manufacturers.	• Requires significant capital investment and reliance on economies of scale for soluble coffee manufacturers.	• Patents. • Trademarks. • Industrial designs. • Trade secrets. • Know-how in blending and roasting for market preferences.	• Usually located in proximity to the consuming market. • Soluble manufacturers may be located elsewhere than the consuming market, thanks to the longer shelf life of soluble coffee products.

Source: WIPO based on Samper et al. (2017).

Note: *denotes new intangible assets due to opportunities in the newer market segments.

Figure 2.2

Coffee-importing countries take most of the income from retail sales

Share of total income from grocery retail coffee going to exporting countries, importers and importing countries, 1965-2013

Income and value distribution of coffee sales (USD/lb)

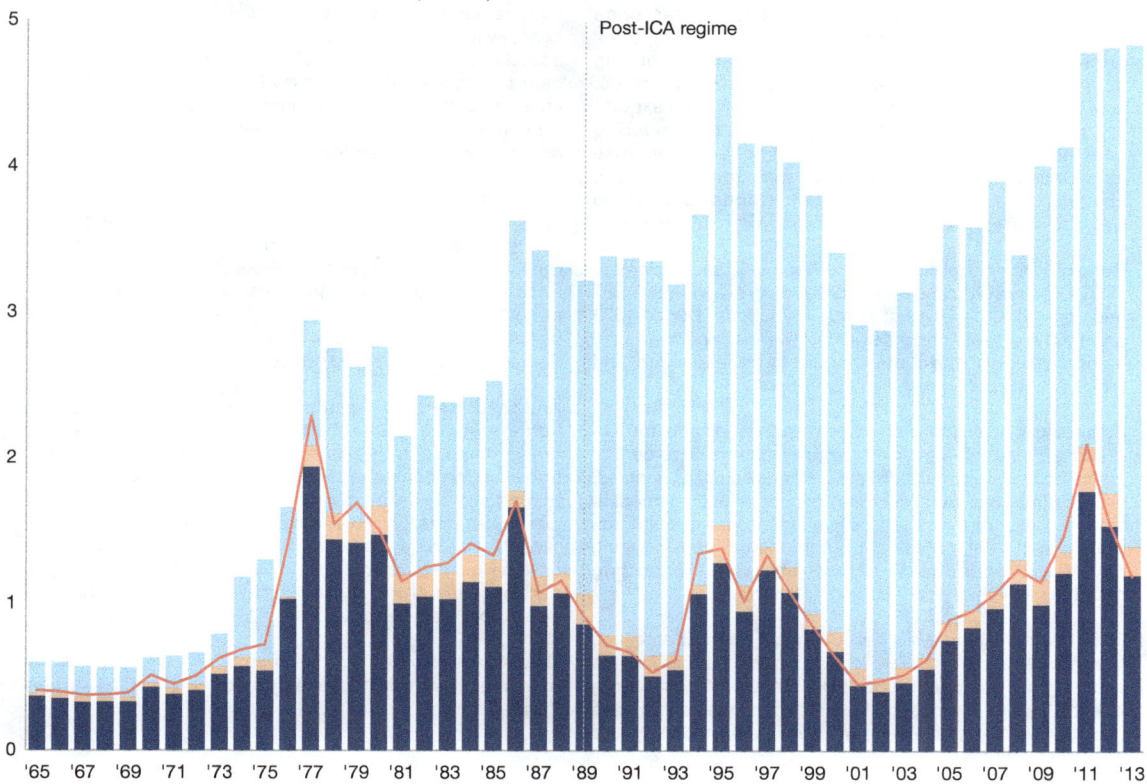

Post-ICA regime

VALUE ADDED AT IMPORTING COUNTRIES   INCOME AT PRODUCING COUNTRIES
IMPORTER INCOME AND WEIGHT LOSS   ICO INDICATOR PRICE

Source: Samper et al. (2017) based on data collected from the FAO and ICO.

Note: Retail prices of grocery sales attributed to coffee-importing countries are based on USD per pound of roasted coffee, while incomes in coffee-producing countries and import prices are USD per pound of green coffee free-on-board (FOB). The weight loss refers to the hulling, drying, export preparation and roasting of green coffee. The ICO indicator price is a benchmark price for green coffee of all major origins and types. The ICA quota regime was generally in force from 1962 to 1989, but was temporarily abandoned because of high coffee prices during the period 1975-1977.

The high degree of competition in the first wave market segment implies that the profit margin upstream – from farmers to exporters in coffee-producing countries, and in certain cases to importers in coffee-importing countries – will tend to be small.[21]

Daviron and Ponte (2005) argue that the roasting, blending, grinding and vacuum packaging processes along the coffee value chain are relatively low-tech and make up a small share of downstream participants' margins. Rather, it is the investments they make to differentiate their coffee products, particularly through branding, that generate a significant share of the high value added in coffee-importing countries.[22]

Box 2.2

The ICA quota restriction and its impact on income distribution

The global coffee trade was heavily regulated by an International Coffee Agreement (ICA) between 1962 and 1989, albeit not consistently.[23]

The aim of the agreement was to reduce coffee price fluctuations and stabilize prices, especially when coffee prices were low. Parties to the agreement, comprising both coffee-producing and coffee-consuming countries, agreed to a target band price for coffee and limited exports of coffee by assigning export quotas to different producing countries. Quotas were relaxed when coffee prices rose above the target band, and tightened when they fell below it. They were abandoned completely when coffee prices rose well above the band, as was the case from 1975 to 1977.

Coffee prices were relatively high between 1963 and September 1972, October 1980 and February 1986, and November 1987 and July 1989, because of quota restrictions. During 1973 and 1980 there was no agreement between the parties to the agreement and so the quota restriction was suspended, and after 1989 the agreement was abandoned.

According to an estimate of income distribution under the ICA quota regime by Talbot (1997), approximately 20 percent of coffee income was retained in the coffee-producing countries, while coffee-importing countries accounted for 55 percent of income.[24] In contrast, when the ICA regime was abandoned, the share of total income attributable to coffee-producing countries dropped to 13 percent and coffee-importing countries saw their share surge to 78 percent.

Talbot cautions that while the ICA quota restriction regime may have been responsible for the higher share of income accruing to the coffee-producing countries, price fluctuations due to changes in global coffee production yields may have had an effect on the income split between producing and importing countries.

A rise in international coffee prices would shift a greater share of income to coffee-producing countries, while a fall would raise the share going to importing countries.

More recent estimates of the income distribution generally concur with the assessment that coffee-importing countries account for a higher share of the income from coffee than before.[25] Two factors explain the lower share of income accruing to coffee-producing countries – a real-terms decline in international coffee prices and an increase in non-coffee related costs in the coffee industry.

There were many problems in maintaining production restrictions under the quota regime. First, coffee-importing countries had to agree to higher prices than they would have received without the regime. Second, efficient producers in coffee-producing countries had to restrict their sales of coffee beans even when prices were high, and so lose potential revenue, in order to comply with the regulation. Some countries destroyed coffee beans in high-yield years.[26]

And third, the quota restriction gave incorrect signals to farmers with regard to their yield and planting decisions. Since the price they received was disconnected from real green coffee consumption needs, they were encouraged to produce more than real market demand, causing further downward pressure on international coffee prices. A more recent study on the effects of the ICA quota restriction on coffee yield argues that coffee harvests are lower today in part because of the lower coffee price in place after the agreement was dissolved.[27]

Despite these problems, the restriction generally met its objective of stabilizing prices for coffee producers when it was in force.

The importance of certification in the second wave

The second wave market segment began in the 1990s when the price of coffee fell sharply after the end of the ICA quota restriction.[28] Soon thereafter, non-governmental organizations (NGOs) started highlighting the impact of the low coffee prices on farmers, calling for action to help alleviate this problem. In response, coffee specialty shops such as Starbucks started offering coffees that met the expectations of their more socially conscious consumers. Sustainably farmed, organic coffees and products that promised higher prices for farmers started appearing in these shops along with their traditional outlets in health-food stores.

Most specialty shops do not have direct access to coffee farmers and so have to rely on intermediaries to ensure that the coffee beans they purchase meet their chosen criteria. Exporters in coffee-producing countries, with relationships with both coffee farmers on the one hand and the importers or roasters in coffee-importing countries on the other, are well placed to arrange for the supply of certified beans that comply with given farming methods and other sustainability criteria. Some NGOs also help provide certifications such as Fair Trade or Rainforest Alliance certifications.[29]

The higher prices for these certified or labelled coffee products – with their emphasis on more value flowing to participants upstream in the value chain – are reflected in a different income level for farmers than in the first wave (see table 2.3). A host of other benefits clearly associated with VSSs have also been observed, ranging from improved resource and environmental conservation to better labor practices.[30]

However, researchers differ on whether farmers receive significantly higher incomes. Some argue that farmers participating in this market segment receive higher prices than those in the first wave; others are less convinced.[31]

The skeptics argue that the cost of implementing a VSS and complying with certification standards may offset the higher gross income received, or that price premiums are declining.[32]

Knowing the origin of your third wave coffee

The third wave market segment places high importance on appreciating the coffee beverage. Information about upstream activities – such as the origin of the coffee beans, how they were farmed and the climate conditions – is seen as almost as important as the downstream coffee activities of roasting, blending and brewing.

Table 2.3

Coffee farmers receive higher incomes in the newer market segments

		First wave		Second wave		Third wave	
		USD/lb (453g)	Index	USD/lb (453g)	Index	USD/lb (453g)	Index
Coffee farmer to exporter	Producer/farm gate	1.25 (a)	86	na		4.11	80
	Exporter	na		na		0.45 (d)	
	Dry milling	na		na		0.4	
	Packaging	na		na		0.11	
	Cooperative services	na		na		0.07	
Importer	Green FOB	1.45 (b)	100	2.89	100	5.14	100
	Logistic costs and importer margin			0.24			
	Green coffee at warehouse	na		3.13	108.3	6.58	128
Roaster	Weight loss and delivery to roaster	na		3.91		na	
	Packaging and direct labor	na		0.84		na	
	Other wages	na		1.00		na	
	Other fixed costs	na		2.00		na	
	Fair Trade USA fee for maintaining certification	na		0.04		na	
	Traveling to origin	na				0.35	
	Gross margin	na		0.71		na	
	Total roaster sale price	4.11 (c)	283	8.50	294	17.45	340

Source: ICO (2014), SCAA (2014) and Wendelboe (2015).

Notes: (a) Simple average from all ICO countries that submitted data; (b) average exdock indicator minus 10 cents for ex-dock FOB conversion; (c) simple average from all ICO countries that submitted data on retail prices minus 30 percent to cover channel markup, (d) producer–exporter breakdown based on 2012 figures. Index FOB = 100. Data for the market segments are based on 2014 prices.

This market segment arguably has the highest potential to increase participants' income along the global value chain. First, there is direct trade between coffee farmers and independent retailers. This vertical integration shortens the supply chain and ensures that farmers earn higher wages for their green coffee. The average price differential between coffees that identify the grower and those that do not can reach USD 8 per pound.[33] Moreover, one study focusing on the U.S. market estimates that single-origin coffee protected using IP instruments fetches at least three times the average U.S. retail price for roasted coffee.[34]

Table 2.3 illustrates the different incomes that coffee farmers receive in the different market segments. The farm-gate price per pound of coffee that a farmer supplying the second or third wave market segments receives is higher than in the first wave. In particular, the average third wave farmer's income per pound is triple that in the first wave. While this jump in income is impressive, it reflects the differentiation strategies employed upstream in the supply chain. In the second wave, differentiation is achieved through participation in a VSS, while third wave farmers look to differentiate both by emphasizing the quality of coffee bean and through direct trade with roasters in coffee-importing countries.

The closer relationship between upstream and downstream supply chain participants means there is more interaction between them. Roasters are able to learn more about how coffee is farmed and may help farmers improve their farming methods as well as their marketing, while the farmers are able to supply the high-quality coffee that roasters need.

In this context, both upstream and downstream coffee participants increase the value they derive from their activities – the coffee farmers by upgrading their farming in line with roasters' needs, the roasters by using the enhanced knowledge they gain about the farmed coffee to help them produce very high-quality beverages.

Figure 2.3 presents the income distribution in the market segments in a more graphic way. Whereas figure 2.2 above showed the historical trend of income distribution for the first wave market segment, figure 2.3 is a snapshot of the three different waves based on prices in 2014.

Figure 2.3

Coffee farmers gain better remuneration from third-wave coffee

Share of total income from coffee going to participants in producing and importing countries by market segment, 2014

Distribution of income by market segments (USD/lb)

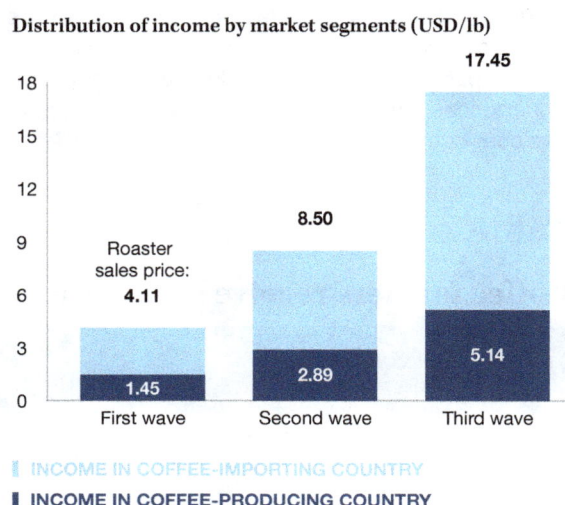

INCOME IN COFFEE-IMPORTING COUNTRY
INCOME IN COFFEE-PRODUCING COUNTRY

Source: ICO (2014), SCAA (2014) and Wendelboe (2015).

Note: See notes on table 2.3.

2.2.3 – Ownership of intangible assets can help participants capture value

The distribution of income along the coffee value chain can in part be explained by the ownership of intangible assets. As seen in the previous subsection, investments in innovation and branding are likely factors in explaining the high value added toward the tail end of the chain.

One way to measure innovative activities is examining the ownership of patents, utility models and industrial designs for coffee-related inventions, while branding activities can be measured through registered and unregistered trademarks and GIs, where applicable.[35]

Most coffee-related IP is owned by participants in coffee-importing countries

As mentioned in part 2.2.1, coffee-importing countries tend to own most of the related formal intangible assets. Figure 2.4 compares the use of IP by the top five producing countries, on the one hand, and the top five importing countries plus China on the other.[36]

Not surprisingly, the figures show that participants in importing countries account for large numbers of the IP rights related to coffee.

The United States, Switzerland and Italy are the top three countries of origin of participants filing for patents related to coffee. For trademarks filed at the United States Patent and Trademark Office (USPTO), European countries – specifically, Italy, Germany and the United Kingdom – are the top three filers, other than U.S. nationals.[37]

China, however, is a stark exception to the general picture in figure 2.4. IP filings related to coffee from China-based applicants rival those from the top five coffee-importing countries. Prior to 1995, the number of coffee-related patents from applicants in China was in the same low range as those for many coffee-producing countries such as Brazil, Colombia and Mexico. But since 1995, China has ranked among the important markets where patent protection is sought, along with traditional coffee-importing countries such as the United States and several European countries (see box 2.3).

Figure 2.4

Participants in importing countries own most of the IP related to coffee

Totals of different IP rights owned by participants based in the top coffee-importing countries versus equivalent rights owned in coffee-importing countries and China, 1995-2015

Coffee-importing countries

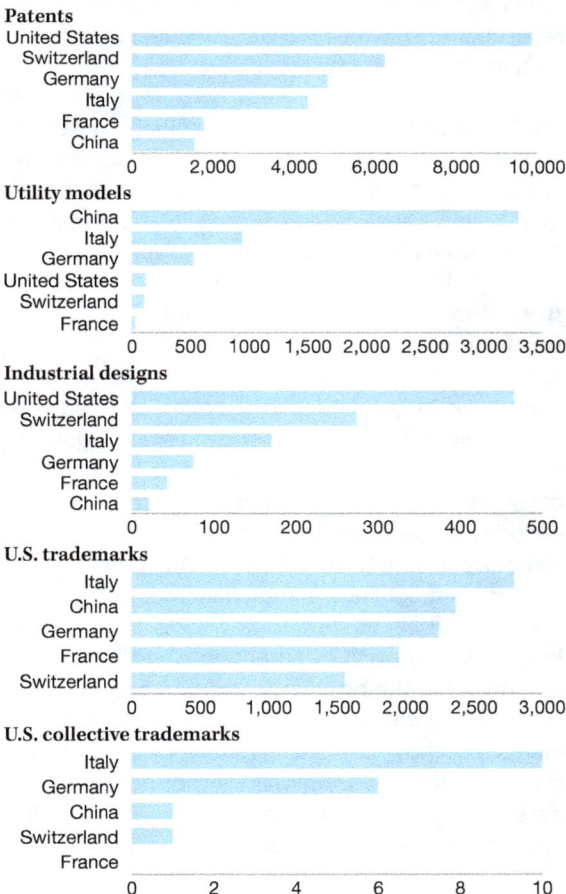

Coffee-producing countries

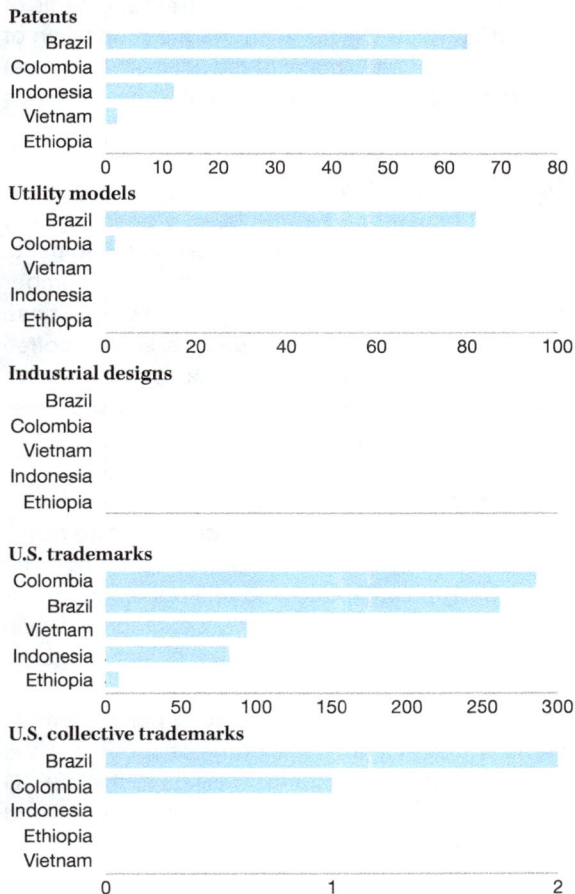

Source: WIPO based on PATSTAT and USPTO; see technical notes.

Note: Data on patents, industrial designs and utility models come from the PATSTAT database, while data on trademarks come from the USPTO (see note 36).

Box 2.3

China – huge growth potential both in production and as a market

China is one of the newer coffee-producing countries, producing Mild Arabica coffee in the Yunnan province.[38] China's production of coffee has doubled every five years over the past two decades. It is a market with high growth potential for coffee consumption; its consumption pattern is similar to the evolution of demand for coffee in Japan 50 years ago.[39]

China's IP activities seem to coincide with its increase in coffee production. It has seen a leap in both patent and trademark filing activities over the past decade, rivalling the higher-income coffee-importing countries.

Since 1995, applicants in China have filed nearly the same number of coffee-related patents as those in France, and more than those in the United Kingdom.[40] In addition, nearly 3,300 coffee-related technologies are protected through utility models.[41] However, most Chinese patent filings are made in China only and do not have a foreign orientation is in contrast to those from France, Italy and the United Kingdom.

But China filed nearly 2,400 trademarks at the USPTO in relation to coffee-related goods and services, ahead of Germany's filing of approximately 2,200. This suggests that Chinese companies have a significant presence in the U.S. coffee market.

IP ownership mirrors the distribution of income along the value chain

Figure 2.5 compares the distribution of patenting activities and firms across the different segments of the coffee value chain.[42] It shows the proportion of participants at each stage of the chain (in light blue) and their share of total coffee-related patent filings (in dark blue).

Over 90 percent of all coffee-related patenting activities are concentrated in the bean processing and final distribution segments.[43] These two segments account for nearly two-thirds of the total number of firms in the coffee industry worldwide. These participants typically include roasters, soluble coffee manufacturers and retailers that also do their own roasting such as specialty coffee shops and independent coffee retailers.

In contrast, the activities that usually take place in coffee-producing countries such as coffee farming, harvesting and post-harvesting do not see much patenting. The farming and harvesting/post-harvesting segments together account for less than 2 percent of overall coffee-related patent filings.

Branding activity is growing among participants at the final distribution stage of the chain. Figure 2.6 plots the number of trademark filings at the USPTO by U.S. coffee retail brands in the first, second and third waves.

While trademark filings relating to coffee-related goods and services have generally been on the rise since 1980, the number of applications filed by second and third wave participants nearly tripled between 2000 and 2016. Filings from independent retail operators in the third wave account for a significant share of this growth.

This increasing reliance on trademark filings reflects the importance placed on branding activities for the coffee industry in general, but particularly for the second and third waves. These market segments started gaining traction from 2000 and 2010, respectively.

Branding activities are increasing, unlike patenting

Trademark filings in relation to coffee-related goods and services have risen over the years. Figure 2.7 shows that the ratio of coffee trademark filings to all other trademark categories has increased in recent decades. Notable jumps in coffee-related trademark filings occurred in 1991, 2000 and 2010, coinciding with the birth and uptake of the second and third waves.[44]

In contrast, growth in patenting of coffee-related technologies during this period has been uneven. While the number of coffee-related patents has increased, they have declined as a proportion of all patents since 2005. Annual filing of coffee-related patents peaked that same year, with more than 1,500 applications filed worldwide.

Figure 2.5

More than half of all coffee-related patents relate to final distribution

Percentage share of firms in the coffee industry and share of coffee-related patent applications by value chain segment

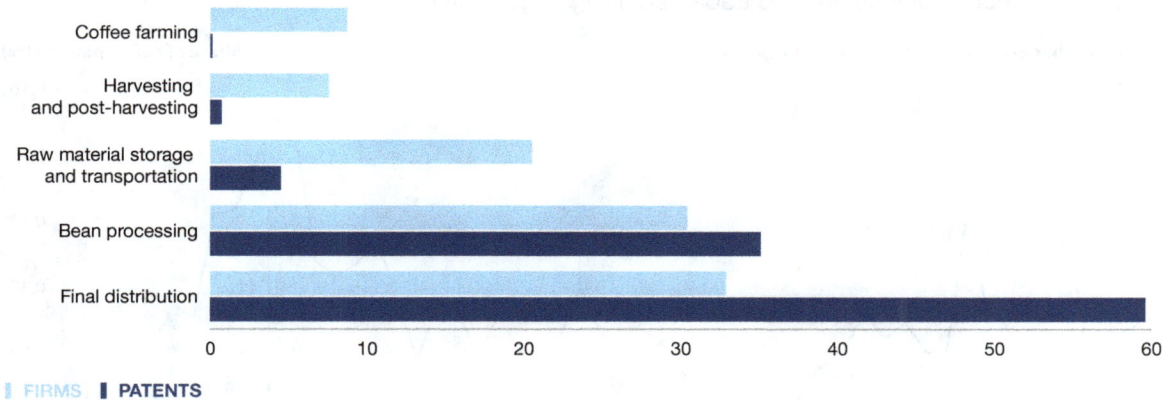

FIRMS   PATENTS

Source: WIPO based on PATSTAT and Ukers (2017); see technical notes. The classification of value chain segments is based on Samper et al. (2017).

Note: The bars in light blue represent the share of all firms in the coffee industry operating in each particular segment of the value chain. The dark blue bars indicate the share of coffee-related patents attributable to each chain segment. The share of coffee participants for the coffee-farming segment is likely an underestimate as the list of coffee participants retrieved from the Ukers directory only includes registered firms.

Figure 2.6

Trademark filings are rising, particularly for the second and third waves

Total coffee-related trademark filings at the USPTO by market segment, 1980-2016

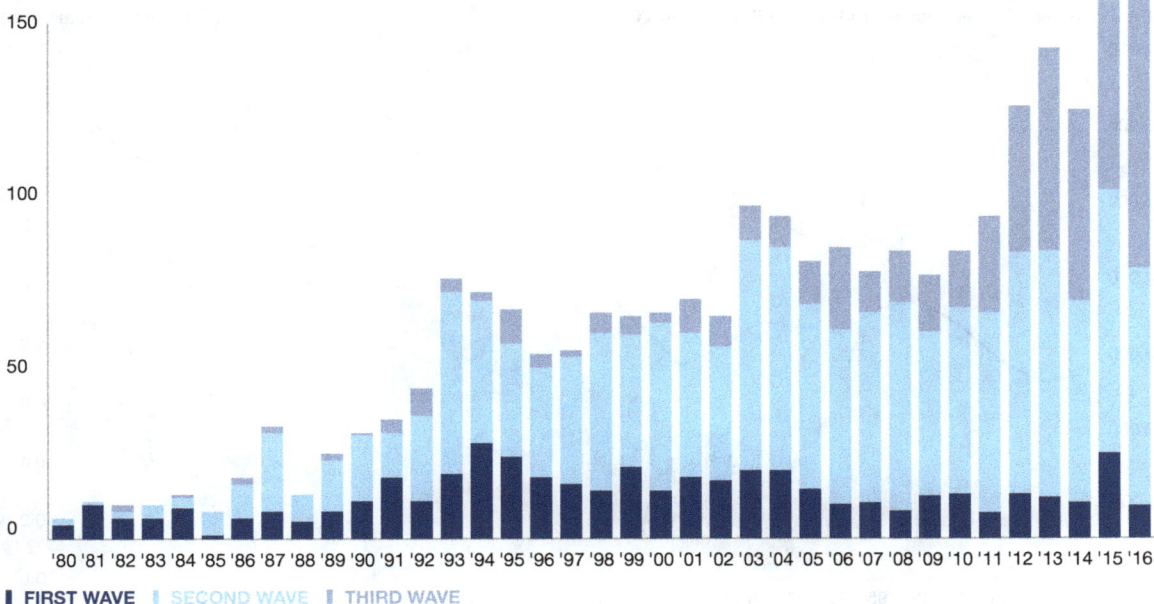

FIRST WAVE   SECOND WAVE   THIRD WAVE

Source: WIPO based on the USPTO and PQC; see technical notes.

Notes: U.S. coffee brands have been classified by Premium Quality Consulting (PQC) according to the three different coffee market segments. PQC's list was used to identify trademark filings at the USPTO for each market segment or wave.

Figure 2.7

Coffee participants are increasingly using branding as a means of differentiation

Annual coffee-related patent and trademark filings (left axis) and percentage share of coffee patents and trademarks in total patent and trademark filings (right axis)

Total number of coffee-related patent filings

Share of coffee patents (%)

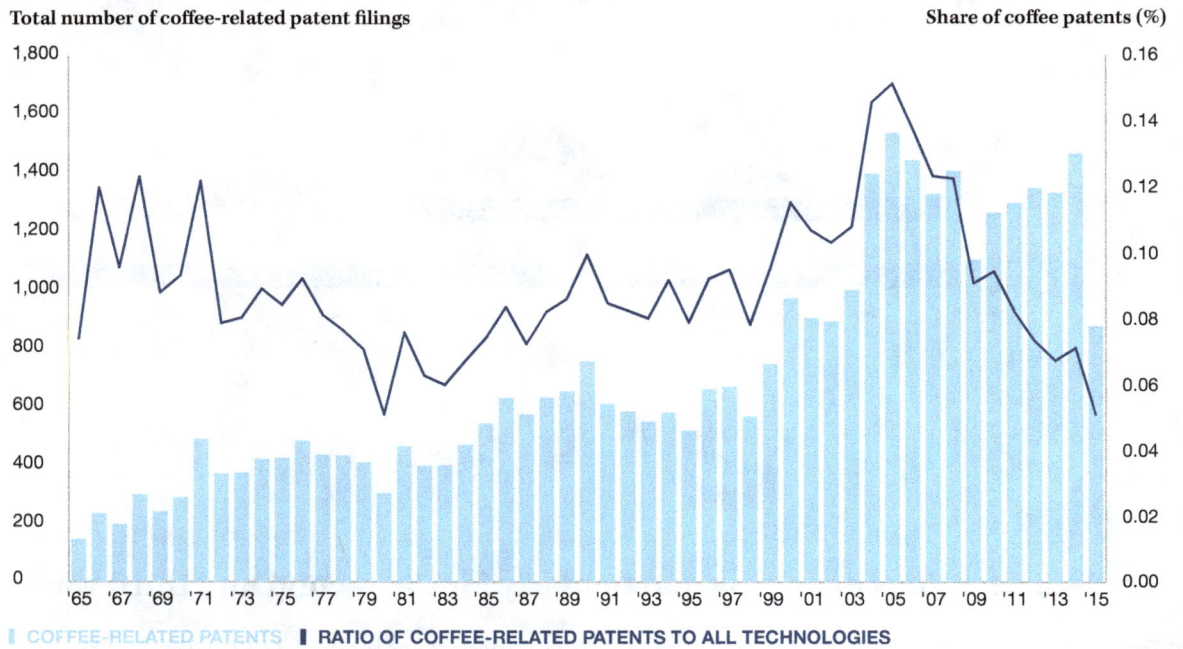

COFFEE-RELATED PATENTS ■ RATIO OF COFFEE-RELATED PATENTS TO ALL TECHNOLOGIES

Total number of coffee-related trademark filings at USPTO

Share of coffee trademarks (%)

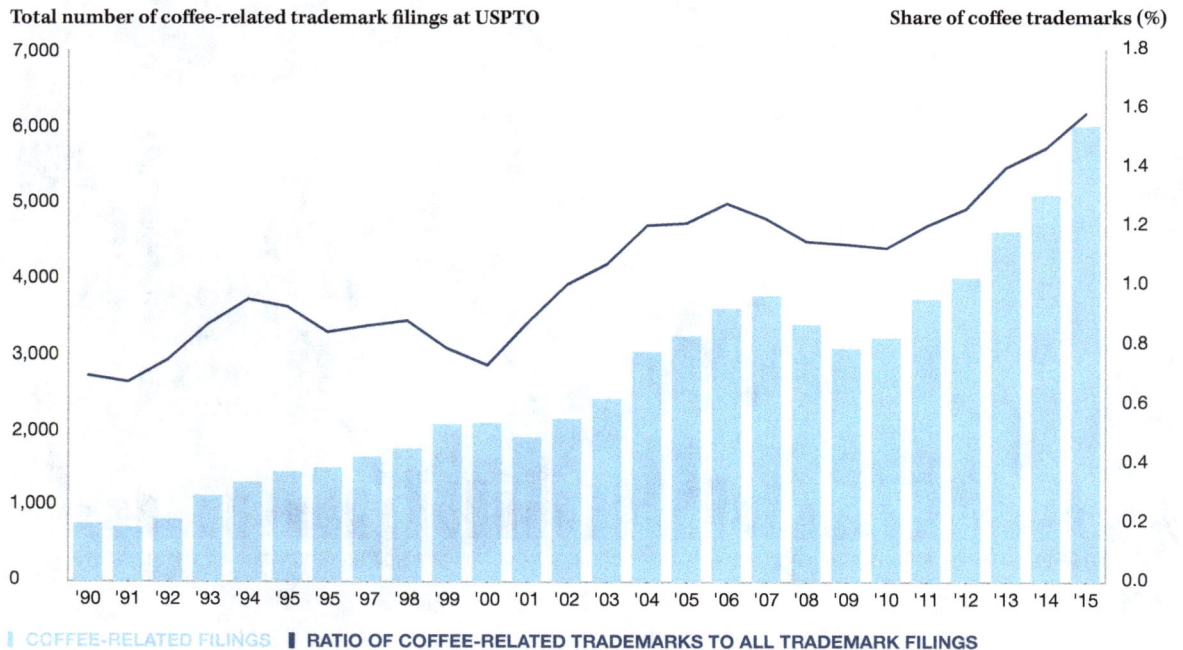

COFFEE-RELATED FILINGS ■ RATIO OF COFFEE-RELATED TRADEMARKS TO ALL TRADEMARK FILINGS

Source: WIPO based on PATSTAT and the USPTO; see technical notes.

2.3 – Managing intangible assets in the coffee value chain

Participants in the global value chain for coffee protect and manage their intangible assets in four main ways: (i) protecting their patentable technologies where competitors are located, (ii) using differentiation strategies and especially branding to separate themselves from their rivals, (iii) building more direct connections to coffee farmers, and (iv) securing coffee yield by addressing climate change and coffee disease issues.

2.3.1 – Protecting coffee in important markets

As noted above, most of the formal intangible assets in the coffee global value chain are owned by participants in the more developed, coffee-importing economies. These participants protect their intangible capital in countries where they face competitors, usually other more developed coffee-importing economies.

Figure 2.8 shows where patented technologies were protected worldwide in the periods 1976-1995 (top) and 1996-2015 (bottom).

Figure 2.8

The important markets for coffee-related patents

Percentage share of total worldwide coffee-related patent families for which applicants sought protection in a given country in 1976-1995 (top) and 1996-2015 (bottom)

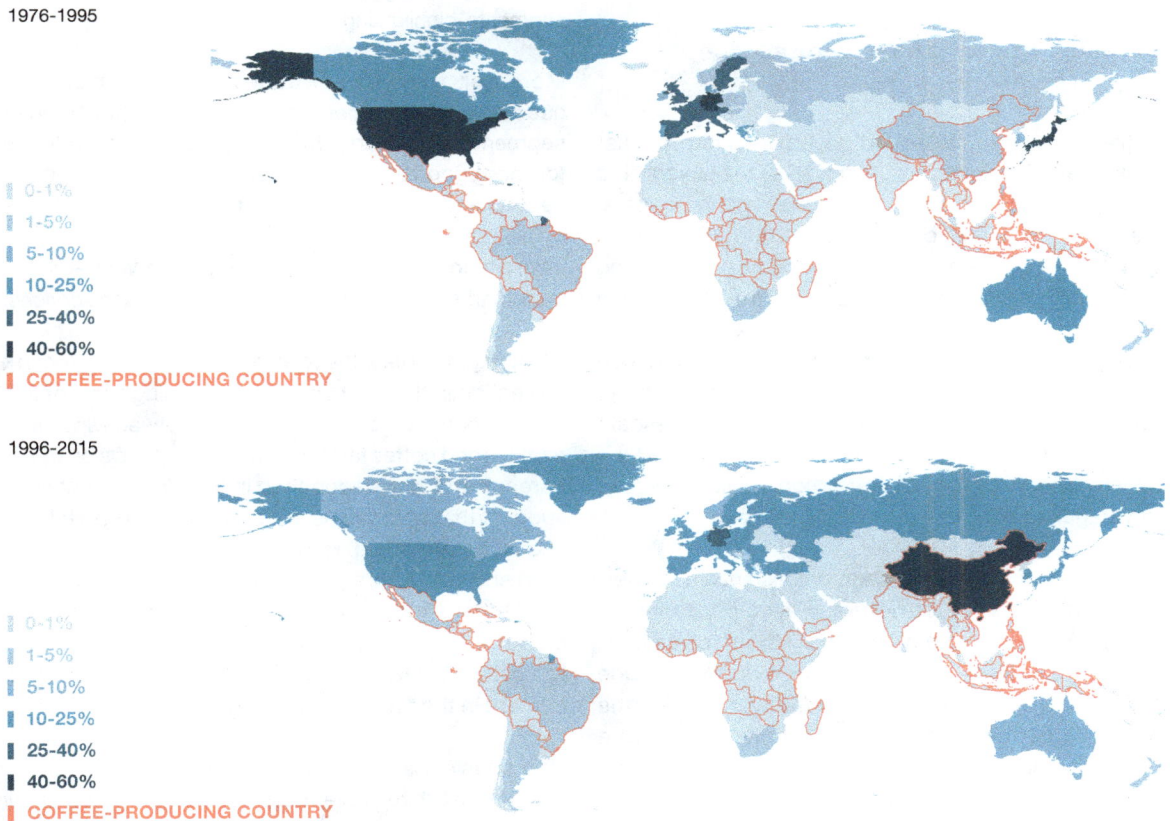

1976-1995

- 0-1%
- 1-5%
- 5-10%
- 10-25%
- 25-40%
- 40-60%
- COFFEE-PRODUCING COUNTRY

1996-2015

- 0-1%
- 1-5%
- 5-10%
- 10-25%
- 25-40%
- 40-60%
- COFFEE-PRODUCING COUNTRY

Source: WIPO based on PATSTAT; see technical notes.

Notes: Patent families included in the figure have at least one patent document granted by an IP office.
The countries outlined in red are ICO member countries identified as coffee-producing countries plus China.

Two points stand out. First, coffee-related technologies are protected mainly in more developed economies; that was true in 1995 and remains true today. Brazil, China and Mexico are the only coffee-producing countries where patent protection is being sought for coffee-related inventions. Second, however, IP offices in sizable markets like China and Russia now receive a higher share of coffee-related patent filings than they did in the period before 1996, likely reflecting the growth of coffee consumption in those countries.

But the rise in patenting activity in China is unique. Most filings at the State Intellectual Property Office of the People's Republic of China (SIPO) are filed only in China and nowhere else, while patents filed in other countries tend to be protected in more than one jurisdiction.

2.3.2 – Using branding as a differentiation strategy

Branding strategies differ across the three market segments

In the first wave, market-led governance implies that most intangible assets are controlled by the buyers, that is, coffee roasters and soluble coffee manufacturers. Here, long-term relationships with distributors, investments in introducing newer technologies and branding activities continue to ensure buyers' market share in a competitive marketplace. A prime example of the importance of branding is Nestlé and its introduction of at-home, single-portion espresso coffee machines and capsules through Nespresso and the Nescafé Dolce Gusto brands. These machines introduced the novelty of consuming single-portion quality espresso beverages at home.

The second wave market segment also has a market-based governance structure. Participants invest heavily in branding to differentiate themselves from their competitors. Starbucks, for example, is one of the biggest coffee brands in the world.[45] But the specialty coffee shops in the second wave have a different business model from the first wave which connects them directly to their consumers. These coffee shops pay close attention to consumption trends and often position themselves to cater to specific lifestyle images.

The second wave's emphasis on certification and labelling is being adopted by first wave roasters and soluble coffee manufacturers. More and more coffee packaging now includes third-party certification labels to indicate how the beans were farmed and reassure consumers that the farmers were adequately remunerated.

Figure 2.9 plots the number of trademarks filed in the U.S. by retail coffee brands in the first, second and third waves. Almost all of the retail coffee brands in the first wave have a trademark filed. While the second and third waves have more filings than the first wave in total, there is less likelihood that a brand in these two market segments will have trademark protection than a first wave brand. Only 12 percent of brands in the first wave have no trademark, while nearly 30 percent and 45 percent respectively of second and third wave brands are not protected through trademark registration.

In other words, participants in the first wave are more likely to use trademarks than those in the newer market segments, highlighting the value of the underlying brands.

Moreover, the types of trademark application vary according to the target consumers in the three market segments. Retail brands in the first wave tend to file for more goods-related trademarks than those in the second and third waves, reflecting the former's focus on at-home consumption. The two newer markets have a higher share of applications for services-related trademarks, reflecting their focus on in-person services.

What might explain the relatively low use of trademark protection in the third wave? The defining traits of this market segment – close connections between specialist retailers and coffee farmers, greater emphasis on transparency and knowledge than in the older segments – suggest that branding is crucial intangible capital that should be protected. However, the data on trademark filing show that barely half of third wave retailers have applied for a trademark. The share of third wave retail brands with no trademark is 45 percent in comparison to nearly 30 percent in the second wave and just 12 percent in the first wave.

One possible explanation for this apparent anomaly is that most third wave retail brands tend to be small niche brands that may not need to rely on trademark protection for brand recognition. By contrast, first and second wave brands are more likely to be bigger and target the global coffee market, so may need to rely on more formal IP protection.

Figure 2.9

Newer market segments file for more trademarks in the United States

Count of retail coffee brands and their related trademark filings by coffee market segment (left);
distribution of different trademark filing types by coffee market segment (right)

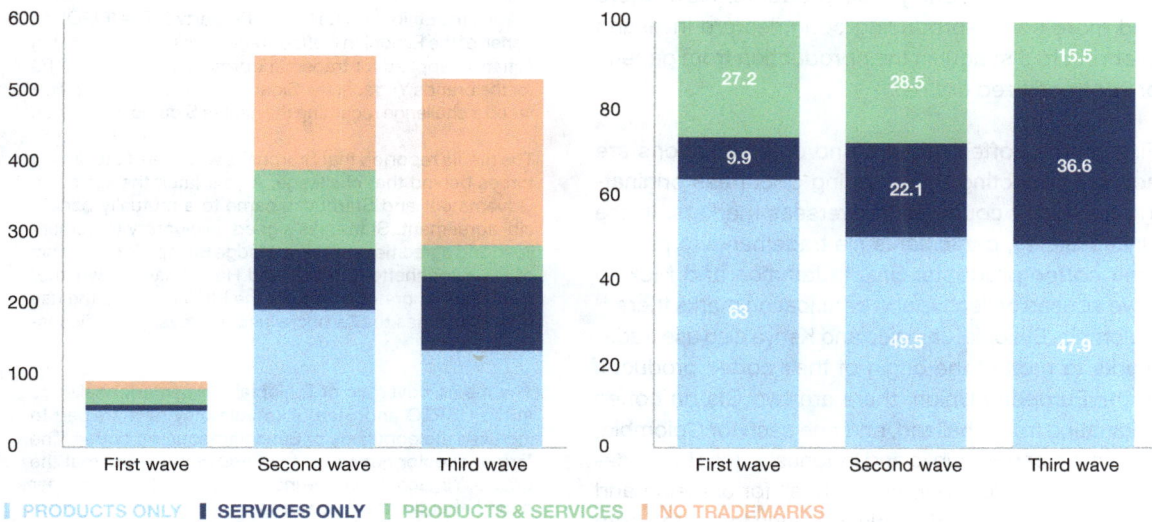

| PRODUCTS ONLY | SERVICES ONLY | PRODUCTS & SERVICES | NO TRADEMARKS

Source: WIPO based on PATSTAT and PQC; see technical notes.

While the third wave remains small in terms of traded volume, it has already had an impact on how business is being conducted in the other two market segments.

2.3.3 – The third wave gives coffee growers opportunities to upgrade

The third wave, with its relational governance, has influenced how intangible assets are managed in the coffee industry. Its shortened value chain, which allows for direct trade with farmers, has opened up new opportunities for participants to upgrade, particularly farmers and buyers in the form of independent coffee shop retailers.

First, information on the origin and variety of coffee beans, how they were farmed and processed, and if the farmers are adequately compensated has become an integral part of selling coffee. This information and knowledge translates into higher prices for coffee, which can be reinvested to upgrade coffee farms.

Second, sourcing high-quality coffee beans is increasingly important for many buyers. Direct trade is one way buyers can ensure they are purchasing high-quality coffee.

In addition, buyers learn more about the coffee and may then be able to communicate its history to their customers. For coffee farmers, direct communication with buyers can sometimes lead to sharing of technology and know-how, helping to upgrade farms and processing.

A case in point is the Italian roaster Illycafé and its relationship with Brazilian coffee farmers since the late 1980s. For Illycafé, partnering directly with coffee growers ensured that it had a relatively stable supply of Brazilian coffee beans that met its high-quality specification. For the farmers, the partnership helped them to upgrade their coffee-growing and post-harvest methods and processing facilities, and included substantial formal training systems.

Third, the origin of the coffee bean has become an important aspect of coffee, and features on the packaging of coffee products. Single-sourced beans are now being offered by roasters, soluble coffee manufacturers and specialty coffee shops in both the first and second wave market segments. This emphasis on the origin of the coffee provides an opportunity for coffee farmers to differentiate themselves from suppliers in other coffee-producing countries.

More coffee-producing countries are adopting differentiation strategies

The second and third wave market segments show that participants in coffee-producing countries may be able to obtain a higher income from the value chain by differentiating their products. Now, more and more coffee-producing countries are investing in efforts to distinguish their production from generic or commoditized coffee.

First, some coffee farmers and/or associations are actively protecting the branding of coffees originating from their countries in overseas markets. In the United States, participants file trademarks to protect their coffee products. Brazil, Jamaica and Mexico have all used collective and certification marks there.[46] Colombia, Ethiopia, Jamaica and Kenya also use trademarks to protect the origin of their coffee products. In the European Union, there are two GIs on coffee originating from Thailand, and one each for Colombia, the Dominican Republic and Indonesia, four EU trademarks related to the word "coffee" for Jamaica and Ethiopia, and five trademarks on logos for coffee from Colombia and Jamaica.

Governments such as those of Colombia and Ethiopia have supported initiatives to secure IP rights like GIs and trademarks to ensure that their countries' products stand out. In Colombia, the Colombian Coffee Growers Federation (FNC) implemented a differentiation strategy that involved actively protecting coffees originating from its regions, compliance with certain VSSs and demonstrating that its coffee beans were suitable for espresso-based beverages. The FNC's efforts include supporting the 100% Colombian Coffee Program, which allows certain coffee blends in the first wave as well as other market segments to be labelled with the 100% Colombian logo.[47]

In Ethiopia, the Ethiopian Coffee Trademarking and Licensing Initiative, a public-private partnership consortium, has been actively branding coffees originating from its regions in an effort to promote them.[48] It has applied for trademark rights in Australia, Brazil, Canada, China, the European Union, South Africa and the United States, to name a few. The consortium has also hired a U.K.-based company to help market its coffees worldwide. Its initiatives have helped to increase the popularity of Ethiopian coffee (see box 2.4).

Box 2.4

How the Ethiopian trademark filing challenge at the USPTO raised its coffees' popularity

In 2005 the Ethiopian Intellectual Property Office (EIPO), on behalf of the Ethiopian Coffee Trademarking and Licensing Initiative, applied for trademark protection at the USPTO for the brands Yirgacheffe, Sidamo and Harrar. However, it faced a challenge regarding the names Sidamo and Harrar.

The media reported that Starbucks was one of the driving forces behind that challenge. A year later, the Ethiopian Government and Starbucks came to a mutually beneficial agreement. Starbucks signed a voluntary trademark licensing agreement to acknowledge Ethiopia's ownership of the Yirgacheffe, Sidamo and Harrar names, whether trademarked or not. In return, the EIPO licensed the use of those names to Starbucks under a royalty-free licensing scheme.

The media coverage of Ethiopia's trademark challenge at the USPTO and Starbucks' role may have helped to increase the popularity of Ethiopian-sourced coffee. The former director general of the EIPO commented that the price of Yirgacheffe coffee increased by USD 60 cents per pound after the media coverage.

Source: WIPO, "Ethiopia and the Starbucks Story", IP Advantage: www.wipo.int/ipadvantage/en/details.jsp?id=2621.

Second, countries like Colombia and Brazil have entered the downstream coffee supply chain by roasting and selling products to markets overseas. Colombia has also entered the coffee retail business by opening specialty shops akin to Starbucks in different parts of the world. These shops carry the Juan Valdez brand and only serve Colombian coffee. By 2016, there were 371 Juan Valdez coffee shops in operation, 120 of them located outside the country. The Juan Valdez brand had accumulated USD 37 million in royalties for the Colombian coffee association by the end of that year.

Third, more and more coffee farmers are liaising directly with coffee buyers by participating in coffee community networks.

Building reputation by mobilizing the coffee community

The coffee community includes a network of baristas and roasters organized into guilds and associations. These guilds and associations hold contests and meetings whereby participants learn from one another and showcase their craftsmanship to gain recognition for their work.

One contest that benefits coffee farmers and buyers is the Cup of Excellence (COE). The COE recognizes coffee farmers for their investments in producing high-quality coffee. It provides an opportunity for the farmers to promote their coffees in an international setting. Coffees that rank among the top 10 of the COE are auctioned off and often receive premium prices. Their farmers and farms gain recognition and usually enter into long-term relationships with coffee buyers.[49] This form of branding confers substantial value on successful competitors.

An independent assessment of the COE programs in Brazil and Honduras put the value generated for these countries at USD 137 million and USD 25 million, respectively. These gains in value were estimated to come from direct auction sales, an upsurge in direct trade and increased access to specialty coffee markets. Successful COE participants saw their profit margins increase by two to nine times those of their conventional counterparts.[50]

The coffee community adheres to standards to simplify the trade between buyers and farmers. Codified quality concepts and measurements such as the cupping and grading standards of the Specialty Coffee Association (SCA) facilitate this trade. These standards motivate coffee farmers to produce higher-quality coffee while also assuring baristas and roasters of the quality of the coffee they purchase. The more coffee participants that recognize a standard, the easier it becomes for transactions to take place directly between coffee suppliers and buyers in the global marketplace.

However, climate change issues and coffee diseases are threatening the production of coffee beans worldwide.

2.3.4 – Creating new coffee varieties through public-private partnerships

Coffee production faces several challenges, including climate change, coffee diseases and pests, labor shortages and land pressures.

These challenges are particularly acute for the production of high-quality Arabica coffee. First, there is little diversity in the Arabica coffee plant species, making it highly susceptible to diseases and climate change.[51] Second, rising temperatures due to climate change are likely to reduce suitable coffee-farming areas.[52]

More resilient coffee plant varieties are needed to ensure the supply of coffee worldwide. Research institutions in certain African coffee-producing countries such as Côte d'Ivoire, Ethiopia, Kenya, the United Republic of Tanzania and Uganda and Latin American countries such as Brazil, Colombia, Costa Rica and Honduras have been able to develop new coffee varieties for their regions.[53] There are also efforts by NGOs to help develop stronger coffee varieties. One notable example is World Coffee Research, which has been working closely with coffee-producing countries to share coffee varieties worldwide in an effort to develop hardier varieties. More recently, private coffee value chain participants such as Starbucks, Nestlé and Ecom Agroindustrial Corporation have been engaging with local research institutes too.

Most of the research outputs in this area are publicly available. Two reasons may explain why. First, research institutions and governments may request that work remain public. Second, plant varieties are specific to a region and its climate, so a coffee variety that has proven successful in one area may not easily be transferred to and used in a different region. In many cases, research institutions in different coffee-producing countries have to develop varieties specific to their environments, multiplying the effort and investment needed.

An initiative by World Coffee Research attempts to save effort and investment in identifying strong coffee plant varieties by sharing these varieties across countries within particular world regions. By closely collaborating with governments and coffee growers, this NGO is helping transfer technology from its research group to farmers.

Another possible way to facilitate this technology transfer is through relying on plant breeders' rights (PBRs). A few countries have relied on the system under the International Union for the Protection of New Varieties of Plants (UPOV) to protect the coffee plant varieties developed. The UPOV system aims to provide incentives to plant breeders to develop new plant varieties and encourage their dissemination.[54]

The first application for PBRs under the UPOV system was in Brazil in 2004.[55] Currently, there are 46 PBRs filed on the coffee plant varieties of Arabica and Canephora, as disclosed to UPOV.[56] These 46 PBRs originated from Brazil (19), Colombia (19), Costa Rica (1) and Kenya (7) and most of them are filed by public research organizations and coffee associations.

2.4 – Conclusion

As with many commodities produced in the Global South and consumed in the Global North, the distribution of income along the coffee value chain is uneven. Roasters, brand holders and retailers downstream in the coffee-importing countries capture the lion's share of the total value of the market.

Intangible assets play an important role in the coffee global value chain. As seen in chapter 1, intangible capital accounts for 31 percent of total income in the food, beverages and tobacco product group. This chapter has shown how the income from coffee is currently distributed along the chain, and how ownership of intangible assets helps explain this allocation.

The first wave market segment dominates due to its consumption volume and market value. Competition in this market is intense and, more importantly, based on keeping the production cost low. Decisions regarding the origin of the coffee and whether Arabica or Robusta beans are used to cater to this market segment are based on price. Until recently, the origin of the coffee has been of minor importance; rather, downstream coffee participants – large roasters, soluble coffee manufacturers and large coffee retailers – rely on branding to differentiate themselves from their rivals. These participants capture a significant share of the total market income, reflecting the economic importance of these activities in the global value chain.

The beginning of the second wave market segment in the mid-1990s revived coffee-drinking culture and reintroduced the social aspect of coffee consumption. This market segment emphasizes higher-quality coffee and personal service and highlights the importance of where and how coffee has been sourced. The rise of this segment coincided with increasing social and ethical awareness among consumers; demands for fair remuneration of coffee farmers and environmental sustainability of coffee farming became relevant as selling points. In responding to these demands, downstream coffee participants in this segment began to focus on issues of transparency, such as providing more information and knowledge about upstream coffee-related activities through certification and VSS compliance.

The third wave market segment has added another layer in terms of quality and knowledge. As well as seeking to address social and ethical concerns about how farmers are paid and the sustainability of coffee farming, this market segment emphasizes direct links between specialist retailers and coffee farmers, and retailers' and consumers' in-depth knowledge of how best to brew beans in order to fully appreciate their flavor, body, aroma, fragrance and mouthfeel.

The newer coffee consumption trends of the second and third waves are changing the coffee industry landscape. First, ways to address social and ethical concerns pioneered by second wave roasters and retailers through various certification and VSS schemes have become a big differentiating point for selling coffee. The price differential between coffees that identify the grower and those that do not can reach up to USD 8 per pound.[57]

Second, direct links between retailers and farmers provide upgrading opportunities for both upstream and downstream coffee participants. This new way of doing business in the coffee industry facilitates learning and technology transfer between participants. It also helps coffee farmers to create awareness of their coffees through branding efforts which may include marketing and/or filing for formal IP protection of trademarks and GIs. The farm-gate prices that coffee farmers receive by supplying to the second or third wave market segments are higher than those in the first wave; farmers' income in the third wave is triple that of first wave farmers.

Third, focusing on activities upstream in the coffee value chain helps to increase the income of both upstream and downstream participants.

The new way of doing business pioneered in the third wave is being assimilated by the first and second waves due to its fast growth and potential to expand coffee consumption. Indications include the recent acquisition by Nestlé – a large first wave roaster – of a notable third wave firm, Blue Bottle, signaling its entry into the third wave. And it is not the only one. Its close competitor, JAB, has purchased brand names Peet's and Stumptown to ride the third wave. Starbucks, from the second wave, recently tested the waters by introducing its Reserve brand.[58]

The adoption of the third wave business strategy in other market segments creates further opportunities for upstream coffee participants to increase their income, particularly by leveraging their brands. The extent to which these participants are able to do so will depend on consumers' recognition and awareness of these brands. This will require more investment to raise awareness among both consumers and large retailers in coffee-importing countries.

The growth potential of the Third Wave is increasingly attractive to traditional roasters and soluble coffee manufacturers, even if it represents a small share of the coffee industry. So far, this business model seems to be highly profitable for every member of the coffee global value chain. If coffee growers are to benefit more from this attention, they must not only focus more on the array of differentiation opportunities, but may also need to consider using IP instruments to retain the value they create.

Notes

1. This chapter draws on Samper et al. (2017).

2. According to a project carried out by Technomic (2015) based on a study commissioned by NCAUSA (2015). In terms of GDP per capita, the United States is the 26th-largest coffee-drinking country. The country with the highest yearly coffee consumption per capita is Finland, followed by Norway, Iceland, Denmark and the Netherlands (Smith 2017).

3. ICO (2015a).

4. The seven countries include Burundi, Ethiopia, Guatemala, Honduras, Nicaragua, Rwanda and Uganda (ITC 2012; ICO 2015c).

5. ICO (2014).

6. The volatility of coffee prices is also influenced by investors' behavior in the commodity markets.

7. Most coffee beans consumed in the world come from the Arabica and Canephora species; the latter is commonly referred to as Robusta coffee. Arabica coffees are considered higher quality and fetch higher prices than Robusta coffees.

8. This differential is a band that stipulates by how much the price may vary, for example from the price of green coffee.

9. Brazil is an exception to this rule. According to the ICO (2014), Brazil increased its coffee consumption by nearly 65 percent, from 26.4 million bags in 2000 to 43.5 million bags in 2012.

10. Samper et al. (2017) value the global coffee industry at between USD 194 billion and USD 202 billion in 2016.

11. ICO (2013) calculates that soluble coffee exports by coffee-producing countries were worth 26 percent less on average than soluble coffee re-exports by coffee-importing countries in the period 2000-2011.

12. Samper et al. (2017).

13. Ponte (2002), Pendergrast (2010), Morris (2013), Elavarasan et al. (2016).

14. ITC (2012).

15. Ukers (1922).

16. Talbot (1997a) writes that soluble (instant) coffee was invented during the American Civil War. However, the first patent granted on soluble coffee was in 1771 in Great Britain on a "coffee compound." The first soluble coffee sold commercially is credited to a New Zealander, David Strang, who was granted a patent on the "Dry Hot-Air" process of making coffee in 1890.

17. The engineer was Max Rudolph Morgenthaler, and the patent was filed in Switzerland in 1937 for a "Process of preserving the aromatic substances of a dry soluble coffee extract."

18. See chapter 3 of WIPO (2013).

19. Giovannucci et al. (2009).

20. The methodology for this estimate of coffee income distribution is based on prior work by Talbot (1997b), and updated by Fitter and Kaplinsky (2001) and Ponte (2002). Lewin et al. (2004), and Daviron and Ponte (2005) have reviewed this methodology.

21. Daviron and Ponte (2005) show this point well in their breakdown of the coffee costs in the Uganda-Italy value chain for Robusta coffee.

22. Daviron and Ponte (2005) refer to these differentiation strategies as investments in "symbolic production." Lewin et al. (2004), call them "non-coffee costs."

23. ICO (2014).

24. Talbot (1997b) was the first to calculate the share of total income distribution in the coffee global value chain. His analysis covered the years from 1971 to 1995.

25. See Fitter and Kaplinsky (2001), Ponte (2002), Lewin et al. (2004) and Daviron and Ponte (2005). These four estimates use different methods of calculating the distribution of income between coffee-producing and coffee-importing countries. However, all four show similar results: a declining share of income accruing to coffee-producing countries.

26. See Long (2017).

27. Mehta and Chavas (2008) captured the evolution of coffee prices at the farm, wholesale and retail levels during and after the ICA regime in the case of Brazil.

28. The low price of coffee was a reflection of the high coffee stock that was dumped on the market, causing an oversupply of green coffee (ICO 2014).

29. See ITC (2011) for the different certification labels and their impact on the coffee trade.

30. COSA (2013) documents the observed benefits associated with VSSs.

31. Wollni and Zeller (2007). Daviron and Ponte (2005) find that farmers under the Fair Trade scheme receive an income similar to those during the ICA quota restriction regime, approximately 20 cents to the dollar, but they caution that when their study was conducted, the Fair Trade scheme covered less than 1 percent of the coffee market. Dragusanu et al. (2014) updated the data and reviewed global evidence to find general but not universal benefits.

32. A recent analysis by García-Cardona (2016) argues that coffee producers that participate in these certification standards do not necessarily receive a higher price for their certified coffee. The cost to farmers of complying with and maintaining the various certification standards is often high. See also IISD (2014) and Samper and Quiñonez-Ruiz (2017).

33. Transparent Trade Coffee (2017).

34. Teuber (2010).

35. A GI is different from a trademark in that it relates to the specific geographical origin of the product, and that product possesses qualities or a reputation associated with that origin, the *terroir*. See box 2.2 in WIPO (2013) for a more detailed explanation.

36. U.S. trademark filings at the USPTO have been excluded from this analysis.

37. The USPTO's trademark data was chosen for two reasons. First, the U.S. market is a big and important market for coffee consumption. Second, the USPTO has a use requirement, which paints a more accurate picture of actual coffee-related product and service competition (see chapter 2 of WIPO (2013) on intention to use versus actual use of trademarks).

38. The Chinese Government revived the coffee production industry in 1988. China also produces some Robusta coffee on Hainan island.

39. ICO (2015b).

40. China has filed approximately 1,500 patents on coffee-related technologies since 1995. Patents filed from France and the United Kingdom in the same period total 1,763 and 1,225, respectively.

41. Refers to the total number of utility models filed by Chinese inventors since 1995.

42. The Ukers (2017) directory has a large database of firms in the coffee industry, from farmers associations to roasters and suppliers of coffee machines as well as other coffee-related services such as coffee-specific packaging companies. Firms are classified according to their respective value chain segment. However, the list of firms does not include individual coffee farmers in different parts of the world, and thus underestimates the size of coffee participants in this particular segment.

43. Participants in these two segments tend to overlap. Most coffee roasters also perform their own bean processing activities.

44. The second wave market segment was introduced in the 1990s but did not take off until the year 2000, while the third wave market segment took off in 2010 after beginning around the year 2000.

45. In 2012, Starbucks was in the news for its transfer pricing and tax activities in the United Kingdom. The company had used international accounting rules to price its intangible capital in such a manner that it had avoided paying U.K. taxes (Bergin 2012). See chapter 1 on transfer pricing.

46. Jamaica and Mexico do not appear in figure 2.4 because they are not among the world's top five coffee producers.

47. See Reina et al. (2008).

48. The consortium included Ethiopian cooperatives, private exporters and the EIPO among other government bodies.

49. See www.allianceforcoffeeexcellence.org/en/cup-of-excellence/winning-farms for more information.

50. ACE and Technoserve (2015).

51. World Coffee Research found that Arabica coffee had only 1.2 percent pairwise genetic diversity. Robusta beans, however, are stronger and more diverse.

52. The model by Moat et al. (2017) predicts that there will be a 40 to 60 percent decrease in suitable farming areas in Ethiopia due to climate change, assuming no significant intervention or other major influencing factors. See also Stylianou (2017).

53. See ICO (2015c) for the African examples and Samper et al. (2017) for the Latin American examples.

54. See Jördens (2009).

55. The registry maintained by UPOV is based on voluntary reporting by national authorities. It is very likely that the list of registrations under the UPOV system is larger at the national offices than those disclosed here.

56. See Chen et al. (2017).

57. Transparent Trade Coffee (2017).

58. See de la Merced and Strand (2017).

References

ACE and Technoserve (2015). *Cup of Excellence in Brazil and Honduras: An Impact Assessment*. Alliance for Coffee Excellence.

Bergin, T. (2012). Special report: how Starbucks avoids UK taxes. *Reuters*. London: Reuters.

Chen, W., R. Gouma, B. Los and M. Timmer (2017). Measuring the Income to Intangibles in Goods Production: A Global Value Chain Approach. *WIPO Economic Research Working Paper No. 36*. Geneva: WIPO.

COSA (2013). *The COSA Measuring Sustainability Report: Cocoa and Coffee in 12 Countries*. Philadephia, The Committee on Sustainability Assessment.

Daviron, B. and S. Ponte (2005). *The Coffee Paradox: Global Markets, Commodity Trade and the Elusive Promise of Development*. London and New York: Zed Books.

de la Merced, M.J. and O. Strand (2017). Nestlé targets high-end coffee by taking majority stake in Blue Bottle. *New York Times (NYT)*, September 14, 2017.

Dragusanu, R., D. Giovannucci and N. Nunn (2014). The economics of Fair Trade. *Journal of Economics Perspectives* 28(3), 217-236.

Elavarasan, K., A. Kumar, et al. (2016). The basics of coffee cupping. *Tea & Coffee Trade Journal*, January, 30-33.

Fitter, R. and R. Kaplinsky (2001). Who gains from product rents as the coffee market becomes more differentiated? A value-chain analysis. *IDS Bulletin* 32(3), 69-82.

García-Cardona, J. (2016). *Value-Added Initiatives: Distributional Impacts on the Global Value Chain for Colombia's Coffee*. Doctoral thesis (PhD), University of Sussex. Brighton: Institute of Development Studies, University of Sussex.

Giovannucci, D., T.E. Josling, W. Kerr, B. O'Connor and M.T. Yeung (2009). *Guide to Geographical Indications: Linking Products and Their Origins*. Geneva: International Trade Centre.

Humphrey, J. (2006). Global Value Chains in the Agrifood Sector. *UNIDO Working Research Papers*. Vienna: United Nations Industrial Development Organization.

ICO (2011). "The effects of tariffs on the coffee trade," International Coffee Organization 107th Session Document No. ICC 107-7. London: International Coffee Organization.

ICO (2013). "World trade of soluble coffee," International Coffee Council 110th Session Document No. ICC 110-5. London: International Coffee Organization.

ICO (2014). "World coffee trade (1963-2013): a review of the markets, challenges and opportunities facing the sector," International Coffee Council 112th Session Document No. ICC 111-5 Rev.1. London: International Coffee Organization.

ICO (2015a). "Employment generated by the coffee sector," International Coffee Council 105th Session Document No. ICC 105-5. London: International Coffee Organization.

ICO (2015b). "Coffee in China," International Coffee Council 115th Session Document No. ICC 115-7. Milan: International Coffee Organization.

ICO (2015c). "Sustainability of the coffee sector in Africa," International Coffee Council 114th Session Document No. ICC 114-5. London: International Coffee Organization.

ICO and World Bank (2015). Risk and Finance in the Coffee Sector: A Compendium of Case Studies Related to Improving Risk Management and Access to Finance in the Coffee Sector. *World Bank Group Report Number 93923-GLB*. Washington, DC: World Bank Group.

IISD (2014). *The State of Sustainability Initiatives (SSI) Review 2014: Standards and The Green Economy*. Geneva: International Institute for Sustainable Development.

ITC (2011). Trends in the Trade of Certified Coffees. *Sustainability Market Assessments Doc. No. MAR-11-197.E*. Geneva: International Trade Centre.

ITC (2012). *The Coffee Exporter's Guide – Third Edition*. Geneva: International Trade Centre.

Jördens, R. (2009). Benefits of plant variety protection. In *Responding to the Challenges in a Changing World: The Role of New Plant Varieties and High Quality Seed in Agriculture – Proceedings of the Second World Seed Conference*. Rome: Food and Agriculture Organisation.

Lewin, B., D. Giovannucci and P. Varangis (2004). Coffee Markets: New Paradigms in Global Supply and Demand. *World Bank Agriculture and Rural Development Discussion Paper 3*. Washington, DC: World Bank.

Long, G. (2017). Coffee sustainability: the journey from bean to barista laid bare. *Financial Times*, September 24, 2017.

Mehta, A. and J.-P. Chavas (2008). Responding to the coffee crisis: what can we learn from price dynamics? *Journal of Development Economics* 85(1), 282-311.

Moat, J., J. Williams, S. Baena, T. Wilkinson, T.W. Gole, Z.K. Challa, S. Demissew and A.P. Davis (2017). Resilience potential of the Ethiopian coffee sector under climate change. *Nature Plants*, 3(17081).

Morris, J. (2013). Why espresso? Explaining changes in European coffee preferences from a production of culture perspective. *European Review of History: Revue européenne d'histoire*, 20(5), 881-901.

NCAUSA (2015). *NCA National Coffee Drinking Trends*. New York: National Coffee Association USA.

Pendergrast, M. (2010). *Uncommon Grounds: The History of Coffee and How it Transformed Our World*. New York: Basic Books.

Ponte, S. (2002). The "Latte Revolution"? Regulation, markets and consumption in the global coffee chain. *World Development*, 30(7), 1099-1122.

Reina, M., G. Silva and L. Samper (2008). *Juan Valdez: The Strategy Behind the Brand*. Bogotá: Ediciones B.

Samper, L. and X. Quiñones-Ruiz (2017). Towards a balanced sustainability vision for the coffee industry. *Resources*, 6(2), 17.

Samper, L., D. Giovannucci and L. Marques-Vieira (2017). The Powerful Role of Intangibles in the Coffee Value Chain. *WIPO Economic Research Working Paper No. 39*. Geneva: WIPO.

SCAA (2014). *Economics of the Coffee Supply Chain: An Illustrative Outlook*. Santa Ana, CA: The Specialty Coffee Association of America.

Smith, O. (2017). Mapped: the countries that drink the most coffee. *The Telegraph*, October 1, 2017.

Stylianou, N. (2017). Coffee under threat: will it taste worse as the planet warms? *BBC News*. London: BBC.

Talbot, J.M. (1997a). The struggle for control of a commodity chain: instant coffee from Latin America. *Latin American Research Review*, 32(2), 117-135.

Talbot, J.M. (1997b). Where does your coffee dollar go? The division of income and surplus along the coffee commodity chain. *Studies in Comparative International Development*, 32(1), 56-91.

Technomic (2015). The Economic Impact of the Coffee Industry. *NCA Market Research Series*. New York: National Coffee Association USA.

Teuber, R. (2010). Geographical indications of origin as a tool of product differentiation: the case of coffee. *Journal of International Food & Agribusiness Marketing*, 22(3-4), 277-298.

Transparent Trade Coffee (2017). Specialty Coffee Retail Price Index – 2016, Q4: www.transparenttradecoffee. org/scrpi.

Ukers (2017). *UKERS Tea & Coffee Global Directory & Buyer's Guide*. 64th Edition. Bell Publishing Ltd.

Ukers, W.H. (ed.) (1922). *All About Coffee*. New York: The Tea and Coffee Trade Journal Company.

Wendelboe, T. (2015). 2014 *Transparency Report*.

WIPO The Coffee War: Ethiopia and the Starbucks Story. *IP Advantage*: www.wipo.int/ipadvantage/en/details. jsp?id=2621.

WIPO (2013). *World Intellectual Property Report 2013: Brands – Reputation and Image in the Global Marketplace*. Geneva: World Intellectual Property Organization.

Wollni, M. and M. Zeller (2007). Do farmers benefit from participating in specialty markets and cooperatives? The case of coffee marketing in Costa Rica. *Agricultural Economics*, 37(2-3), 243-248.

Innovation is transforming the photovoltaic industry

Demand is booming

Prices have plummeted

Western companies used to dominate but now Chinese firms lead production of PV modules.

2005

2012

- China
- Japan
- USA
- Germany
- Others

Leading firms are looking to intangibles for competitive edge, intensifying their investments in R&D and patenting.

Source: World Intellectual Property Report 2017

Chapter 3
Photovoltaics: technological catch-up and competition in the global value chain

New technologies related to renewable energy are a pillar of sustainable economic growth and development. Recent decades have seen increasing global interest and demand for successful innovations capable of transforming solar, wind or geothermal energy – among other sources – into electricity.[1]

This chapter explores how the global value chain for solar photovoltaic (PV) technologies has evolved to meet the demand for sustainable electricity generation. It focuses on the importance of intangible assets as a crucial means of adding value in the different segments of this particular global value chain, where technological innovation and diffusion have played a key role.

As with many technologies, an accidental discovery led to the initial development of solar PV technology for electricity generation. In the late 1930s and early 1940s at Bell Laboratories in New Jersey, United States, Russell Ohl discovered that shining light on a monocrystalline material registered electric potential on a voltmeter. He patented a device that employed this principle in 1941.[2] Ohl was not the first scientist to discover a material that conducted electricity – known as the semiconductive effect – when exposed to sunlight. The earliest documented incident was almost a century earlier in France, when Edmund Becquerel noted that an electric current was produced when two metals immersed in a liquid were exposed to sunlight. Though several scientists had managed to produce PV cells from different materials between the discoveries of Becquerel and Ohl, it was really the scientists at Bell Laboratories who developed the first crystalline PV cell.[3]

Nowadays, two different solar PV cell technologies are being commercialized – wafer-based crystalline and thin-film PV cells – but the former accounts for over 90 percent of the PV market. Present systems based on either PV cell technology can provide electricity similar to a conventional power plant, known as utility-scale generation. Such systems can act as a power plant generating electricity exclusively for the grid. Alternatively, large industrial plants – or other loads such as data storage centers – can generate electricity from PV systems on a large scale solely for their own consumption, thereby potentially offsetting some or all of their electricity consumption from the grid. Smaller-scale PV systems can also be used for residential or commercial uses. These too may be either connected to the grid or used solely for own consumption, particularly in remote, off-grid areas.

Any PV system that is used purely for own consumption needs to rely on batteries or be hybridized with other fuel sources to ensure a consistent supply of electricity throughout the day.

Figure 3.1

Demand for PV is growing exponentially

Annual PV capacity additions (MW), 2000-2015

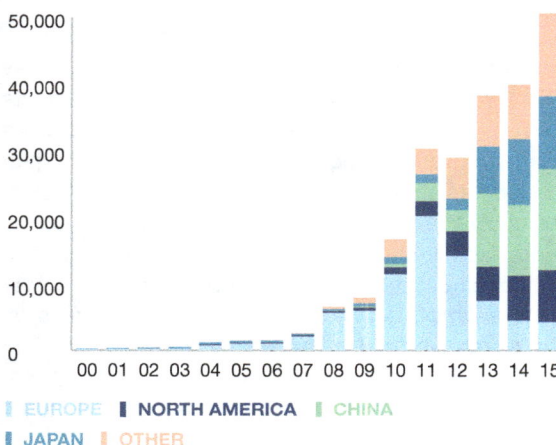

EUROPE   NORTH AMERICA   CHINA
JAPAN   OTHER

Source: IEA (2016).

Demand for PV systems has grown exponentially since 2000 (figure 3.1). In 2016, 34 percent more new capacity was installed worldwide than in the previous year, and growth hit 126 percent in China. Until 2011, growth occurred mainly in Europe. Demand has become more evenly distributed since then, and China is now the largest market. Figure 3.1 shows additions to annual PV capacity by origin of demand from 2000 to 2015. The growth trend is exponential, with an increase from little more than zero in 2000 to 50.6 GW in 2015. Capacity growth in Europe has slowed markedly since 2011, but it remains strong in China, Japan and North America.

Government support policies have been the main drivers of development in the solar PV market (figure 3.2). Historically, regulators have mostly used feed-in tariffs (FITs), which impose guaranteed prices for electricity generated from solar energy sources on grid operators. This mechanism allows solar PV power generated at higher cost to benefit from a higher price than power generated from conventional sources, accelerating investments in PV technology that spread upward through the value chain.

However, such mechanisms limit the price information passed from the supply side to regulators, which in turn to some extent limits the incentives to invest in cost-reducing PV technologies along the value chain. As the price is set by the regulator, supply margins depend on the quality of its information about the costs of generating electricity through PV technology. Experience suggests that regulators have regularly overestimated these costs, as installed capacity has almost systematically exceeded the quantities that were initially planned to be commissioned.

As an alternative, regulators now tend to rely more on auctioning and competitive mechanisms, such as FITs through tender or power purchase agreements (PPAs). These policies rely on clearer price signals from suppliers, giving current suppliers and project developers stronger incentives to reduce their costs. Arguably, PPAs can spread cost-reducing innovations more rapidly along the whole value chain, as solar PV developers submit bids to develop new power generation projects and the government agrees on the purchase for the most cost-competitive bids. However, FITs without tender still accounted for almost 60 percent of the PV market in 2015.

This chapter is organized in three main sections. In section 3.1, the evolution of the global value chain is analyzed. Section 3.2 examines how intangible assets – particularly product and process innovations – have shaped the global supply chain. Section 3.3 explores the role of IP protection, notably patents, in the new business environment that has emerged from major recent changes in the industry. A final section summarizes the main findings.

3.1 – The evolution of the PV global value chain

A linear value chain structure

This section describes the structure of the value chain for wafer-based crystalline PV cells, which constitutes the vast majority of the PV market. Following the taxonomy described in chapter 1, the typical value chain structure for wafer-based crystalline PV technologies is snake shaped, as schematized in figure 3.3. The upstream and midstream segments concern all the processes involved in the production of PV systems. These segments rely heavily on production equipment, which has played a crucial role in technology dissemination in the PV industry.[4] The downstream segments concern the services involved in generating electricity from PV systems.

Figure 3.2

Governments are the main driver of PV market development

Distribution of solar PV market incentives and enablers, 2015

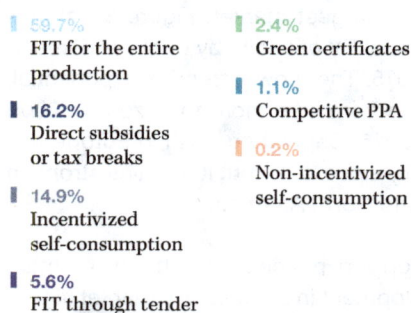

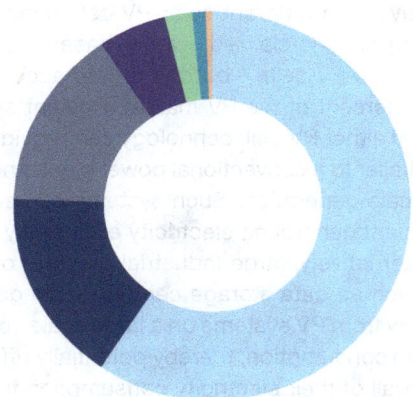

59.7%
FIT for the entire production

16.2%
Direct subsidies or tax breaks

14.9%
Incentivized self-consumption

5.6%
FIT through tender

2.4%
Green certificates

1.1%
Competitive PPA

0.2%
Non-incentivized self-consumption

Source: IEA (2016).

Figure 3.3

The global value chain for crystalline PV is shaped like a snake

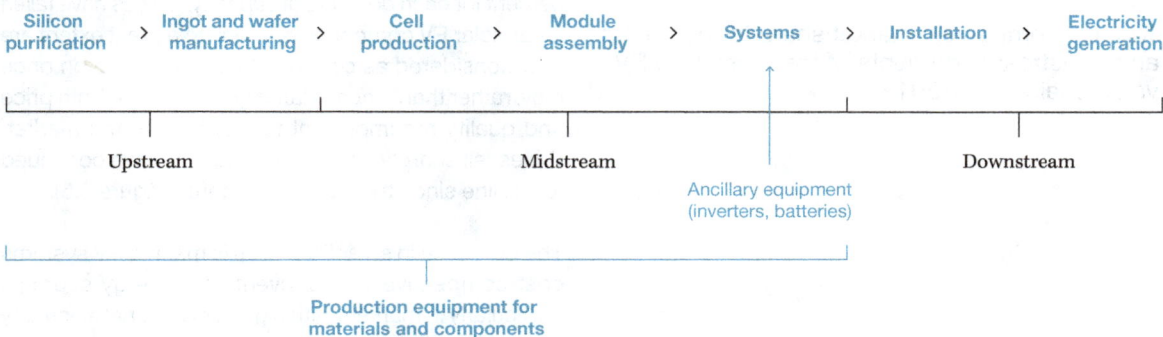

Source: Carvalho, Dechezleprêtre and Glachant (2017).

The production of crystalline PV systems involves five main segments. The first stage is the purification of silicon from silica (SiO_2) found in quartz sand. The ultra-high purity required for the PV industry – greater than 99.999 percent pure – is obtained through a heavy and highly energy-consuming chemical process, resulting in a material called polysilicon. The semiconductor industry also makes use of polysilicon, but the PV industry accounts for 90 percent of polysilicon production.[5] The second stage is the manufacturing of ingots and wafers, which consists of growing cylinders or bricks of pure silicon (ingots) and slicing them into thin layers (wafers). Stage three is the production of crystalline PV cells by assembling two differently doped wafers to form a p-n junction responsible for the photovoltaic effect. Many treatments or process modifications can be applied at this stage to increase the PV efficiency. Stage four is the assembly of modules, where PV cells are soldered together and encapsulated in glass sheets, forming a module which will be cooked in a laminating machine. The fifth stage is integration into PV systems: modules are combined with complementary equipment – such as batteries or inverters – to deliver electricity to devices or to the grid.

Regardless of whether crystalline or thin-film solar PV technologies are used, there are two main downstream segments. The first is installation of PV systems in the end-user market, which includes all market services related to the development of PV projects, financing, logistics, certifications and labor.

The second is the generation of electricity from PV systems, including all services related to operating and monitoring installed PV capacity.

Despite the crisis, the PV industry is booming, with increased market competition

Despite the financial crisis of 2008, demand for PV systems, and consequently production, increased between 2005 and 2011. Demand is still booming, and more production capacity is being created everywhere. As an illustration, between 2005 and 2012 global ingot manufacturing capacity grew by 9,590 percent, and capacity to manufacture wafers grew by 3,991 percent. The traditional main players in the sector – Germany, Japan and the United States – as well as new ones like China and India all multiplied their production capacities in the upstream and midstream segments of the crystalline PV value chain between 2005 and 2011.[6]

This boom also involved market entry of new players, which in turn induced more competition. In 2004, the different production segments were heavily concentrated, with the five largest players supplying most global production. As depicted in figure 3.4, in 2004 the top five producers accounted for between 80 and 100 percent of production in most segments. The only exception was the module segment, and even there the top five accounted for over 50 percent of module production. But by 2012 their share of production in the other four segments had dropped markedly to around 30 percent.

73

Figure 3.4

Competition in the PV market has increased markedly

Top five companies' market share for upstream and midstream segments of the crystalline PV value chain, 2004-2012

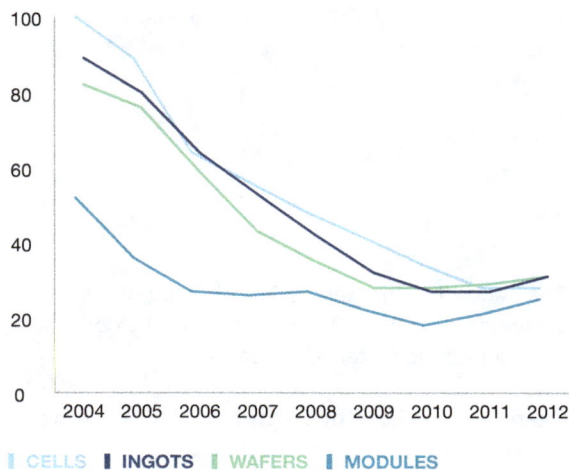

CELLS   INGOTS   WAFERS   MODULES

Source: ENF (2013a, 2013b).

These developments resulted in a dramatic decrease in solar PV prices from 2008. Solar PV module prices are estimated to have decreased by more than 80 percent between 2008 and 2015, with price reductions of 26 percent for each doubling of capacity.[7] Prices have fallen for all solar PV components, which to a great extent are now considered as commodities, competing on price only, rather than differentiated goods, where both price and quality are important for success in the market. Prices fell sharply until early 2012, and have continued to decline since then, but more gently (figure 3.5).

The decrease in solar PV prices is making PV systems cost-competitive with conventional energy sources, particularly in markets with high conventional electricity prices, high levels of solar radiation and low interest rates. These conditions have increased incentives to install solar generation for self-consumption, and so demand in that market has also increased. It is not surprising that the increase in PV demand from regions other than Europe has coincided with the steep price fall observed since 2011. Moreover, the abovementioned government support policies based on tenders are likely to have reinforced the downward price trend. For example, in 2016 Abu Dhabi and Mexico achieved some of the lowest bids for solar PV pricing contracts.

Figure 3.5

PV component prices have fallen dramatically

Spot price of multi-crystalline PV individual components, 2010-2017

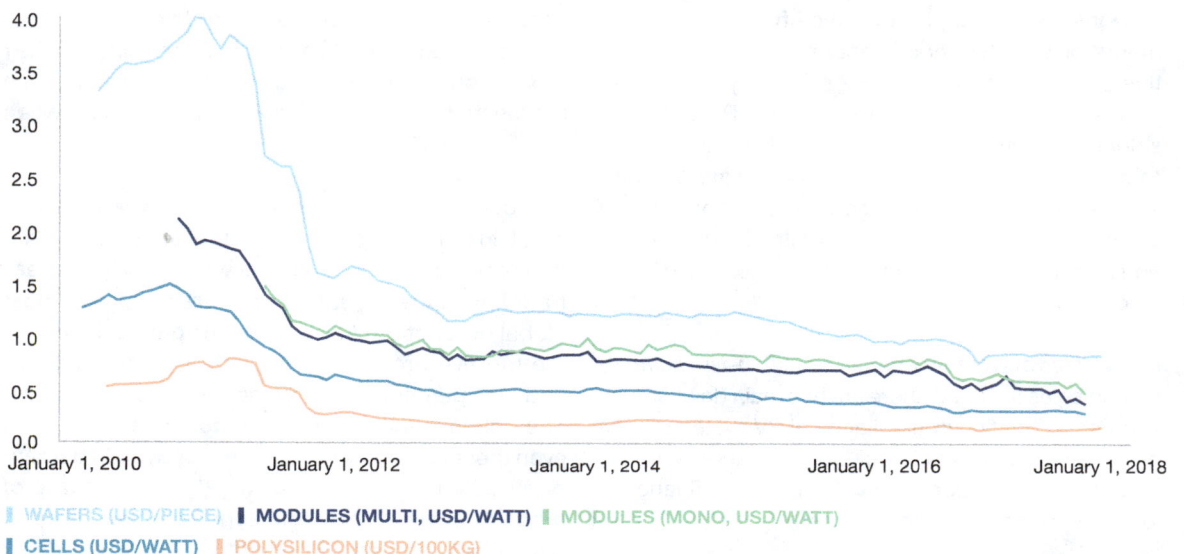

WAFERS (USD/PIECE)   MODULES (MULTI, USD/WATT)   MODULES (MONO, USD/WATT)
CELLS (USD/WATT)   POLYSILICON (USD/100KG)

Sources: WIPO based on BNEF (2017).

China: the new big player in the PV value chain

The global distribution of the PV value chain has changed dramatically in the last decade, with a massive relocation of upstream and midstream activities to China.[8] While traditional producing economies did manage to increase their production output and capacities between 2005 and 2011, growth was much larger and faster in China.

Until 2004, demand and production was largely concentrated in Europe, where governments gave generous support to accelerate the deployment of PV capacities. This created powerful economic signals in countries with a strong semiconductor industry – such as Germany, Switzerland, Japan and the United States – which initially became leaders in providing production equipment for wafer-based crystalline PV technologies. Production and demand then slowly started to catch up in Asian economies, most notably in China. This led to overcapacities, drastic price decreases and the exit of many upstream and midstream Western firms.

By 2015, China had become the main PV market and the lead economy in all upstream and midstream production segments. Figure 3.6 contrasts the evolution of Chinese market shares with those of the leading economy in the production of each segment in 2005. The trend is clear: by 2012 the Chinese economy was the main supplier of the global PV market in all these segments. It concentrated more than 60 percent of production in all segments of the chain except polysilicon production. Chinese companies did enter the polysilicon market and became the main supplier there too, accounting for one-third of production by 2011; but compared to the other production segments, they entered much later and have concentrated appreciably less of the global market.

Trade restrictions: policy actions and economic reactions

The steep price fall mentioned above caused competitive pressures against U.S. and European solar PV companies, which had enjoyed significant profits prior to 2008. This resulted in an increase in bankruptcies and acquisitions in 2011 and 2012.[9]

As a result, solar PV manufacturing associations in both the United States and Europe petitioned their respective governments to impose tariffs against Chinese solar PV products.[10]

Figure 3.6

China is now the top supplying economy in all upstream and midstream PV market segments

Percentage of global manufacturing capacity, 2004-2012

Top supplier economies in 2005

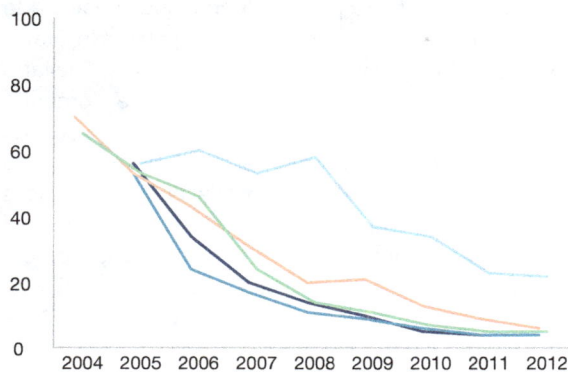

China

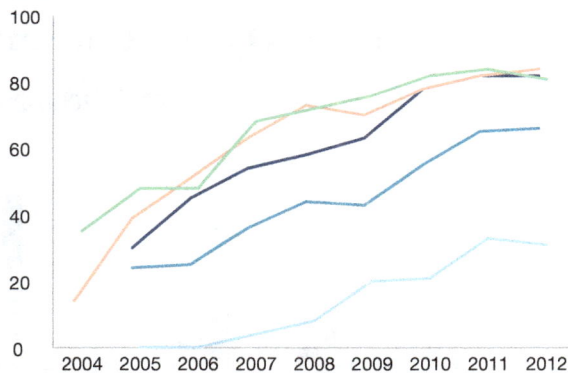

POLYSILICON   CRYSTALLINE PV MODULES
INGOTS   CRYSTALLINE PV CELLS   WAFERS

Sources: ENF (2013b) and BNEF (2013).

Note: Top supplier economies in 2005 were the United States for polysilicon and crystalline PV modules, Europe for ingots and wafers, and Japan for crystalline PV cells.

They argued that Chinese solar PV firms benefited from subsidized loans from their government, allowing them not only to set up production facilities, but also to sustain production even when market prices fell below the cost of production.[11] This led both the U.S. and EU governments to impose anti-dumping duties on different Chinese crystalline PV products in 2012 and 2013. These duties are currently still in place due to extensions in both the United States and the EU.[12]

Furthermore, other countries that have set up market support mechanisms for solar PV have invoked local content requirements, meaning a certain percentage of technologies used in local PV markets must be sourced from local manufacturing facilities. Such requirements were introduced in India, South Africa and Ontario, Canada, although Ontario eventually had to revoke its measures following a ruling by the World Trade Organization.[13]

Chinese firms have partially bypassed these trade barriers by setting up manufacturing plants in Brazil, Germany, India, Malaysia, the Netherlands, Thailand and Viet Nam.[14] These plants serve the domestic markets in these countries, but are also used as export bases to other markets that currently have duties against them. Thus, political economy factors – such as how trade restrictions affect market access – can play an important role in the geographical distribution of the global value chain.

Surviving through vertical integration

The distribution of gains in the PV value chain has changed drastically in the last decade. Before 2011, generous subsidies in Europe maintained prices well above production costs in all segments of the value chain. Following the price downturn in 2011, upstream and midstream players suffered a fall in profit margins that made it difficult for companies to survive (see box 3.1 and figure 3.7).

Although the economic environment has improved since then, several companies operating in different segments continue to face serious difficulties. In general, midstream firms' margins fall short of the average in the semiconductor industry. Low market prices for upstream and midstream segments of the value chain mean that a greater proportion of the value in the chain now lies downstream, in the market development segment. In consequence, many upstream and midstream solar PV companies have consolidated with downstream companies (see table 3.1).[15]

Figure 3.7

PV manufacturers have become much less profitable

Net profits of leading PV firms (USDm), 2008-2012

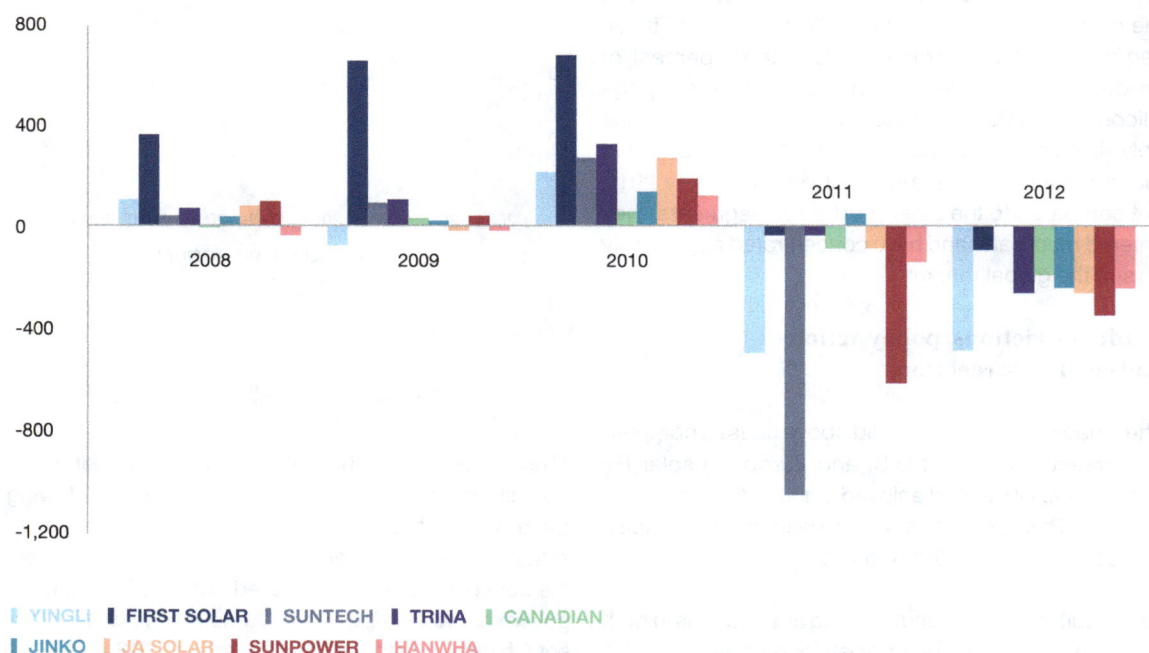

Source: Carvalho et al. (2017).

Box 3.1

Creative destruction in the PV value chain?

All major midstream players started losing money in 2011 or 2012 (see figure 3.7). In 2012, Q-Cells, a German-based cell manufacturer that led the market in most of the 2000s, went bankrupt and was then bought by Hanwha of the Republic of Korea. Chinese PV giant Suntech also defaulted in 2013, leading to a complete restructuring of its activity. Since then, the situation has become less severe, but it remains difficult. Companies like REC Silicon and Centrotherm Photovoltaics, which operate in different segments, continue to face serious difficulties. In general, midstream firms' margins fall short of the average in the semiconductor industry.

Vertical integration has been the solution for many companies in the PV value chain. As can be seen in table 3.1, several upstream and midstream players, such as GCL, First Solar, Canadian Solar, SunPower and Jinko Solar, have also vertically integrated downstream activities.

Many argue that process innovation is the only possible survival strategy for upstream and midstream companies.[16]

First Solar provides an interesting case in point. Specializing in thin-film cells, which account for a minor share of the market – just 7 percent in 2015 – has enabled it to become the most profitable midstream company. What drives its commercial success is being able to manufacture innovative PV components below the market price and production costs of competitors. Its thin-film PV cell has power conversion efficiencies nearing crystalline PV levels, but with production costs substantially below the retail market price for crystalline PV. First Solar can maintain its comparative advantage because other companies do not know how to reproduce its product – a PV cell made from cadmium telluride materials – and because it uses specialized production equipment protected by intellectual property rights.

But how replicable is this example? First Solar was able to attract finance, scale up production and commercialize its technology when solar PV technology prices were high.[17] It is hard to see such a window of opportunity in current market conditions.

Table 3.1

EBITDA margins of main PV companies, 2015-2016

Company	Market segments	EBITDA margin (%)
GCL-Poly Energy	Silicon/wafers/power projects	25 (a)
Wacker	Silicon production/other chemicals	19.8 (a)
REC Silicon	Silicon production	-4 (a)
OCI Company	Silicon production/other chemicals	7.4 (a)
First Solar	Cells/modules/power projects	21.6 (a)
Trina	Ingots/wafers/cells/modules	5.54 (a)
JA Solar	Cells/modules	7.55 (a)
Canadian Solar	Ingots/wafers/cells/modules/power projects	8.01 (a)
Jinko Solar	Wafers/cells/modules/power projects	10.6 (b)
SunPower	Cells/modules/power projects	6.36 (b)
Applied Materials	Production equipment	25.2 (b)
Centrotherm Photovoltaics	Production equipment	-10.7 (a)
Sungrow	Inverter	10.6 (a)
SMA Solar	Inverter	11.3 (a)
SolarEdge	Inverter	10.3 (a)

Source: Carvalho et al. (2017).

Notes: (a) 2015; (b) 2016.

Solar PV manufacturers are increasingly moving downstream by getting involved in market development. This trend was initially observed during the financial crisis of 2008, when orders for solar PV technologies were cancelled due to the inability of solar PV project developers to obtain financing support.[18] Prior to the crisis, most developers financed their solar PV projects through bank loans. Banks were willing to finance solar PV projects – along with other renewable energy projects – because governments' FIT policies provided guaranteed prices for at least 20 years. However, the financial crisis hit the liquidity of banks and their capacity to provide loans to project developers.

As a result, project developing companies had to cancel their projects, which in turn meant cancelled orders for PV products upstream in the value chain. Solar PV manufacturers that had enjoyed high profits up to this time faced cancellation of their orders and could not resell them to other project developers. Those companies with strong balance sheets started moving downstream to project development in order to generate demand for their own upstream products.

3.2 – How do intangibles add value in the PV global value chain?

As described in the previous section, the past decade has seen a striking relocation of most upstream and midstream activities to China. As a direct consequence, a significant share of the economic activities related to the PV value chain – including total value added – has also been transferred to that country.

But the story in regard to the creation and returns to PV intangible assets is less straightforward.[19] First, knowledge assets in the PV value chain were not necessarily tied to either the main production location (China) or demand locations (Europe). Second, as suggested in the previous section, knowledge assets relate not only to product innovations, but also to cost-reducing process innovations. Third, it is important to understand how China acquired the knowledge assets needed to reshape the current global PV value chain.

This section explores how knowledge assets have shaped the current structure of the PV value chain. The role of reputational assets in downstream segments is explored in the next section.

Box 3.2

The photovoltaic revolution

There are now four different families of solar PV cell technologies: (i) wafer-based crystalline, (ii) thin-film, (iii) high-efficiency (often referred to as Group III-V) and (iv) organic PV cells. Only the first two are currently commercialized, while the latter two show great promise. Wafer-based crystalline PV cells account for over 90 percent of the PV market.[20]

Newer PV technologies have to overcome two challenges to reach the market. First, the technology has to generate electricity reliably and stably in non-laboratory settings, and second, production costs have to be lower than competing market prices for existing PV technologies. As of today, certain types of thin-film and high-efficiency PV cells have achieved higher power conversion efficiencies than commercialized technologies, but they struggle to meet the prices of the marketed technologies, partly because they are produced on a smaller scale.[21]

This makes process innovation along the value chain crucial for the PV industry (see figure 3.3). Two major production processes are used for polysilicon production: the Siemens process and the fluidized bed reactor (FBR) process.[22]

Since the production of polysilicon is electricity-intensive, a large part of decreasing costs lies in improving the energy efficiency of these processes, with the FBR process being more efficient than the Siemens one. Companies in the United States, Canada and Norway are trying alternative and proprietary metallurgical processes to reduce the energy and production costs of polysilicon. Another way in which companies attempt to reduce electricity costs is relocating plants to regions where electricity is cheap. Cost-reducing innovations in the production of ingots and wafers have also been achieved through innovations in the production equipment installed in those factories. For ingots, this is done by growing larger crystals and improving the seed crystals needed to reduce process time and increase yield.[23] Other production equipment improvements include cutting ingots into thinner wafers, reducing loss of unused ingot material (known as kerf), increasing recycling rates and reducing consumables.[24] Other process innovations include reducing the amount of metallization pastes/inks containing silver and aluminum, which are the most process-critical and expensive non-silicon materials used in current crystalline silicon cell technologies.[25]

Where are PV knowledge assets created?

Since 1975, the National Renewable Energy Laboratory (NREL) has been tracking the stakeholders – companies and academic institutions – achieving the world's highest power conversion efficiencies of PV cells in any of the different PV cell technologies (see box 3.2). Over that period, world records have been broken frequently within each PV cell family. Moreover, record power conversion efficiencies across all PV cell technologies have been achieved almost every year since 2010, after two decades of very slow progress. There has also been fast progress in all alternative technologies to crystalline PV, such as multi-junction, single-junction, thin-film and emerging PV cell technologies.[26]

Who is behind these current and alternative PV product innovations? As shown in table 3.2, the United States achieved 56 percent of the 289 observed world efficiency records, followed by Germany (12 percent), Japan (11 percent) and Australia (6 percent). These four countries account for most of the documented PV product innovations. The United States dominates the best-in-class landscape across all PV cell types, with particular strength in the alternative thin-film and multi-junction PV cell innovations. Australia is second in terms of breaking records for the current crystalline PV cells, but has not achieved any record for alternative PV technologies. Conversely, other countries such as the Republic of Korea, Canada and Switzerland have set records only in alternative PV technologies.

Table 3.2

Best-in-class product innovations by PV cell type and economy, 1976-2017

Economy	Crystalline silicon cells	Thin-film technologies	Multi-junction cells (two-terminal, monolithic)	Single-junction GaAs	Emerging PV	Total
United States	23	72	36	10	20	161
Germany	9	11	6	3	5	34
Japan	12	7	6		7	32
Australia	16					16
Rep. of Korea		1		2	5	8
Canada					7	7
Switzerland		1			6	7
China	2	3				5
France		2	2			4
Netherlands				3	1	4
Austria					3	3
India		3				3
Sweden		3				3
Hong Kong, China					1	1
Spain			1			1
Total	62	103	51	18	55	289

Source: Carvalho et al. (2017).

It seems that frontier innovation has not driven the market dominance of Chinese firms. The greatest product innovations – in terms of improved conversion efficiencies of different PV cell families – still appear to occur in other countries. In contrast to these economies, China has achieved global best-in-class technology only five times, including three records in thin films, a technology that is not yet commercialized.

A similar but more detailed picture can be seen when patent applications for PV-related technologies are analyzed (see figure 3.8). Growing market demand for solar PV installations has been accompanied by parallel growth in the number of patent applications worldwide. First patent filings increased from less than 2,500 in the early 2000s to over 16,000 in 2011. Until 2008, most of these technologies originated in Japan and the United States. Since then, China has seen rapid growth in PV patenting, becoming the top PV filing economy by 2010 and accounting for the majority of filings by 2014.

Figure 3.8

China – the new PV innovation champion?

First filings of PV-related patents by origin, 2000-2015

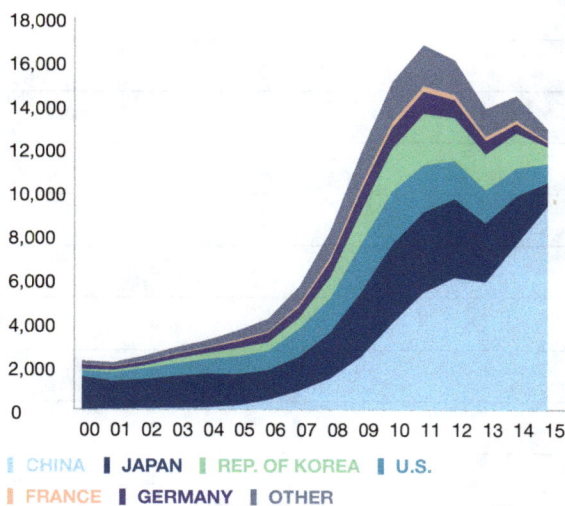

Source: WIPO based on PATSTAT; see technical notes.

With over 46 percent of the world's first filings in the period 2011-2015, China has now become the global leader in PV-related patent filings (figure 3.10). It ranks first in first filings for technologies related to each PV segment, and has the majority of these in the case of silicon, ingots/wafers and modules. But when the specialization of Chinese firms between current (crystalline) and alternative cell-related technologies is considered, a different picture emerges. As observed for the world's efficiency records, China seems to have specialized more in alternative cell technologies than crystalline ones. Indeed, China holds the largest share of alternative cell patent filings, while still behind Japan, the United States and the Republic of Korea in filings for crystalline technologies. These figures contrast with China's current competitive advantage as regards crystalline PV cell production.

Figure 3.9

PV modules and cells dominate patent filings for PV innovations

First filings of PV-related patents by segment, 2000-2015

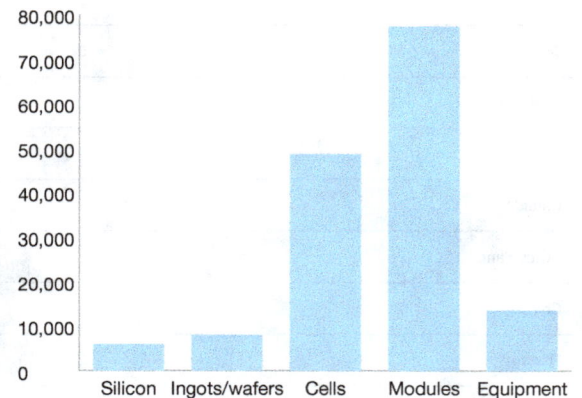

Source: WIPO based on PATSTAT; see technical notes.

Most patenting activity happens in the two midstream segments. More than half of all PV-related patents filed in the period 2000-2015 concerned module technologies, and almost a third related to cell ones (see figure 3.9). Technologies related to silicon, ingots and wafers accounted for less than 10 percent of patents.

Figure 3.10

China has become a major PV technology stakeholder

Percentage distribution of PV-related patents by origin and value chain segment, 2011-2015

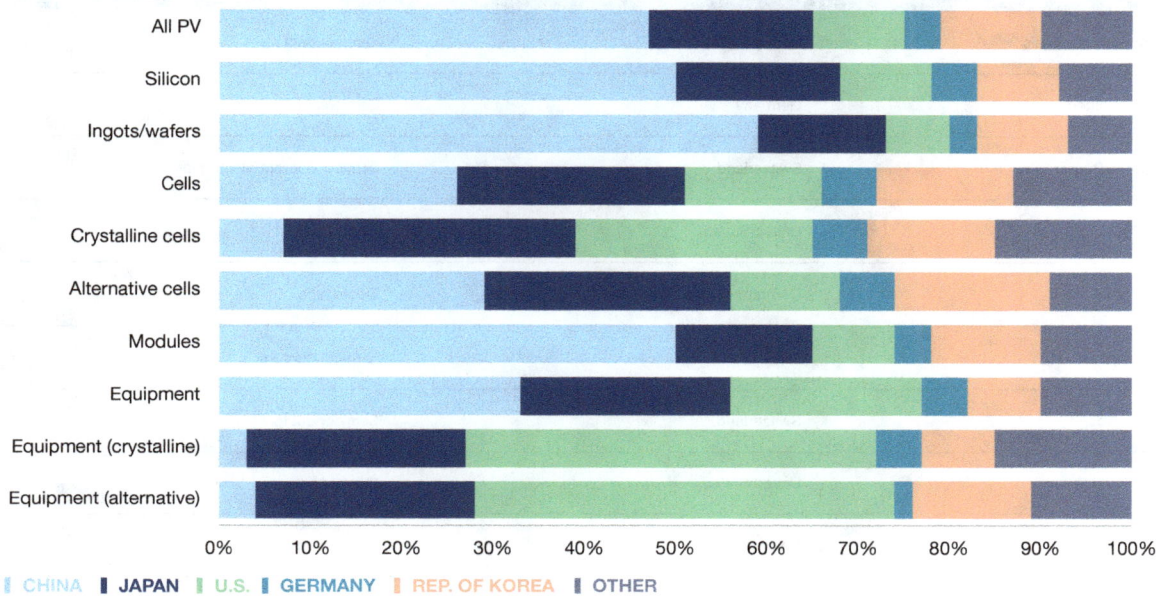

CHINA   JAPAN   U.S.   GERMANY   REP. OF KOREA   OTHER

Source: WIPO based on PATSTAT; see technical notes.

This is not to say that innovation is less frequent in the upstream and production equipment segments. Indeed, field studies have found that companies patent minor inventions intensively – particularly in China – but critical inventions are usually kept secret. Many of these critical innovations focus more on process, which is often not carried out in specific R&D departments but directly on production lines, and protected by secrecy rather than patenting. This is the case not only for new-entrant Chinese companies, but also for major Western and Japanese silicon producers, which have developed advanced know-how on purifying silicon at reasonable cost that they keep secret.[27]

Cost-reducing process innovations

Neither power conversion records nor patents can ensure the successful introduction of PV product innovations. As noted in box 3.2, for a new PV technology to achieve success, it needs to be both reliable and competitively priced, and while certain alternative PV cell technologies have achieved impressive results in the laboratory, they are not yet being offered on a competitive scale.

Moreover, the products already in the market along the PV value chain – from purified silicon to solar panels – are highly standardized. Market competitiveness of these mainly derives from the capability to manufacture products that satisfy a standard level of quality at an affordable cost. In this context, successful entry into and survival within each market segment requires access to state-of-the-art production technology, which in turn requires international markets for production equipment that are competitive.

This means that process innovations are instrumental for introducing new PV products into the market and maintaining existing ones. New technologies can only be introduced into price-competitive markets if they achieve large-scale production and are supported by complementary process innovations to reduce costs. In fact, several companies in the upstream and midstream segments of the crystalline PV cell value chain have only survived through high-level process innovations that allowed them to reduce their production costs faster than their competitors operating in the same segment.[28]

Table 3.3

Top production equipment companies, 2011

Company	Headquarters country	Sector of origin
Applied Materials	United States	Semiconductors
Centrotherm	Germany	Semiconductors/electronics
MeyerBurger	Switzerland	Semiconductors/electronics
GTAT	United States	Electronics
Schmid	Germany	Electronics
Komatsu-NTC	Japan	Semiconductors
Oerliko	Switzerland	Semiconductors
APPOLLO	United States	Electronics
RENA	Germany	Electronics
JGST	China	Solar

Source: Carvalho et al. (2017) and Zhang and Gallagher (2016).

Who generates PV production equipment innovations? Production equipment for crystalline PV initially came from companies specialized in producing equipment for the semiconductor and electronics industry. These companies applied their technological capabilities in the semiconductor industry to produce equipment suited for manufacturing ingots, wafers, cells and modules. Semiconductor companies based in the United States, Germany and Japan consistently featured as the top companies in terms of market share and quality of equipment for solar PV production equipment (see table 3.3).

Patent mapping complements this picture. Until 2012, the United States and Japan largely dominated the landscape of patent filings relating to production equipment. Since then, such filings have declined sharply; they fell by around 60 percent between 2012 and 2015 (see figure 3.11). The drop was higher for the United States and Japan, allowing China to claim the largest share in this segment in 2012.

China accumulated one-third of the patents filed during the period 2011-2015. Nevertheless, the United States still accounted for almost half of all patent filings relating to production equipment for crystalline or alternative cells in that period (see figure 3.10). Japan and the Republic of Korea also rank higher than China, which holds a very low proportion of such patents.

How did China catch up technologically?

What has been the role of intangible assets in shaping the current global PV value chain? Addressing this question primarily entails understanding how Chinese upstream and midstream firms acquired the necessary knowledge assets to enter at different stages of the value chain. There were two main channels for technology transfer to China: production equipment and skilled human capital.

Table 3.4

Distribution of headquarters of solar PV technology equipment producers, 2016

Economy	Number of companies	Share of total number of companies (%)
China	381	41
United States	152	16
Germany	125	13
Japan	70	7
Rep. of Korea	53	6
Taiwan (Province of China)	44	5
Italy	18	2
Switzerland	15	2
Rest of world	81	8
Total	939	100

Source: Carvalho et al. (2017).

Table 3.5

Top six solar module/cell companies in China, 2015

Company	World rank	Share of total global revenue (%)	Creation	FDI/JV links
Trina Solar	1	10	1997	None
JA Solar	2	8	2005	Australia (through JingAo)
Jinko Solar	3	7	2006	None
Yingli	5	5	1998	None
Canadian Solar	6	5	2001	Canada
Shungfeng-Suntech	8	3	2001	None

Source: Carvalho et al. (2017).

Chinese companies mostly acquired PV technologies by purchasing production equipment from international suppliers.[29] Pioneering Chinese firms entered the market by purchasing production equipment from Western providers.[30] But technological knowledge diffusion to China went beyond the transfer of such equipment. Indeed, evidence of technological catch-up is apparent from the progressive emergence of equipment goods suppliers that are solely Chinese. By 2016, almost half the world's production equipment firms were headquartered in China, with the next most significant headquarter locations being the United States, Germany and Japan (see table 3.4).

The circulation of a skilled workforce has been another factor aiding the success of Chinese firms in upstream and midstream segments of the value chain.[31] When entering the industry in the 2000s, Chinese PV companies benefited strongly from the arrival of highly skilled executives who brought capital, professional networks and technology acquired in foreign companies and universities to China.

For instance, the founder and CEO of Suntech, China's largest PV company until 2013, studied at the University of New South Wales in Australia and then worked for the Australian company Pacific Solar. Three of the largest Chinese companies – Shungfeng Suntech, Yingli and Trina – were created by Chinese nationals who had formerly been researchers in Australia, and nearly two-thirds of the board members of the four largest Chinese PV firms in 2016 – Trina, GCL Poly, Jinko Solar and Canadian Solar – had studied or worked abroad. All big companies have recruitment programs to attract senior management from abroad.

Conversely, there is little evidence to support the hypothesis that investment by multinational firms was a decisive factor in the emergence of the Chinese industry.[32] Table 3.5 presents the top six cell or module manufacturers located in China. Only two of them have investment links with foreign companies. Moreover, these FDI-based firms turn out to be late entrants whose creation has followed in the footsteps of strictly Chinese pioneer firms.

3.3 – What is the role of IP in the PV industry?

This section looks in more detail at the role of IP in protecting knowledge and reputational assets. It will first consider how IP has been used to protect knowledge assets and its role in future technological appropriation by China, then examine recent trends in the use of IP to protect reputational assets and ornamental features of PV products.

How the PV value chain protects its knowledge assets

Throughout the first decade of the 21st century, there was a growing tendency to use patents to protect knowledge assets for all the technologies in the PV value chain (figure 3.11). The largest increases were observed for cells and modules, which peaked in 2011 at around 15,000 and 20,000 patent applications, respectively.

Figure 3.11

PV-related patent filings have been falling since 2011

PV-related patent applications worldwide by value chain segment, 2000-2015

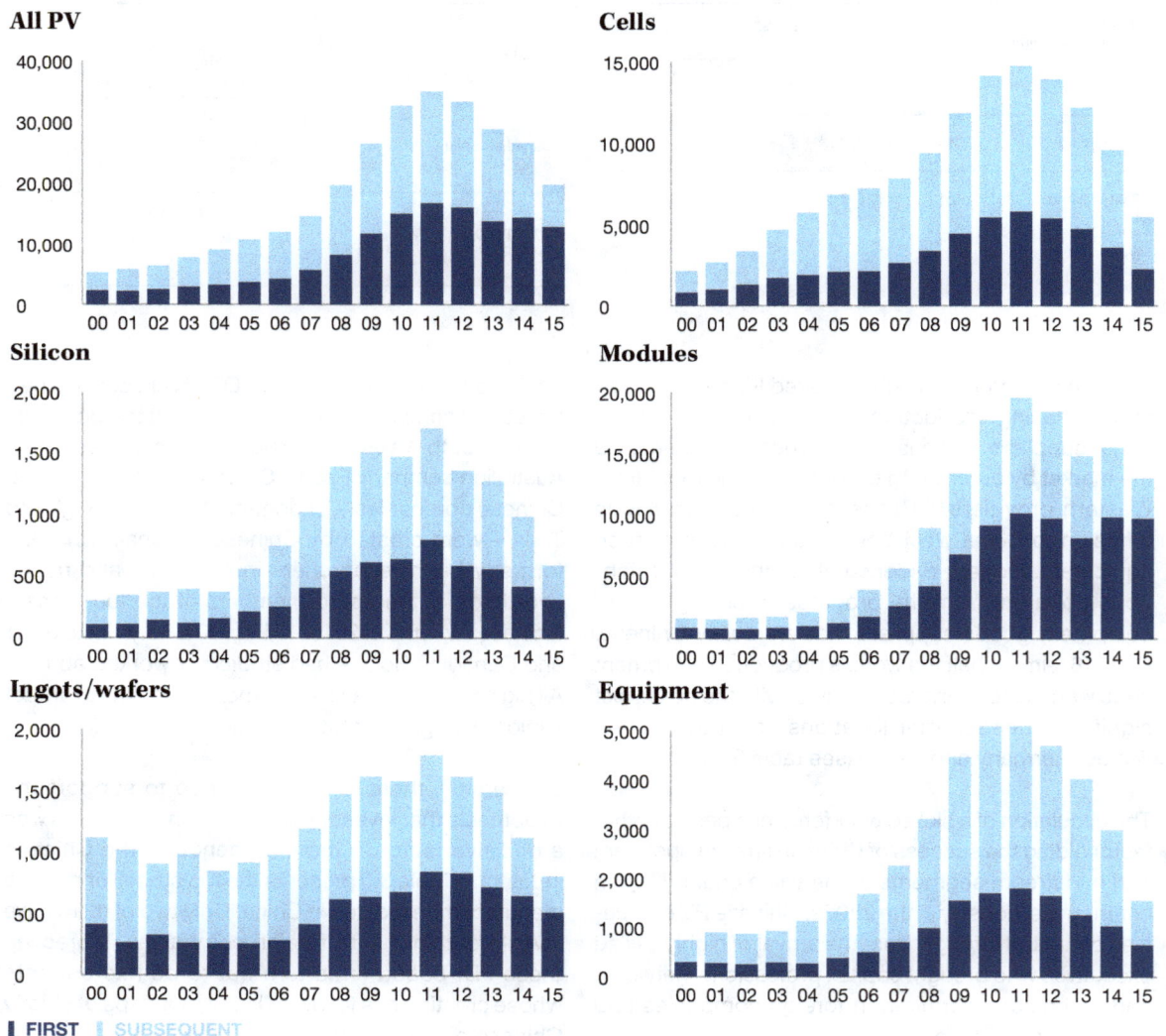

All PV

Cells

Silicon

Modules

Ingots/wafers

Equipment

■ FIRST ■ SUBSEQUENT

Source: WIPO based on PATSTAT; see technical notes.

The growth in PV patenting activity has reversed recently. Between 2011 and 2015, the number of PV-related patent applications fell by 44 percent. PV patent filings have also fallen as a share of global patenting activity, decreasing 30 percent in just four years. The fall has occurred across all segments of the value chain, from silicon to module technologies, but is particularly pronounced for silicon, cells and equipment (figure 3.11).

There has also been dramatic change as regards the country of origin of patent applications. PV-related patent filings have fallen in all major innovating countries with the notable exception of China (see figure 3.8).

At first sight, the downward trend in global PV patenting since 2011 suggests that the outlook for technological innovation in the sector is gloomy. Is patenting becoming less attractive in the PV industry?

Table 3.6

R&D intensity and patent filings by top PV companies

Company	Country	R&D intensity* (%)		Average first patent filings per year		Average annual R&D expenditure (USDm)*	Average PV patent filings per USDm R&D expenditure*
		2010	2015	2005-2009	2010-2014		
Silicon							
GCL-Poly Energy	CN		1.12	5	3.4	20.5	0.20
Wacker	DE	2.90	3.30	6	18.6	146.5	0.08
REC	NO	2.10	2.50	3.4	11.6	11.65	0.64
OCI Company	KR			1	1.75		
Cells							
First Solar	US	3.70	3.60	5.6	52.2	112.8	0.26
Trina	CN	1	3.50	6	41.8	26.05	0.92
JA Solar	CN	2.50	3.20	3	9.4	16.5	0.38
Canadian Solar	CN	0.45	0.50	1	2.75	12.5	0.15
Jinko Solar	CN	0.38	2.30	0	19.75	15.1	0.65
SunPower	US	4.10	6.30	13.8	38.4	74	0.35
Hanwha Q CELLS	KR-DE		6.80	12.75	14.8	28	0.49
Equipment							
Applied Materials	US	12.00	15.40	45.6	40.8	1297.5*	
Centrotherm Photovoltaics	DE	6.80	5.30	4.4	11.8	20	0.41
Meyerburger	CH	5	17.20	0	1.3	49.5*	
Inverters							
Sungrow	CN		4.3	2	13		
SMA Solar	DE			9	26.2	78.5	0.22
SolarEdge	Israel		6.10	6.3	5.6	22	0.27

*Note: includes non-PV R&D.

Source: Carvalho et al. (2017).

In fact, it appears that the decrease is driven by two different forces. First, the number of applicants has collapsed.[33] Between 2011 and 2014, the number of applicants from the United States, Germany, Japan and the Republic of Korea declined, and entry of new applicants fell even more sharply. This also implies that, on average, the number of patent applications filed per applicant has increased, particularly in the main PV-producing countries. These trends are even more marked for alternative types of PV cells, where the decline in patent filings has been much lower.

The evolution of R&D intensity at major PV firms is consistent with these patent figures (see table 3.6). Almost all major players increased their R&D intensity between 2010 and 2015 – sometimes substantially – but their patenting activity grew even more. While the relation between R&D expenditure and patents is not straightforward, the disproportionate increase in patenting activity compared with R&D intensity suggests an increase in patenting intensity among surviving firms across the industry.

In other words, what seems to be happening is the following. Many players have exited the market and entry is becoming even more difficult. However, surviving firms are reacting by increasing their innovation efforts and filing more patents. In addition, these players are reacting to the industry shake-up by focusing their innovation efforts on the next generation of technologies. This suggests that IP-protected knowledge assets may become more valuable in this time of sectoral recomposition.

The second driving force is a reduction of the internationalization of PV patents. Patent applications can be divided into first applications for patent protection of an invention (known as first filings) and extensions of protection to another country for existing patent applications (known as subsequent filings). Both first and subsequent filings grew rapidly in the PV industry in the 2000s, but since 2011 both have fallen, with subsequent filings falling even faster than first filings. In the mid-2000s, each PV invention was filed on average in three different patent offices; by 2015, that average was only one-and-a-half.

This reduction suggests that more and more PV patent applicants opt out of seeking international protection. Virtually all PV patent applications from the main origins are filed domestically first. But the internationalization

of PV technologies differs substantially across origins and destinations (table 3.7). U.S. applicants are the most foreign oriented across the main origins. Although they file less than 40 percent of their applications in any of the other main patent offices, the proportion is even lower for applicants from Europe, Japan and the Republic of Korea. Chinese applicants are the least likely to file for foreign protection, which reinforces the overall statistical trend away from internationalization as they are the only ones increasing their PV-related patent applications.

Table 3.7

Percentage share of patent families filed at major patent offices by origin, 1995-2015

Origin	WIPO	USPTO	EPO	JPO	KIPO	SIPO
United States	51.8	96.2	38.3	33.3	22.5	37.8
Europe	48.8	51.8	58.4	32.1	20.7	33.3
Japan	28.6	45.8	21.5	99.2	17.7	26.2
Rep. of Korea	15.2	31.7	10.1	13.9	99.5	17.1
China	2.0	1.7	0.7	0.6	0.3	99.7
Other	12.3	47.4	10.7	11.3	5.4	30.1
Total	20.0	32.8	16.9	31.0	21.3	55.5

Source: Carvalho et al. (2017).

Worldwide extension of patent protection for PV-related innovations is very limited. Indeed, a handful of economies – notably China, the United States, Japan, the Republic of Korea and European countries – are among the few locations where some patent protection is sought. Figure 3.12a shows that PV technologies are virtually unprotected in all remaining economies, including Australia, the Russian Federation, Latin America, Africa and the Middle East. The huge number of recent Chinese PV patent applications – most protected only domestically – may affect these results (see figure 3.12b). But the general distribution remains qualitatively the same when these are excluded, as shown for the distribution of PV patent families from the United States in figure 3.12c.

Figure 3.12

Patent-protected PV technologies are concentrated in a few economies

Share of world, Chinese and U.S. PV patent families by protected country, 1995-2015

(a) World

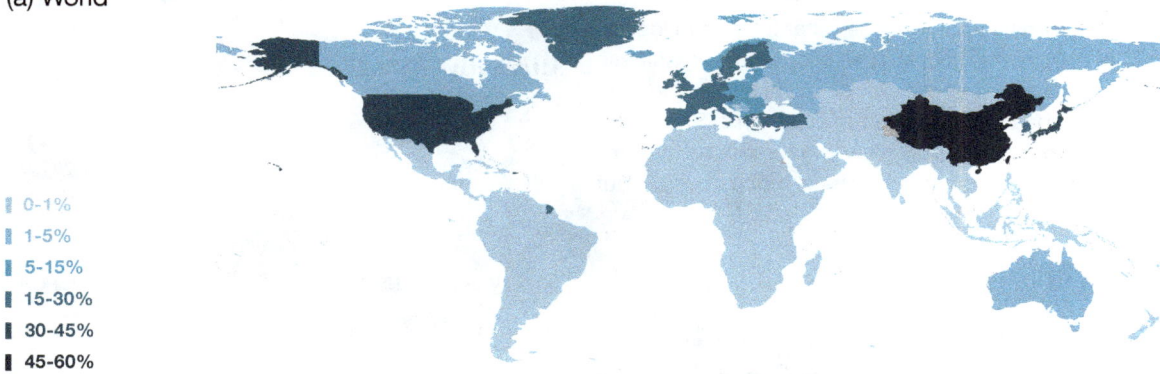

0-1%
1-5%
5-15%
15-30%
30-45%
45-60%

(b) China

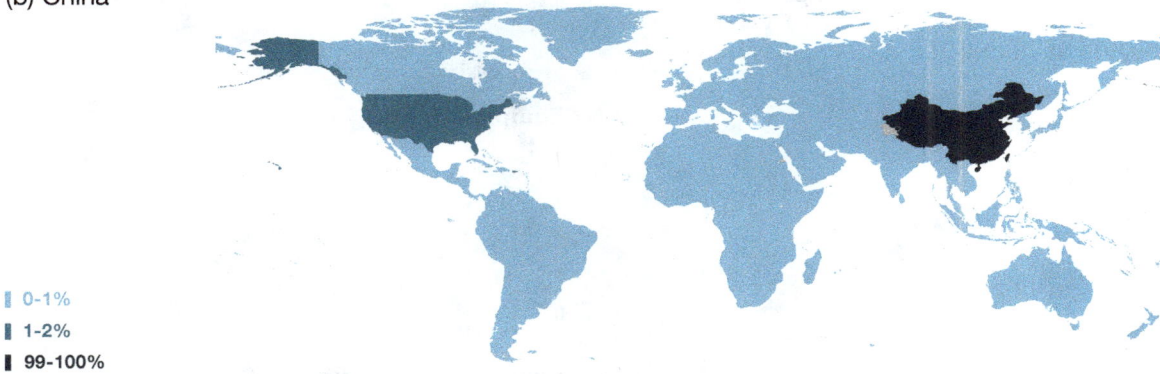

0-1%
1-2%
99-100%

(c) United States

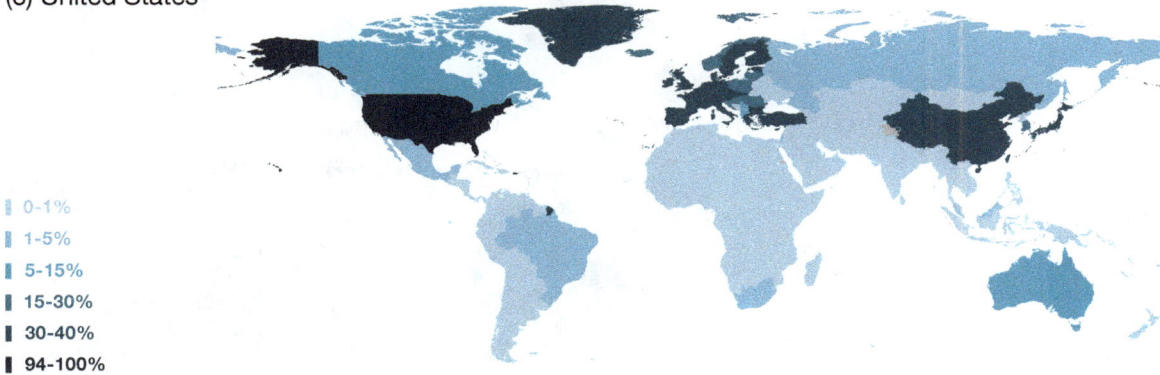

0-1%
1-5%
5-15%
15-30%
30-40%
94-100%

Source: WIPO based on PATSTAT; see technical notes.

Can China sustain its position in PV production without IP protection?

A striking finding from the patent analysis is the relative absence of Chinese applications at major patent offices. This is a phenomenon that is not unusual in terms of Chinese patenting activity generally; most foreign extensions of Chinese patents are confined to ICT-related technologies. The proportion of Chinese PV-related patent applications filed at all main foreign IP offices has never exceeded 2 percent. Shares for PV technologies are slightly higher than those for Chinese applications filed in these offices overall, but still remarkably low.

Figure 3.13

Chinese applicants tend not to seek patent protection for PV technologies in other markets

Percentage share of Chinese patent families filed at major patent offices by PV value chain segment, 1995-2015

Silicon

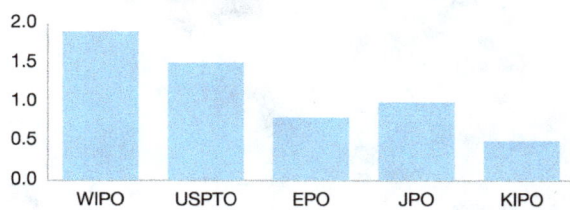

Ingots/wafers

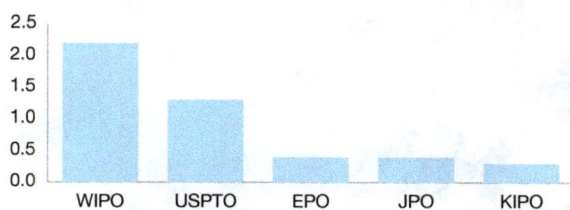

Cells

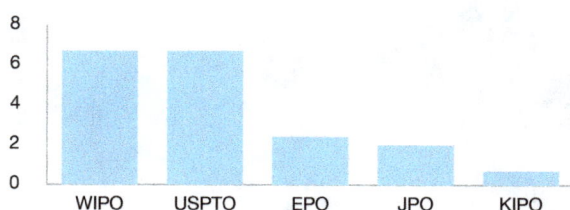

Crystalline PV cells

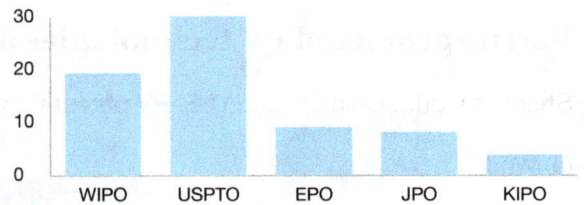

Alternative PV cells

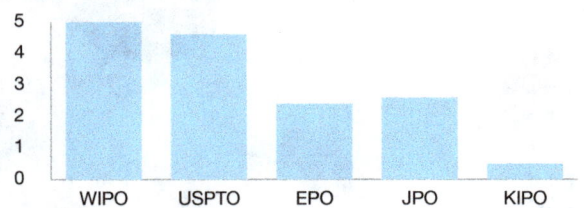

Modules

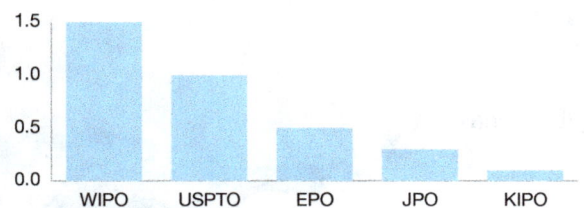

Equipment

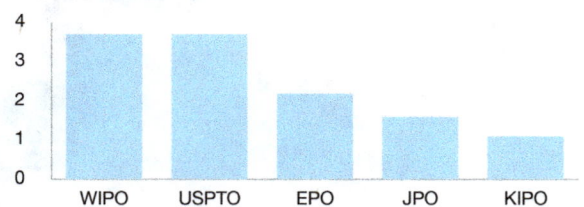

Equipment for crystalline PV cells

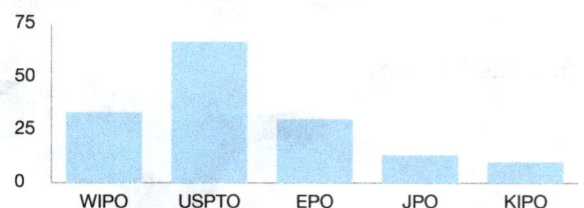

Equipment for alternative PV cells

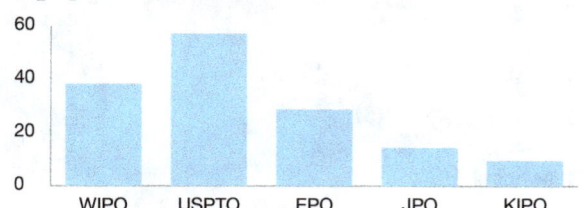

Source: WIPO based on PATSTAT; see technical notes.

As shown in figure 3.13, there is some variation in the internationalization of Chinese patent protection across PV segments. Patents are more likely to be filed internationally in relation to PV cells than for any other PV segment. In particular, international filings related to PV cells peak at roughly 7 percent in both the United States and through the Patent Cooperation Treaty (PCT) System. The generally very low internationalization rates for Chinese PV patenting contrast with Chinese companies' market share of around 80 to 90 percent in most segments of the PV value chain.

There are, however, some differences across the type of PV technology. The internationalization rate is significantly higher for Chinese patent filings related to crystalline cell technologies and production equipment for both crystalline and alternative cells (figure 3.13). China has a relatively small number of patents in these three technologies, but they are remarkably likely to have foreign extensions, especially in the United States.

It remains to be seen what the long-term impact of the absence of international protection for most Chinese-owned PV technologies will be. Will protecting them in China only be enough to maintain Chinese producers' commercial success, or does it give other industry players an opportunity to come back? Only time will tell.

This is particularly the case if alternative technologies to crystalline PV cells finally make their way to market. In this respect, a few highly innovative firms and research institutes with large patent portfolios and highly efficient cells – such as Fraunhofer ISE, Sharp, IPFL and Boeing Spectrolab – may be better positioned to exploit PV products currently on the shelf.

A brand new PV world?

There is increasing evidence of a growing role for reputational assets in downstream segments. This is very relevant for at least two reasons. First, these are the more profitable segments, where value added must to a great extent be produced locally. Second, these segments have a broader geographic distribution than upstream or midstream ones, remaining located largely in industrialized economies such as Europe and the United States.

A sign of consolidation in the PV industry is the increasing importance of branding-related activities. As demand for PV technologies and their capacity have grown exponentially in the past 10 years, so too has the use of trademark protection for PV products and services.

Figure 3.14 illustrates this trend. All the main sources of trademark data – the USPTO, WIPO's Global Brands Database and the Madrid System – support this finding, with figures for 2016 four to six times higher than those for 2005.

Figure 3.14

Brand protection is increasingly important in the PV market

PV-related trademark applications, 1990-2016

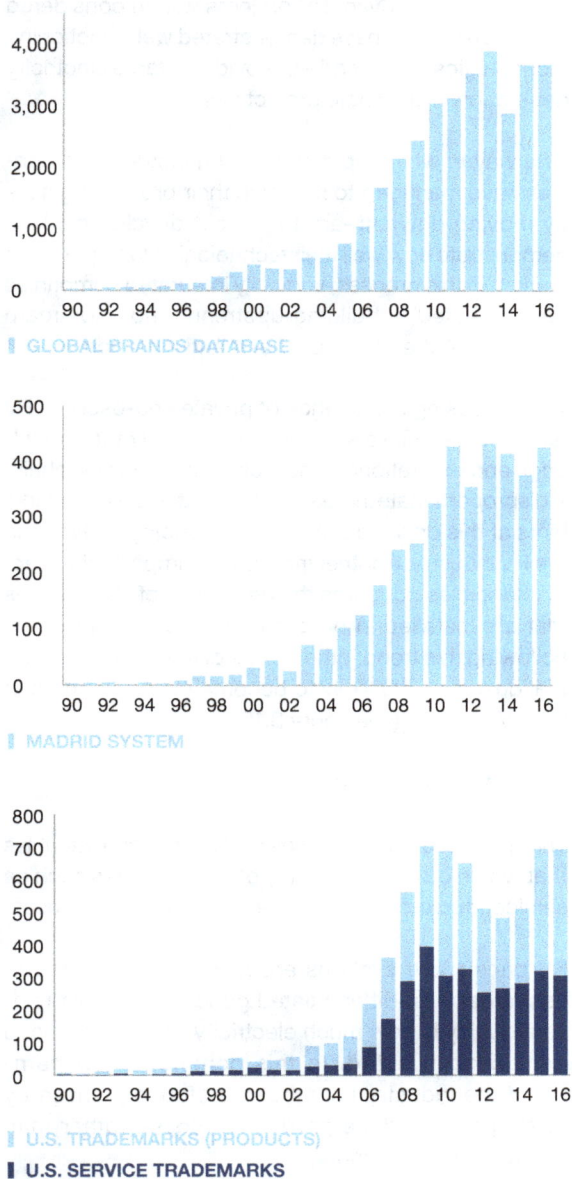

GLOBAL BRANDS DATABASE

MADRID SYSTEM

U.S. TRADEMARKS (PRODUCTS)

U.S. SERVICE TRADEMARKS

Source: WIPO based on the USPTO, the Global Brands Database and the Madrid System.

What lies behind this trend? One direct cause is simply the rapid growth of the market. A complementary explanation relates to the tight margins and vertical integration discussed above. Most solar PV projects are financed through debt financing from banks, meaning that interest rates account for a significant part of the project cost. Interest rates are determined not just by market risk, but also by technological risk, making it particularly important for solar PV project developers to source technologies from recognized players. The bank has to have confidence in both the project developer's reputation and the technological inputs that will be employed. PV projects will be considered "bankable" if they have demonstrated well-functioning technologies in the market, providing stable electricity generation and reliable project yields.

One way in which upstream and midstream companies have managed to maintain their profit margins is by moving downstream to project development, to demonstrate how well their technologies function in the market. In this process, vertically integrated companies have invested in building upstream and midstream reputation – the so-called Tier 1 and 2 brands.

The increasing importance of private end-users of PV technologies may also change the role of other knowledge and reputational assets along the PV value chain. A disproportionate increase in PV-related service marks hints at this downstream pull for branding activities in the PV industry. Another increasingly important aspect of intangibles concerns the aesthetics of PV modules that are installed in private consumers' residences. Following this trend, other forms of IP – notably industrial designs – are likely to become more important in the PV industry (see figure 3.15).

3.4 – Conclusion

The spatial evolution of the solar PV value chain resembles that which occurred in many other industries such as semiconductors, electronics and domestic appliances.

PV panels and systems are now mostly commodities rather than differentiated goods: their most relevant quality is how much electricity can be produced per dollar invested. In this context, the dynamics of the industry have been profoundly driven by strategies to reduce production costs, rather than by product innovation.

An indication is that the market is still dominated by the most mature technology – crystalline PV – while alternative PV technologies bore great hopes in the early 2000s, when market demand and prices for solar PV technologies were high due to policy support mechanisms in Europe.

As a result, PV products initially invented in the Western world decades ago were no longer protected by patents, and Chinese firms needed only to acquire the knowledge to manufacture their components efficiently along the value chain. This highlights two channels of technology transfer. First, Chinese firms got access to production equipment and turnkey fabrication lines supplied by U.S., European and Japanese firms. The production equipment was protected by patents to some extent, but there was enough competition in international markets to maintain reasonable prices. Second, Chinese firms also relied on knowledge transmission through human capital, in the form of their founders and workers who studied abroad in regions that engaged with innovation in solar PV technologies. The PV industry is a case study of a complete form of technology transfer to an emerging economy, as indicated by the fact that Chinese firms have now also become the leaders in PV production equipment.

Understanding how channels of knowledge transfer affect the spatial distribution of the value chain has implications for future innovation. The solar PV market is now saturated with an incumbent technology whose depressed prices provide tight profit margins for companies. Firms can dedicate their R&D efforts either to high-level process innovations that will reduce production costs in the dominant technology, or to new solar PV product innovations whose production prices are below those for the incumbent technology.

The major changes undergone by the global PV industry during the last decade have been accompanied by a renewed interest in intellectual property protection, as is illustrated by the fact that companies that survived the collapse in PV prices worldwide seem to have increased their patenting propensity recently.

As this chapter has documented, IP protection of intangible assets was not a key determinant in the success of Chinese companies, but it may well nevertheless become a key ingredient for commercial success in the coming decades.

Figure 3.15

Solar panel designs are becoming more creative

Selected solar panel industrial designs filed via the Hague International Design System

Source: Hague System, WIPO.

Notes

1. This chapter draws on Carvalho et al. (2017).

2. US patent 2402662, filed on May 27, 1941.

3. See Fraas (2014) and Perlin (1999).

4. See Carvalho (2015b), de la Tour, Glachant and Ménière (2011), Fu and Zhang (2011) and Wu and Mathews (2012).

5. Schmela et al. (2016).

6. BNEF (2014).

7. BNEF (2017).

8. See BNEF (2014) and ENF (2012, 2013a, 2013b).

9. Wesoff (2015).

10. Ghosh (2016).

11. Goodrich et al. (2011).

12. Schmela et al. (2016).

13. Johnson (2013).

14. Schmela et al. (2016).

15. See IEA (2016).

16. IEA (2016) and SEMI PV (2017).

17. See Carvalho (2015a).

18. See BNEF (2013).

19. See the general discussion in chapter 1, section 1.4.

20. See IEA (2016), SEMI PV (2017) and Schmela et al. (2016).

21. Ekins-Daukes (2013) and NREL (2017).

22. SEMI PV (2017).

23. IEA (2016).

24. IEA (2016) and SEMI PV (2017).

25. SEMI PV (2017).

26. NREL (2017).

27. de la Tour et al. (2011).

28. IEA (2016) and SEMI PV (2017).

29. de la Tour et al. (2011), Fu and Zhang (2011) and Wu and Mathews (2012).

30. de la Tour et al. (2011) and Wu and Mathews (2012).

31. Luo et al. (2017).

32. de la Tour et al. (2011).

33. See Carvalho et al. (2017).

References

BNEF (2013). *PV Market Outlook Q1 2013*. London: Bloomberg New Energy Finance (BNEF).

BNEF (2014). *Q1 2014 Solar Market Outlook*. London: BNEF.

BNEF (2017). *Solar Price Indexes*. London: BNEF.

Carvalho, M.D. (2015a). How does the presence – or absence – of domestic industries affect the commercialisation of technologies? In *The Internationalisation of Green Technologies and the Realisation of Green Growth*. London: London School of Economics and Political Science, chapter 5.

Carvalho, M.D. (2015b). *The Internationalisation of Green Technologies and the Realisation of Green Growth*. London: London School of Economics and Political Science.

Carvalho, M.D., A. Dechezleprêtre and M. Glachant (2017). Understanding the Dynamics of Global Value Chains for Solar Photovoltaic Technologies. *WIPO Economic Research Working Paper No. 40*. Geneva: WIPO.

de la Tour, A., M. Glachant and Y. Ménière (2011). Innovation and international technology transfer: the case of the Chinese photovoltaic industry. *Energy Policy*, 39(2), 761-770. doi.org/10.1016/j.enpol.2010.10.050.

Ekins-Daukes, N.J. (2013). Silicon PV. In *SEF MSc Lecture*. London: Imperial College London.

ENF (2012). *Taiwan Cell and Panel Manufacturers Survey*. London: ENF Ltd.

ENF (2013a). *Chinese Cell and Panel Manufacturers Survey*. London: ENF Ltd.

ENF (2013b). *Global Ingot and Wafer Manufacturers Survey*. London: ENF Ltd. Fraas, L.M. (2014). History of solar cell development. In Fraas, L.M. (ed.), *Low-Cost Solar Electric Power*. Switzerland: Springer. doi.org/10.1007/978-3-319-07530-3.

Fu, X. and J. Zhang (2011). Technology transfer, indigenous innovation and leapfrogging in green technology: the solar-PV industry in China and India. *Journal of Chinese Economic and Business Studies*, 9(4), 329-347. doi.org/10.1080/14765284.2011.618590.

Ghosh, A. (2016). Clean energy trade conflicts: the political economy of a future energy system. In T. Van de Graaf, B.K. Sovacool, A. Ghosh, F. Kern and M.T. Klare (eds), *The Palgrave Handbook of the International Political Economy of Energy*. Basingstoke: Palgrave, 397-416. doi.org/10.1057/978-1-137-55631-8.

Goodrich, A., T. James and M. Woodhouse (2011). *Solar PV Manufacturing Cost Analysis: U.S. Competitiveness in a Global Industry*. Stanford, CA: NREL. www.nrel.gov/docs/fy12osti/53938.pdf.

IEA (2016). *Trends in Photovoltaic Applications 2016: Survey Report of Selected IEA Countries between 1992 and 2015*. Paris: International Energy Agency.

Johnson, O. (2013). Exploring the Effectiveness of Local Content Requirements in Promoting Solar PV Manufacturing in India. *German Development Institute Discussion Paper No. 11/2013*. Bonn: German Development Institute: www.die-gdi.de/uploads/media/DP_11.2013.pdf.

Luo, S., M.E. Lovely and D.C. Popp (2017). Intellectual returnees as drivers of indigenous innovation: evidence from the Chinese photovoltaic industry. *World Economy*, 00, 1-31. doi.org/10.1111/twec.12536.

NREL (2017). *NREL Best Research-Cell Efficiencies 2017*. Oak Ridge, TN: NREL.

Perlin, J. (1999). *From Space to Earth: The Story of Solar Electricity*. Ann Arbor, MI: Aatec Publications.

Schmela, M., G. Masson and N.N.T. Mai (2016). *Global Market Outlook for Solar Power, 2016-2020*. Brussels: Solar Power Europe.

SEMI PV (2017). *International Technology Roadmap for Photovoltaic (ITRPV): 2016 Results*. Milpitas, CA: VDMA Photovoltaic Equipment.

Wesoff, E. (2015). The mercifully short list of fallen solar companies: 2015 edition. *GTM Solar*. Greentech Media. www.greentechmedia.com/articles/read/The-Mercifully-Short-List-of-Fallen-Solar-Companies-2015-Edition.

Wu, C.-Y. and J.A. Mathews (2012). Knowledge flows in the solar photovoltaic industry: insights from patenting by Taiwan, Korea, and China. *Research Policy*, 41(3), 524-540. doi.org/10.1016/j.respol.2011.10.007.

Zhang, F. and K.S. Gallagher (2016). Innovation and technology transfer through global value chains: evidence from China's PV industry. *Energy Policy*, 94, 191-203. doi.org/10.1016/j.enpol.2016.04.014.

Success in the smartphone industry is based on intangibles

Samsung Galaxy S7

Global average price
$ 708

Cost of materials
23%
Distribution and retail
20%
Other
23%
Samsung's value capture
34%

Apple iPhone 7

Global average price
$ 809

Cost of materials
22%
Distribution and retail
15%
Other
21%
Apple's value capture
42%

Huawei P9

Global average price
$ 449

Cost of materials
20%
Distribution and retail
15%
Other
23%
Huawei's value capture
42%

Leading firms use **technology, design and branding** to secure a huge share of market value.

Up to 35% of all patents filed worldwide since 1990 may relate to smartphones.

Designs of user interfaces are also heavily protected.

Source: World Intellectual Property Report 2017

Chapter 4
Smartphones: what's inside the box?

Smartphones are cellular telephones with an operating system that allows consumers to tap into increasingly rich mobile applications. They are produced by global value chains composed of a few handset manufacturers that draw on a large range of communications technology, component and software suppliers.

This chapter takes a look inside the smartphone global value chain. It quantifies the value capture for three recent top-end smartphones from market leaders Apple, Huawei and Samsung, with a focus on the creation and valorization of intangible assets.[1] Section 4.1 details the characteristics of the underlying global value chain; section 4.2 identifies who captures the value of smartphone sales; section 4.3 assesses the role of intangible assets and intellectual property in value capture; and section 4.4 discusses the process of technological learning.

4.1 – The smartphone global value chain

Despite the leadership of a few firms in terms of consumer market shares, a vast network of firms operating in the electronics and software industry is ultimately responsible for the conception and production of smartphones.

4.1.1 – The evolving nature of the smartphone market

Over the last 20 years, cellular communications have shifted from basic phones used for voice communications to smartphones used also for data-intensive content applications. The smartphone industry has grown from 124 million units sold in 2007 to 1.47 billion unit sales in 2016 with a total market value of USD 418 billion.[2] Globally, there are 3.8 billion users today, and that figure is expected to reach 5.8 billion by 2020, with growth mainly driven by uptake in developing countries.[3]

While growth in the smartphone market has been steady and strong, the handset providers leading the industry have changed over time. The brands initially dominating global smartphone sales were Nokia and BlackBerry, but Apple and Samsung have taken their place since 2011. The market continues to experience exit and entry (table 4.1). Huawei, which only entered in 2010, took third place in 2015.

Table 4.1

Global smartphone market shares, in percentage of units sold

Company	2007	2010	2013	2016
Samsung Electronics	1.8	7.5	31.1	21.1
Apple	3.0	15.6	15.1	14.6
Huawei	–	0.6	4.8	9.5
LG	–	–	4.7	3.7
Xiaomi	–	–	1.8	3.6
Lenovo	0.0	0.2	4.5	3.5
Motorola	6.1	4.6	1.2	*
HTC	2.4	7.2	2.2	1.0
Nokia	49.2	32.8	3.0	*
BlackBerry	9.9	16.0	1.9	.05

Note: *Nokia's smartphone business was bought by Microsoft, and Motorola's by Lenovo.

Source: IDC Worldwide Mobile Phone Tracker, 2017.

Apple (57 percent) and Samsung (25 percent) dominate the market for high-end phones – those costing more than USD 400.[4] The average selling price (ASP) of a smartphone has declined from USD 425 in the period 2007-2011 to USD 283 in 2016, and phones fitted with the Android mobile operating system are now significantly cheaper than Apple devices running iOS (see table 4.2). The proportion of high-end smartphones sold as a share of the entire smartphone market is also declining, due partly to competition in the high-end segment and partly to the rise of cheaper Chinese brands in the mid- to low-end segment.[5] While Chinese smartphone makers Xiaomi, Oppo and Vivo are still relatively unknown to the average consumer outside China, they are now among the top 10 in terms of global smartphone sales.[6]

Table 4.2

Average selling price of smartphones by mobile operating system, in USD

Operating system	2007	2010	2013	2014	2015	2016
iOS (Apple)	594	703	669	680	716	690
Android (Google)	–	441	272	237	217	214

Source: IDC Worldwide Mobile Phone Tracker, 2017.

Figure 4.1

The smartphone global value chain is shaped like a spider

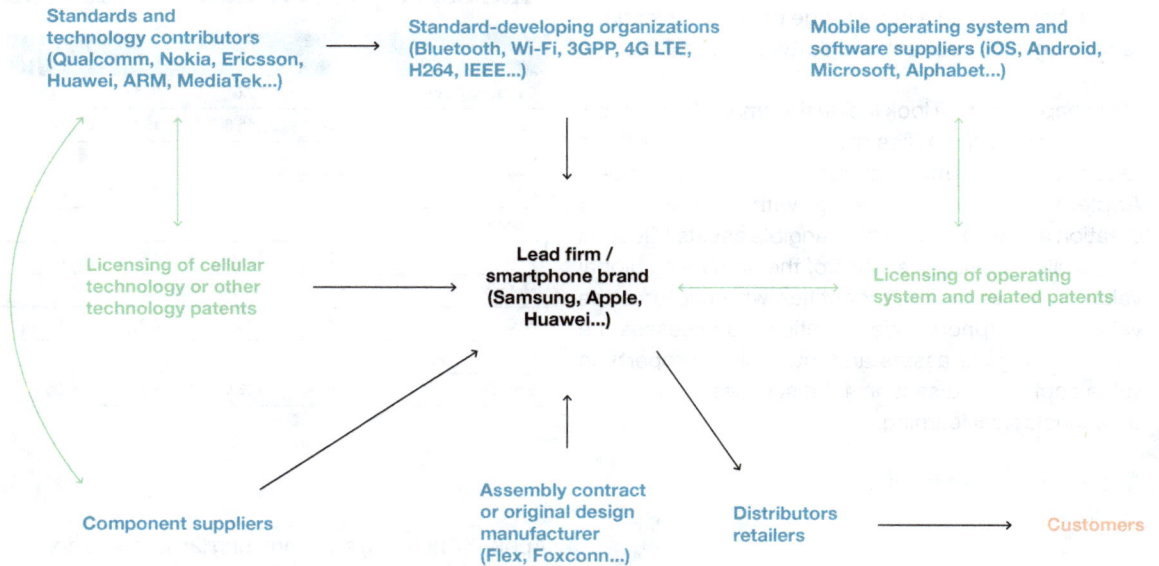

Standards and technology contributors (Qualcomm, Nokia, Ericsson, Huawei, ARM, MediaTek...)

Standard-developing organizations (Bluetooth, Wi-Fi, 3GPP, 4G LTE, H264, IEEE...)

Mobile operating system and software suppliers (iOS, Android, Microsoft, Alphabet...)

Licensing of cellular technology or other technology patents

Lead firm / smartphone brand (Samsung, Apple, Huawei...)

Licensing of operating system and related patents

Component suppliers

Assembly contract or original design manufacturer (Flex, Foxconn...)

Distributors retailers

Customers

Note: Black lines represent the flow of parts or components through the value chain, green lines the licensing of technology and IP.

4.1.2 – Innovation in and the shape of the global smartphone value chain

The smartphone global value chain involves the usual stages of research and development (R&D), design, manufacturing, assembly, marketing, distribution and sales. It is organized not as a linear value chain, but rather – to use concepts introduced in chapter 1 – in a producer-driven "spider" form (see figure 4.1).

In this set-up, the lead firm operates under a strong brand and is responsible for considerable R&D, product design and product specifications. But Apple, Huawei and Samsung source components and technology from third parties, who are sometimes equally innovative and active in producing intangible assets.

First, these lead firms require components and access to standards-related technology. Apple sources mainly from outside suppliers whereas Huawei and Samsung source mainly from within their firms. Certain inputs are commoditized, for example resistors and wiring, while other, high-value, components such as phone casings and chipsets are highly specialized.

All these components also have their own global supply chains. For example, a chip may be designed by a specialized U.S. company for a smartphone supplier; it is then manufactured in China and packaged in Malaysia to reach the end-consumer.

Second, smartphone producers require access to technology employed in interoperability and connectivity standards, such as the fourth-generation (4G) Long-Term Evolution (LTE) cellular standard or the 802.11 Wi-Fi standard. Large companies such as Nokia, Ericsson, Qualcomm, InterDigital, Huawei, Samsung, NTT DoCoMo and ZTE contribute patented technologies to the development of such standards, which are defined by standard-setting organizations. Typically, these technologies are licensed separately, entailing the payment of licensing fees.

Third, smartphone firms require software – not only a mobile operating system, but also other dedicated mobile software applications, often from third parties. Samsung, Huawei and others use Android, developed by Google; Apple produces its own system, iOS.

Table 4.3

R&D expenditures of smartphone technology firms and their ranking among top global R&D spenders

Rank among top company R&D spenders worldwide	Name	Economy or country	Industrial sector	R&D 2015/16 in EUR million	R&D three-year compound annual growth 2014-16 (%)	R&D intensity, 2015/16 (% of revenues)
2	SAMSUNG ELECTRONICS	Rep. of Korea	Electronic and electrical equipment	12,527.9	10.7	8.0
3	INTEL	U.S.	Technology hardware and equipment	11,139.9	5.1	6.1
4	ALPHABET	U.S.	Software and computer services	11,053.6	22.4	22.2
5	MICROSOFT	U.S.	Software and computer services	11,011.3	-0.5	4.8
8	HUAWEI INVESTMENT & HOLDING CO.	China	Technology hardware and equipment	8,357.9	26.3	15.0
11	APPLE	U.S.	Technology hardware and equipment	7,409.8	33.6	3.5
17	CISCO SYSTEMS	U.S.	Technology hardware and equipment	5,701.3	4.2	12.6
25	QUALCOMM	U.S.	Technology hardware and equipment	5,042.7	11.9	21.7
35	ERICSSON	Sweden	Technology hardware and equipment	3,805.6	2.7	14.2
54	NOKIA	Finland	Technology hardware and equipment	2,502.0	-15.6	18.4
57	ALCATEL-LUCENT	France	Technology hardware and equipment	2,409.0	-0.4	16.9
65	ZTE	China	Technology hardware and equipment	1,954.1	12.4	13.8
70	TAIWAN SEMICONDUCTOR	Taiwan (Province of China)	Technology hardware and equipment	1,826.7	17.5	7.8
85	SK HYNIX	Rep. of Korea	Technology hardware and equipment	1,543.0	21.2	10.5
90	HON HAI PRECISION INDUSTRY	Taiwan (Province of China)	Electronic and electrical equipment	1,462.9	4.8	1.2
95	MICRON TECHNOLOGY	U.S.	Technology hardware and equipment	1,414.5	18.8	9.5
98	MEDIATEK	Taiwan (Province of China)	Technology hardware and equipment	1,380.3	30.3	23.2
106	LENOVO	China	Technology hardware and equipment	1,284.7	31.3	3.1
112	NVIDIA	U.S.	Technology hardware and equipment	1,222.6	5.4	26.6
120	STMICROELECTRONICS	The Netherlands	Technology hardware and equipment	1,149.1	-18.7	18.1
141	MARVELL TECHNOLOGY	U.S.	Technology hardware and equipment	968.4	-0.1	38.7
142	BROADCOM	Singapore	Electronic and electrical equipment	963.5	46.3	15.4
162	INFINEON TECHNOLOGIES	Germany	Technology hardware and equipment	817.0	16.9	14.1
457	TCL COMMUNICATION TECHNOLOGY	China	Technology hardware and equipment	231.4	25.7	6.8

Source: WIPO based on the EU Industrial R&D Investment Scoreboard, European Commission, Joint Research Center.[7]

Fourth, the assembly of the final product is often undertaken by large original design or contract manufacturers such as Flextronics, Foxconn and Wistron. These assemblers compete for high-volume – but often low-margin – opportunities. Samsung, however, mostly internalizes the assembly in its own factories, whereas Huawei does both.

Finally, to distribute and retail its phones, Apple is vertically integrated with its own online and physical stores, whereas Samsung operates more through regular distributors. Huawei operates a growing number of exclusive retail outlets, not only in Asia. Other Chinese brands still lack international distribution channels.[8]

As shown in table 4.3, the global value chain is made up of some of the most R&D-intensive firms in the world. These firms also regularly top the rankings of innovative firms, including one of the newly emerging Chinese smartphone brands, Xiaomi.[9] Innovation occurs throughout the above smartphone value chains, including both product innovation (i.e., the introduction of new product features) and product differentiation (i.e., the extent to which existing products differ along a set of characteristics).[10] These innovations occur in all parts of the global value chain: (i) in cellular technology; (ii) in the various smartphone components, in particular in the field of semiconductors as well as in batteries and displays; (iii) in the design and functionality of smartphones, including graphical user interfaces (GUI); and (iv) in the area of software and applications. Even firms traditionally associated with simple assembly, such as Foxconn, spend considerable sums on R&D and own large patent portfolios (see table 4.3).

This highly innovative smartphone global value chain, composed of exclusive technology providers, is far from stable. As the experiences of BlackBerry and Nokia have shown, changing technology and consumer tastes can lead former top brands to drastically lose market share. And as evidenced in the daily press, change also occurs frequently within the supply chain. Lead firms often decide to shift away from established component suppliers; for example, Apple recently shifted its purchases from Qualcomm to Intel.[11] They often also attempt to build high-value components and IP internally, as seen in Huawei's and Xiaomi's quest to develop their own chipsets and Apple's efforts to build graphics processing units (GPUs), turning away from its former supplier, Imagination Technologies Group.[12]

Even the assembly of smartphones is shifting constantly, with lead firms often struggling to meet high demand, leading to experiments with new manufacturers or assembly locations such as India in the case of Apple and Viet Nam in the case of Samsung.

4.2 – Value capture along the smartphone value chain

Who captures most of the value from innovation along the smartphone value chain?

This section addresses this question at the level of specific phones and companies, for the Apple iPhone 7, Huawei P9 and Samsung Galaxy S7. For these phones, released in 2016, estimates are produced by subtracting the costs of purchased intermediate inputs and direct labor costs along the various stages of the global value chain from the wholesale price of each phone (see box 4.1). The residual balance – referred to as "value capture" or gross profits here – accrues to Apple, Huawei or Samsung as lead firms in the smartphone global value chain and as compensation for their intangible assets.

Value capture at the product and firm level is the closest one can get to the concepts of the global value chain residual calculation and "returns to intangible assets" developed in chapter 1. The underlying work in Chen et al. (2017) discussed in that chapter can be seen as the macro-equivalent of the calculations by Dedrick and Kraemer (2017) presented here.

According to this approach, smartphone lead firms and suppliers of high-end components capture a vast part of the value generated from the sale of these three top-of-the-line phones.

4.2.1 – A look inside a smartphone

Smartphones consist of anywhere between 1,500 and 2,000 physical parts. The most expensive input – up to 20 percent of the total cost – is the touchscreen module (see table 4.4). In decreasing order, the other most expensive items are processors, memory and storage, casing, camera, battery, printed circuits, sensors, and assembly.

The location of core activities is depicted in table 4.5. R&D and design usually occurs near the company's headquarters. Development is done jointly by the lead firm and engineers from contract manufacturers.

Table 4.4

Cost of intermediate inputs as a percentage of total material costs

Function	Apple iPhone 7	Samsung Galaxy S7	Huawei P9
Display/touchscreen	15.9	20.5	16.8
App processors/baseband	10.2	18.1	14.3
Storage	4.5	5.2	4.2
Memory	6.1	10.1	7.3
Casing	8.2	8.6	7.8
Subtotal for key components	72.7	71.3	63.6
Hundreds of other components	13.0	18.2	21.8
Assembly	2.2	1.6	2.4
Total factory cost	88	88.9	88
Software	iOS	Android	Android
IP licenses for standard-essential patents (SEPs)	12.0	11.1	12.0
Cost of goods sold	100	100	100

Sources: Dedrick and Kraemer (2017) based on IHS Markit teardown report.

Table 4.5

Location of activities in the global value chain of the smartphone industry

Activity	Standard setting	R&D, design, sourcing	Development and engineering	Manufacture of key components	Production/ final assembly
Apple	International standard-setting organizations	U.S.	U.S./Taiwan (Province of China)	U.S./Japan/Republic of Korea/Taiwan (Province of China)/China	China, India (as of 2017)
Samsung	International standard-setting organizations	Republic of Korea	Republic of Korea	Republic of Korea/Japan/U.S./China	Republic of Korea, Viet Nam, China, India, Brazil, Indonesia
Huawei	International standard-setting organizations	China	China	China/Republic of Korea	China, India

Suppliers of electronic components, whether low or high end, are mostly located in the United States, Japan, the Republic of Korea, Taiwan (Province of China) and China.

Specifically, the role of U.S.-based suppliers ranges from 29 percent to 45 percent of value capture for handsets from the U.S. and the Republic of Korea, but only 9 percent for Huawei's P9 phone. Republic of Korea-based suppliers account for 31 percent of the value capture of suppliers for Samsung, while Chinese-based suppliers make up 34 percent of all suppliers for Huawei. The leaders are in the U.S. (Apple, Google, Qualcomm, Intel and a number of other component makers), the Republic of Korea (Samsung, LG and SK Hynix), Singapore (Broadcom), Taiwan (Province of China) (Taiwan Semiconductor Manufacturing Company, TSMC and some smaller chip and component makers), Japan (Japan Display, Sony, Murata) and China (Foxconn, Huawei and its subsidiary HI Silicon, plus Xiaomi, Oppo, Vivo and Lenovo).

Assembly is left to turnkey suppliers, mostly in China, Japan and East Asia, and with little activity in other world regions except incipient activity in Brazil and India.

4.2.2 – Value capture for high-end smartphone models

Only a few country locations, mostly the United States and a few Asian countries, capture the vast majority of value in smartphone production. Besides the cost of materials, a significant share goes to retailing, to IP, and directly as value capture to the lead firm. Indeed, the "lead firm advantage" – associated in earlier studies only with Apple – also extends to other high-end smartphone manufacturers.

The breakdown of smartphone retail prices shows that the value capture of the lead firm is far more than the combined value captured by, or gross profits of, all the suppliers; USD 283 for Apple as compared to USD 71 for suppliers; USD 228 for Samsung as compared to USD 76 for suppliers; and USD 188 for Huawei as compared to USD 47 for suppliers (see box 4.1).

Applying the above methodology, figure 4.4 shows the value captured in USD terms as a percentage of the smartphone retail price. The results underline the advantageous position of the lead firms in general, and Apple in particular. At the macro-level, the electronics sector saw an increase in the share

of intangible asset income as a percentage of total value over the period 2000-2014 (see chapter 1). It also confirms that in producer-driven global value chains, the returns do indeed rest with activities before the final production stage.

As a proxy for value capture, Apple keeps 42 percent of the retail price of each iPhone sold (or USD 270), Huawei 42 percent (USD 203) and Samsung 33 percent (USD 221.76). Huawei's selling price is lower, thanks to its reliance on low-cost components in part produced internally by its subsidiary Hi-Silicon, and reflecting its pricing strategy as it competes with a large number of other Android phone makers. Samsung's value capture is hurt by its greater reliance on retailers and carriers to sell its products. The figures for value capture include wages and salaries for R&D, design, management, marketing and whatever these lead firms do to generate a competitive advantage.

Figure 4.2

How to arrive at the value capture estimate

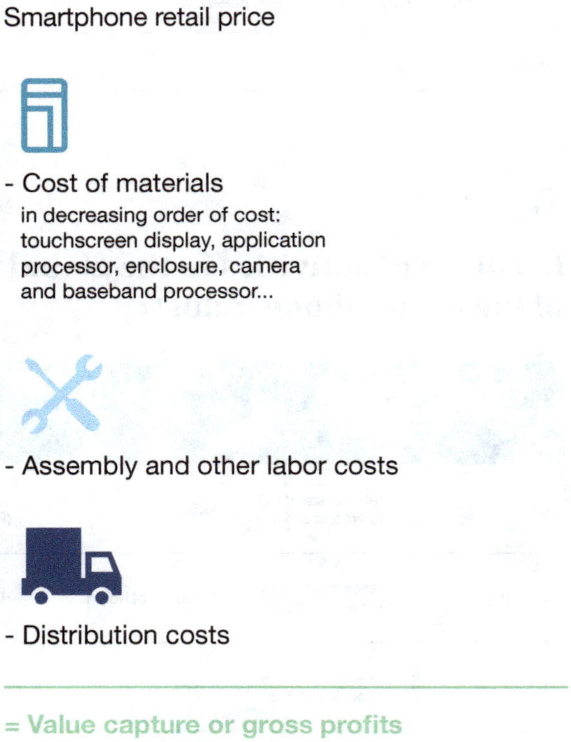

Smartphone retail price

- **Cost of materials**
  in decreasing order of cost: touchscreen display, application processor, enclosure, camera and baseband processor...

- **Assembly and other labor costs**

- **Distribution costs**

= Value capture or gross profits

Box 4.1

The smartphone value capture model – analytical approach and limitations

Value capture at each stage of the global value chain is calculated by subtracting the costs of purchased intermediate inputs and direct labor costs along the various stages of the global value chain and the distribution costs from the selling price of the specific phone (see figure 4.2 and figure 4.3). This amount includes the direct cost of materials used in creating the product along with the direct labor costs used to produce it – including assembly and testing – defined as "cost of goods sold" (COGS).[13] Teardown reports from IHS Markit are used to estimate these costs to arrive at the residual value capture.[14]

The value capture pays for selling, general and administrative expenses (SG&A), R&D and other indirect costs, with the rest being the return to the firm or ultimately the shareholders, which also ultimately constitutes the lead firm's return on its tangible and intangible capital. Figure 4.3 compares the concept of value capture to value added. Five limitations are noteworthy.

First, the supplier and component lists in teardown reports are incomplete, and prices – so-called "rack rates" – may be overestimates when firms are able to negotiate bulk discounts or they produce these components internally. For example, the display in the Samsung S7 – the most expensive component – is sourced from Samsung Display by Samsung Electronics. In the teardown reports the market value of USD 55 is applied, whereas the actual cost may be lower.[15]

Second, independently of the country in question, firm-level information about pure value added is not readily available because publicly listed companies do not generally reveal the amount of their wages for "direct labor." Instead, the wage bill for assembly by third parties is hidden within "cost of goods sold" or "cost of sales." As a result, the difference between "net sales" and "cost of goods sold" is used as a proxy for value capture.

Third, it is assumed that R&D and other intangible asset-related value capture originates and accrues to the company headquarters, including in the form of R&D staff wages.

Today, these multinational companies arguably conduct a share of such functions abroad. The "stickiness" of value or profits to the headquarters location that is assumed in such accounting-based studies – and thus the assumption that all value captured by Apple, for example, is generated and kept in its main location, the U.S. – may thus be exaggerated. Indeed, Apple's 2017 Annual Report shows that the U.S. has less than one-half of its global operating income, and less than two-thirds of its long-lived assets. Furthermore, since Apple's public stock is owned by global investors, its profits distributed as dividends or capital gains are widely distributed globally. So more information is needed to better measure key metrics for affiliated entities within a global value chain of a multinational corporation, and more data to test or specifically analyse the geographic location of economic activity, including profits from IP, across jurisdictions.

Fourth, teardown reports focus on physical components; they do not cover intangibles, including payments for IP. To get a sense of the total return to intangible assets, obtaining estimates for IP-related value is necessary. This is challenging as IP-related transactions are often undisclosed and sometimes indirect.[16] As a proxy, in this exercise the licensing royalties for SEPs are calculated as 5 percent of the phone's cost on average (section 4.2.2). Other IP-related value or payments are even harder to trace, notably those related to internally developed or externally sourced software. For example, the actual cost of using third-party software is unknown. This may well inflate the value capture of the lead firm, though without reducing the estimate for overall returns to intangible capital. In addition, some IP-based transactions such as cross-licensing do not leave a monetary trace, but are still very valuable.[17]

Finally, this methodology abstracts from the large interconnected revenues of the telecommunications operators, and the increasing share of lead-firm revenues driven by accessories, content and services.[18]

Figure 4.3

The difference between value capture and value added

Source: Dedrick et al. (2010) and Dedrick and Kraemer (2017) for more details.

Figure 4.4

Smartphone lead firms capture a large chunk of the value in the chain

Value captured at each stage of the chain as a percentage of smartphone sale price

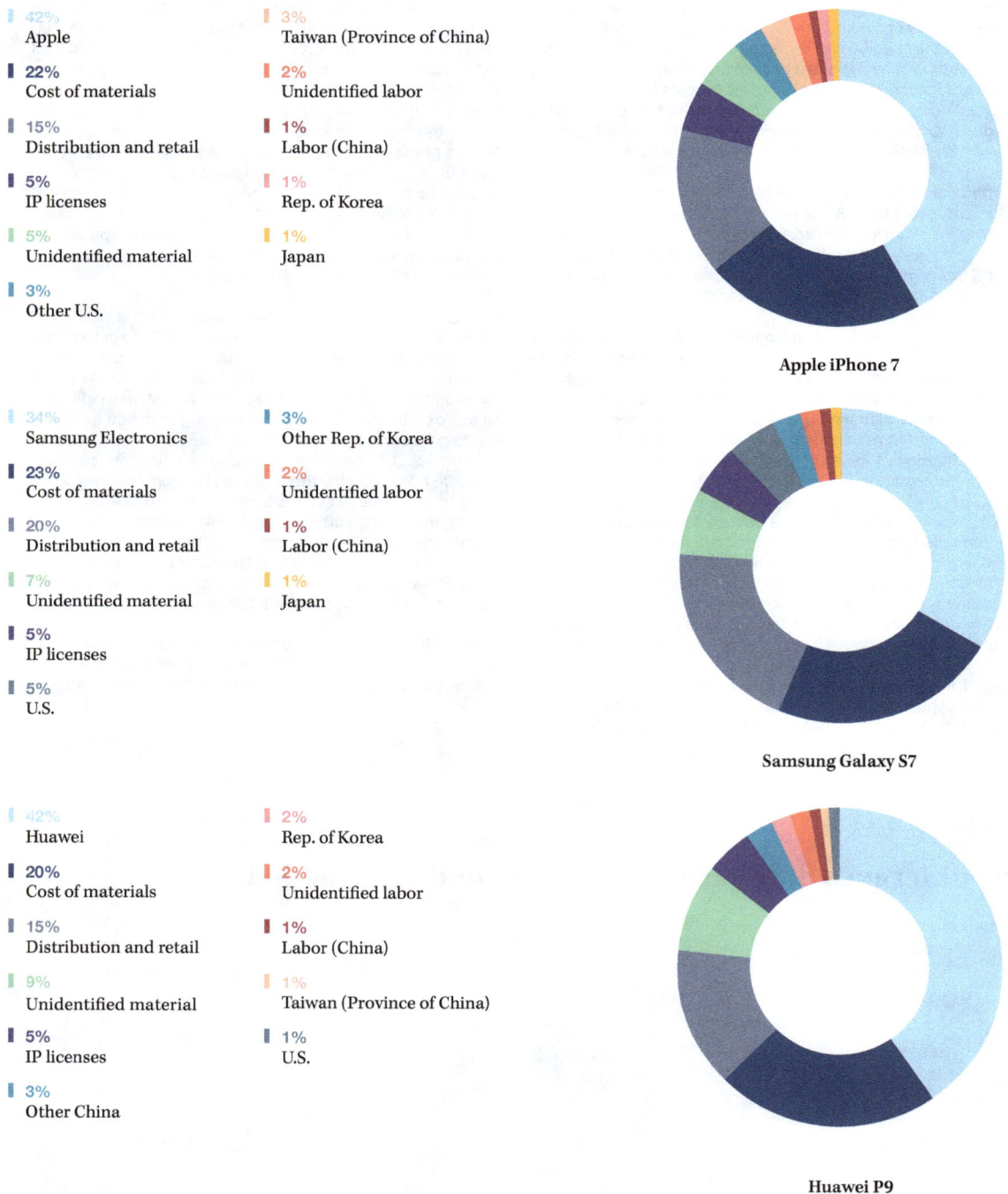

42%
Apple

22%
Cost of materials

15%
Distribution and retail

5%
IP licenses

5%
Unidentified material

3%
Other U.S.

3%
Taiwan (Province of China)

2%
Unidentified labor

1%
Labor (China)

1%
Rep. of Korea

1%
Japan

Apple iPhone 7

34%
Samsung Electronics

23%
Cost of materials

20%
Distribution and retail

7%
Unidentified material

5%
IP licenses

5%
U.S.

3%
Other Rep. of Korea

2%
Unidentified labor

1%
Labor (China)

1%
Japan

Samsung Galaxy S7

42%
Huawei

20%
Cost of materials

15%
Distribution and retail

9%
Unidentified material

5%
IP licenses

3%
Other China

2%
Rep. of Korea

2%
Unidentified labor

1%
Labor (China)

1%
Taiwan (Province of China)

1%
U.S.

Huawei P9

Sources: Dedrick and Kraemer (2017).

Note: The numbers in some charts do not add up to exactly 100% because some numbers have been rounded up.

Figure 4.4 also shows the value captured by other firms in selected countries. For example, other U.S. firms capture 3 percent of the retail price of an iPhone.

As outlined in box 4.1, it is important to remember that the full value capture may not accrue to the headquarters location; subsidiaries in other countries may share in the benefit.[19] Apple is a multinational company with entities spread throughout the world (e.g., Ireland). To enable more detailed, country-specific breakdowns, more information would be needed to better measure key metrics for affiliated entities within a global value chain of a multinational corporation, and more data to analyze the geographic location of economic activity, including profits from IP, across jurisdictions.

Finally, figure 4.4 shows that the amount paid for IP to third parties varies from USD 34 per phone for Samsung to USD 32 for Apple to USD 24 for Huawei. In the following discussion, these costs are subtracted to ultimately yield the value capture of the lead firm, but for our broader analysis these sums constitute an important part of the return to intangible assets across the global value chain, earned here by the owners of cellular technology. Firms such as Qualcomm and others which do not generate revenues from the sale of smartphones spend considerable amounts on communication-technology-related R&D, thereby enabling the functionality of smartphones. These payments help to finance these high R&D costs, and allow for specialization in the marketplace.

4.2.3 – Who reaps most of the value of high-end smartphone sales?

For all three phones, capture of value added is largely detached from the flow of physical goods.[20]

While the value capture shares of the three firms are comparable at the level of the product (the individual phone), at the firm level Apple accounts for a large chunk of overall profits in the industry. By selling only high-end phones, Apple is able to capture a whopping 90 percent of the profits of all smartphone makers, according to third-party estimates, even though it only accounts for 12 percent of all smartphones sold.[21]

Apple captures most of the industry profits thanks to its high prices, large profit margins and the volume of iPhone sales worldwide (see table 4.6).

Its value capture in U.S. dollars is much larger than Samsung or Huawei's, as Apple sells significantly more high-end phones (over 215 million units, compared to 88 million for Samsung and 25 million for Huawei; see table 4.6). When the three companies' high-end phone sales for 2016 are compared, Apple walks away with 83 percent of the combined profits generated by the Apple iPhone 6, Huawei P8 and Samsung Galaxy 6 (see table 4.6). These exceptionally large benefits for Apple are a function of its investments in R&D, design and other intangible assets. They also allow it to spread its significant marketing and overhead costs over a higher volume of sales.

Samsung and Huawei capture high value on their most expensive phones, but their overall margins are reduced by the large number of low-cost products they sell.

Furthermore, this calculation abstracts from the smartphone content and services revenues generated on the basis of the handheld device after its sale. Apple's strategy to integrate everything from the supply of the phone to the delivery of content and services and related standards plays a significant role in its value capture outside, driven by platform lock-in, network externalities and the ability to bundle products efficiently.[22] And, although omitted here, these revenues are on the rise in absolute terms and as a share of Apple's revenues.[23] Other lead firms, however, see these added value and profits accrue to other providers as they do not partake in the added revenues generated in the sale of digital items, online content and services.

Yet Apple is not alone in capturing high profits and value. Component suppliers reap significant revenues and margins too, in particular when linked to proprietary technologies. As opposed to volume effects, smartphone suppliers experience significant variance in their margins. Qualcomm, for example, stands out for its significant value capture, a result of the performance of its baseband chipsets.[24] Qualcomm's value capture is far higher than that of MediaTek, reflecting the fact that it sells to premium-tier phone makers whereas MediaTek sells to low-price phone makers. In markets such as displays and memory, too, the dominant player, Samsung, earns 60 percent margins, while memory maker Micron Technologies settles for 20 percent.[25]

This high variance continues to the level of the contract manufacturers. Most earn low margins while still benefiting from high-volume activity and an important opportunity for technological learning (discussed further in section 4.4).

Table 4.6

Comparison of value capture for premium phone models in 2016

Smartphone model	Global average sales price (USD)	Value capture/ margin (%)	Value capture/ gross profit (USD per phone)	Worldwide shipments (units shipped in 2016)	Total 2016 value capture/gross profits (USD bn)
Apple iPhone 6	748	42	314	199,614,814	62.4
Apple iPhone 7	809	42	339	15,871,584	5.4
Apple total					67.8
Samsung Galaxy 6	732	34	248	52,892,898	13.1
Samsung Galaxy S7	708	34	240	35,701,806	8.6
Samsung total					21.7
Huawei P8	298	42	125	15,418,859	1.9
Huawei P9	449	42	188	9,986,811	1.9
Huawei total					3.8

Sources: Dedrick and Kraemer (2017) based on IHS Markit teardown report.

4.3 – The role of intangible assets in value capture

How do intangible assets, and IP in particular, relate to the value capture discussed above?

The ability to sell a smartphone at a profit depends largely on its performance, features, brand name, design and applications. In this chapter, value capture is a measure of the return to the firm's intangible assets. To protect their intangible assets and reap some related dividends, the actors in the smartphone industry which benefit from high value capture – as set out in section 4.2 – make extensive use of the full spectrum of IP rights.[26]

But is IP the main cause of value capture?

A leading study on the Apple iPhone calculates the value of patentable technologies in the iPhone as a part of Apple's total stock market value.[27] Estimates of brand value, smartphone design and their value as driver of a firm's market value also exist (discussed further below in sections 4.3.2 and 4.3.3).

But these studies rest on a number of strong assumptions. Despite a high correlation between value capture and the use of IP, a direct causal relationship between these two factors is hard to estimate, as is the specific value captured by selected IP assets. IP is usually only a source of competitive advantage when combined with complementary assets such as organizational expertise and human capital plus management skills and effective firm strategies.[28] When enforceable without excessive costs, the value of IP is both direct (i.e., with revenue impacts) and indirect (i.e., it produces defensive or strategic value). In light of these complexities, even smartphone makers themselves are unlikely to have full evidence of the specific value of their different IP assets.

The next sections shed light on the role of intangible assets and IP in value capture. Less formal appropriation schemes such as trade secrets play an important role, but are not included in the analysis as they are even harder to measure.

4.3.1 – Smartphone inventions drive a significant number of patent filings

Most industry experts and academics agree that a vast number of patents are part and parcel of modern smartphones.

One widely used source states that 27 percent of patents granted in the U.S. were related to mobile phones, up from 20 percent in 2012 and 10 percent in 2002.[29] The following calculations show that this is potentially an underestimate, if a broad definition of smartphone-related patents is used (see figure 4.5).

Another frequently cited source dating back to 2012 claims that one in every six patents in force – or about 16 percent of all active patents filed at the United States Patent and Trademark Office (USPTO) – are smartphone-related; other estimates argue that the number of active patents relevant to today's smartphones has increased from 70,000 in the year 2000 to 250,000 now, mainly due to the expanded set of features and functionalities.[30] The methodologies by which these sources arrive at these figures are mostly undisclosed and unverifiable.

Mapping the exact number of smartphone-related patents is a ferociously complex task (see box 4.2 on the approaches taken in this chapter). No simple technology field in international or national patent classifications easily corresponds to the smartphone product, and several issues further complicate the smartphone patent mapping.

First, a smartphone consists of many different technological components, some of which might not be unique to smartphones alone. Instead the components identified in section 4.2 range from semiconductors to memory, to other types of computer or communication technologies. While these items are integral to smartphones, they are also core to most other information and communication technology (ICT) products, and increasingly also to other product types which have connectivity as a built-in component, e.g., cars, fridges and medical technology. Assigning them to smartphones uniquely would be wrong.

Second, a number of inventions are core to the smartphone but are not found in the technology fields most strictly related to modern smartphone technology, for example patent classifications which relate directly to "portable communication terminals" or "telephone sets."

Some are inventions in traditional sectors, outside the ICT industry, such as glass-related patents providing for more durable smartphone casing. Others are inventions in high-technology fields such as navigation displays, sensors and fingerprint technology. If one opens the door to software and other mobile applications which relate to e-commerce, social networks, payment, fitness, or health, the number of potentially relevant patents is even higher. Consequently, it is challenging to identify all relevant patents by traditional search methods which rely on patent classifications or keywords such as "smartphone"; in any case, the related inventions are also typically not unique to smartphones alone.

In the patent-mapping exercise conducted for this report, both a "narrow" and a "broad" smartphone grouping were calculated (see box 4.2). Invariably, the approaches chosen in smartphone patent-mapping exercises will be too constricted in the narrow category or too comprehensive in the broad category. The gap between the two estimates does, however, give a good sense of the sheer number of potential smartphone patents involved.

That said, by any account, smartphone-related patents have increased steadily in recent years, including as a share of total patents.

In the aggregate data, in 2016 patent applications under the Patent Cooperation Treaty (PCT) at WIPO related to digital communication accounted for the largest share of total PCT applications, followed by computer technology (17,155).[31] In fact, digital communication overtook computer technology – which held the top position in 2014 and 2015 – to become the top technological field in 2016. It has been experiencing some of the fastest growth in terms of new PCT filings. In 2014, the latest year for which national patent filing data are available, the field of digital communication also saw its fastest annual growth of any year since 2005.[32]

The patent mapping performed for this chapter shows that between 1990 and 2013 the number of smartphone first patent filings worldwide grew from about 100 patents in the early 1990s to about 2,700 patents in the narrow category in 2013, and from about 230,000 first filings (or about 350,000 patents overall) in the early 1990s to more than 650,000 first filings (or about 1.2 million patents overall) in the broad category. In the broad category – and bearing in mind that many of these patents are not exclusive to smartphones – this represents about 30-35 percent of patents filed worldwide between 1990 and 2013.

Box 4.2

Mapping smartphone patents

To mitigate the complexity of identifying smartphone patents, two approaches were chosen for the patent-mapping analysis discussed in this chapter. One uses a narrow choice of applied patent classifications as relevant to smartphones, the other a broader combination of more comprehensive lists of pertinent patent classifications plus company names and keywords.

1. The narrow approach

A list of restricted Cooperative Patent Classification (CPC) codes was used – mainly H04M 1/72519 ("Portable communication terminals with improved user interface to control a main telephone operation mode or to indicate the communication status") and H04M 1/247 ("Configurable and interactive telephone terminals with subscriber controlled features modifications"), plus a number of related sub-codes.[33] As the figures in this chapter show, these narrow choices necessarily lead to a gross underestimate of smartphone patents.

2. The broad approach

This involved the application of a broad list of International Patent Classification (IPC) codes generated by the identification of the most pertinent IPC categories in:

Section F: mechanical engineering, including lighting or cooling technologies;

Section G: physics, including measuring and navigation, optics, camera, controlling technologies, computing such as data and image processing, communication-related categories, cryptography, digital speech and information storage; and

Section H: electricity, including in telecommunications and digital communication processes, semiconductors and printed circuits and, for example, batteries.[34]

Some of these IPC classes are strictly related to smartphones and mobile communication in general. Others were generated by conducting keyword searches within the IPC classes and in patent databases – mostly Espacenet and the database of the German patent office – with the help of patent examiners.[35] A list of companies involved in the smartphone global value chain was compiled for further checks of the data. The objective was to single out IPC codes which might cover smartphone-related technologies, going beyond a narrow subset, but also covering the multiple technology areas highlighted later in figure 4.10, for example. This search strategy yielded patents in fields such as vehicles, cameras and some of the fields mentioned above, but the problem with this approach is that it yields a large number of patents, and some IPC classes such as semiconductors or cameras are essential but not exclusive to smartphones.

Figure 4.5

The number of smartphone patent filings is large and growing

First filings and all filings worldwide for smartphone-related patents (narrow and broad definitions), 1990-2013

Narrow

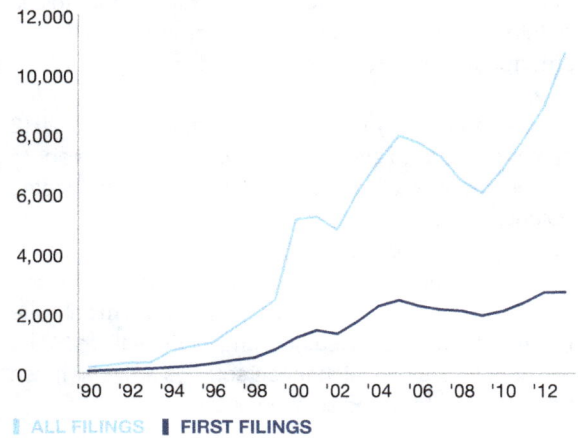

ALL FILINGS   FIRST FILINGS

Broad

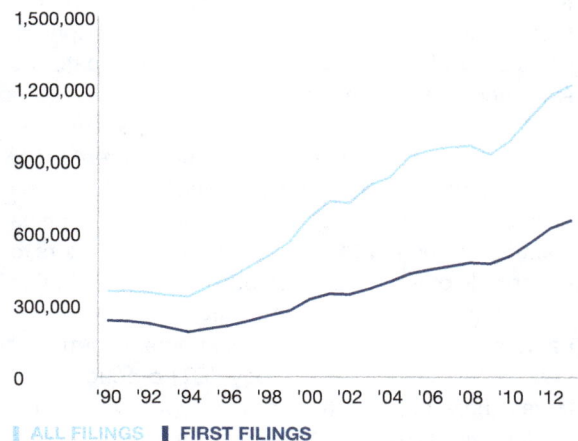

ALL FILINGS   FIRST FILINGS

Notes: For the narrow and broad approaches to mapping smartphone patents, see box 4.2. "First filings" represent unique inventions protected by a unique patent. The same invention can then be patented in additional jurisdictions through secondary filings, leading to multiple patents on the same underlying invention ("all filings").

Source: WIPO based on PATSTAT database.

Figure 4.6

The top origins of smartphone patent filings have changed over the past decade

First filings worldwide by origin for smartphone-related patents (narrow and broad definitions), 1990-1999 versus 2005-2014

Narrow

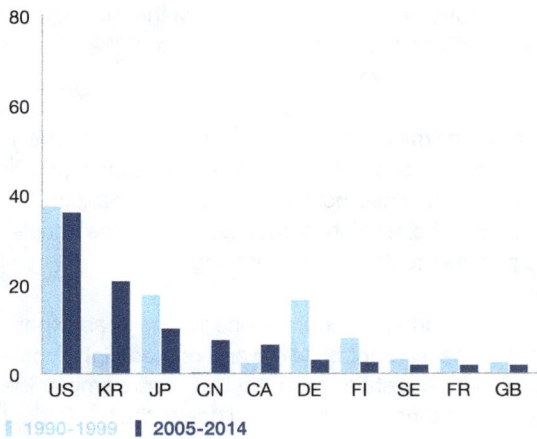

1990-1999   2005-2014

Broad

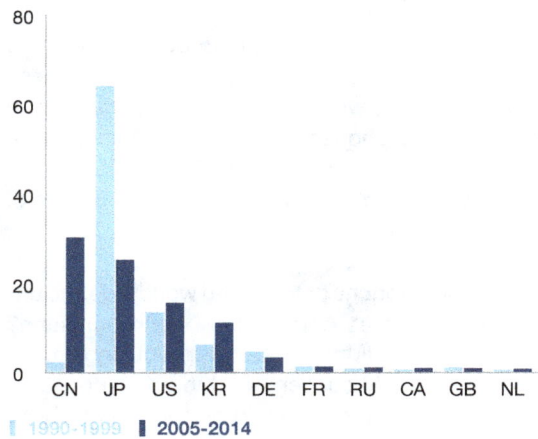

1990-1999   2005-2014

First filings at the USPTO by origin for smartphone-related patents (narrow and broad definitions), 1990-1999 versus 2005-2014

Narrow

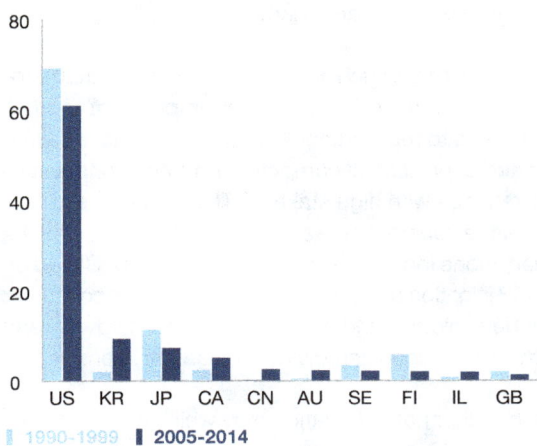

1990-1999   2005-2014

Broad

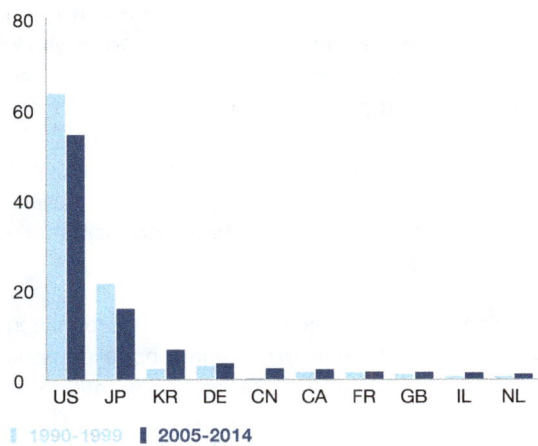

1990-1999   2005-2014

Notes: The use of origin data at the USPTO in the bottom graph introduces a "home bias" at the expense of non-U.S. patent applicants, who tend to file fewer applications abroad or at the USPTO than in their own jurisdiction. Country codes as follows: AU = Australia, CA = Canada, CN = China, DE = Germany, FI = Finland, FR = France, GB = United Kingdom, IL = Israel, JP = Japan, KR = Republic of Korea, NL = Netherlands, RU = Russian Federation, SE = Sweden, US = United States.

Sources: WIPO based on PATSTAT and the USPTO database.

On both the narrow and broad definitions, the U.S., China, Japan and the Republic of Korea are the leading origins of smartphone patents worldwide, followed by patent filers based in Canada, Germany and Finland in the narrow category, and Germany, France, the Russian Federation and Canada in the broad category. Across both definitions, two trends stand out: (i) the shares of Japan and Germany (and in the narrow category, Germany and Finland) declined between 1990-1999 and 2005-2014; and (ii) the shares of China and the Republic of Korea rose markedly – mostly at the expense of Japan but not the U.S., whose share is increasing in the broad category. These trends correspond with the finding that IP capacity in relation to smartphones has built up significantly in these two economies (see figure 4.6). The U.S., Japan and the Republic of Korea are the leading origins of smartphone patents at the USPTO.

Where are smartphone patents filed worldwide, including by firms such as Apple, Huawei and Samsung? Although the lead firms involved in producing smartphones are heavily concentrated in a few countries such as the U.S., the Republic of Korea and China, smartphone inventors seek protection in multiple destinations; see figure 4.7, depicting smartphone patent families.[36] The U.S. is the most sought-after destination, followed by Europe, Japan and China, the Republic of Korea and, to a significant but lesser extent, Canada and Australia. Additional jurisdictions across the world also receive smartphone patent applications, including many economies in Latin America, the Russia Federation and Central Asia, other parts of Asia including Indonesia, but also South Africa, other parts of Africa and Australia.

The strong growth in smartphone-related patenting is first and foremost a reflection of the desire of inventors to appropriate the returns to their considerable innovation investments.[37]

In addition, the use of IP goes beyond the appropriation of innovation rents alone. In the smartphone industry, IP is also an important enabler of collaboration.[38] A smartphone would not see the light of day without extensive vertical and horizontal partnerships, and these are often enabled by IP. In the case of certain technologies, hundreds or sometimes thousands of patent holders, both firms and universities, supply inventions to form a new technology.

In the case of Bluetooth 3.0, which enables short range connectivity between the smartphone and other devices, more than 30,000 patent holders have contributed, including 200 universities.[39]

The use of IP also allows specialization. While most smartphone-related patents are held by large firms, including for defensive purposes, smaller and/or specialized component suppliers make extensive use of the IP system, affording scope for market entry.[40] For example, Corning, the producer of the Gorilla glass in Apple iPhones and a leading glass maker, files a significant number of patents.

In addition, major technologies relevant for smartphones are published via the patent system years, or sometimes decades, before actual commercialization of the knowledge, leading to effective knowledge transfer and possible technological learning.[41]

At the same time, the smartphone industry has experienced quite a patent build-up and related high-profile disputes in recent years. In the U.S., for example, the Apple-Samsung case produced one of the five largest initial adjudicated damages sums in the period 1997-2016, attracting considerable media attention.[42] In this context one may ask: do the increasingly strategic use of IP and the increase in legal disputes harm the smartphone industry?

In truth, the exact litigation costs to firms and the system-wide costs are unknown.

On the one hand, such disputes and their eventual resolution are a means for firms to attempt to appropriate the returns to their intangible assets. They are a reflection and byproduct of competition in a highly innovative marketplace with high stakes.[43] They are also a reflection of the substantial use of IP in this industry. And the smartphone industry is by no means special. Based on U.S. IP litigation data, other industries such as consumer products, biotech and pharma, computer hardware and software are considerably more litigation intensive.[44]

On the other hand, litigation may well impose considerable costs on firms without necessarily creating legal certainty. The Apple-Samsung case provides a prominent example – ongoing in multiple jurisdictions, and with heterogonous and fluctuating outcomes. In this respect, a related source of concern is the amount of litigation and the possible dead-weight losses in legal expenditures.

Figure 4.7

The United States is the biggest destination for smartphone patent filings

Total foreign-oriented smartphone patent families filed, 1995-2014 (narrow definition)

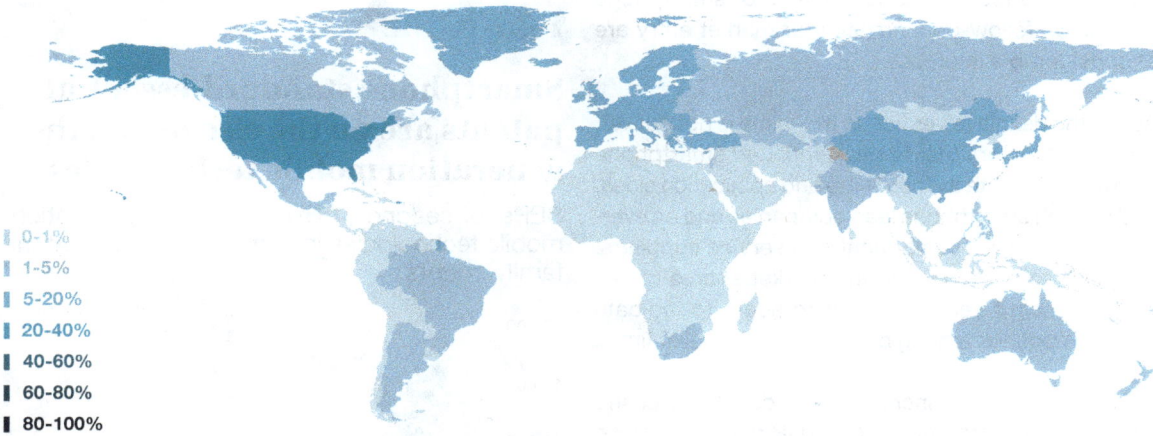

- 0-1%
- 1-5%
- 5-20%
- 20-40%
- 40-60%
- 60-80%
- 80-100%

Total foreign-oriented smartphone patent families filed, 1995-2014 (broad definition)

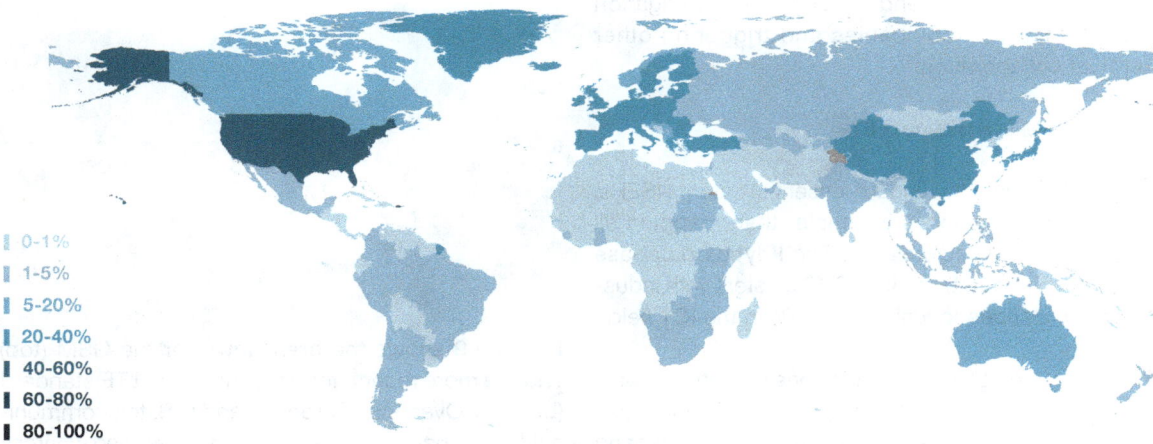

- 0-1%
- 1-5%
- 5-20%
- 20-40%
- 40-60%
- 60-80%
- 80-100%

Note: For the narrow and broad approaches to mapping smartphone patents, see box 4.2.

Source: WIPO based on PATSTAT.

An important question arises from an economic point of view: does the large number of smartphone patents truly incentivize investment in discovery and innovation? Or do these patents instead facilitate anti-competitive behavior by allowing incumbent firms to block key technologies, thereby reducing competition rather than rewarding continued innovation? In other words, the effects of large volumes of smartphone patents on follow-on innovation or market entry are of considerable interest.

Again, the definitive verdict on this issue is not out yet, but recent history testifies to continued smartphone innovation on both the hardware and application sides, and by both smartphone lead companies and an ever-changing array of component and service suppliers. And the rapid changes in the market shares of key firms in recent years would also seem to indicate solid competition among both large and smaller firms.

Moreover, firms have increasingly used market-based strategies to overcome scattered IP rights and solve disputes. Firms engage in collaborative IP strategies involving technology cross-licensing, patent pools, patent clearing houses and other collaboration. IP disputes have often been the effective trigger for amicable solutions – a recent example being the patent licensing deal signed by Nokia and Apple in the first half of 2017, ending all IP-related litigation between the two companies and triggering other forms of collaboration.

Standard-essential patents

The identification of standard-essential patents (SEPs) related to smartphones is simpler than mapping all smartphone-related patents. The IPlytics database was used; this combines IPC/CPC clusters with industry concordances focusing on SEPs in the ICT field.

A relatively high share of smartphone patenting relates to SEPs in the field of communication technologies (see figure 4.1).[45] These IP-enabled standards expand the potential licensing markets, encouraging investment in R&D.[46]

Over time, and as faster cellular and more complex technologies are developed, SEPs associated with these technologies have increased.

As illustrated in figure 4.8, the fourth-generation LTE cellular standard is associated with almost four times as many declared SEPs than the earlier, less complex, second-generation Global System for Mobile Communications (GSM) standard, and almost double the number for the third-generation Universal Mobile Telecommunications System (UMTS).

Figure 4.8

Smartphone standard-essential patents are on the rise in fourth-generation mobile technologies

SEPs for second-, third- and fourth-generation mobile technologies in number of unique patent family counts

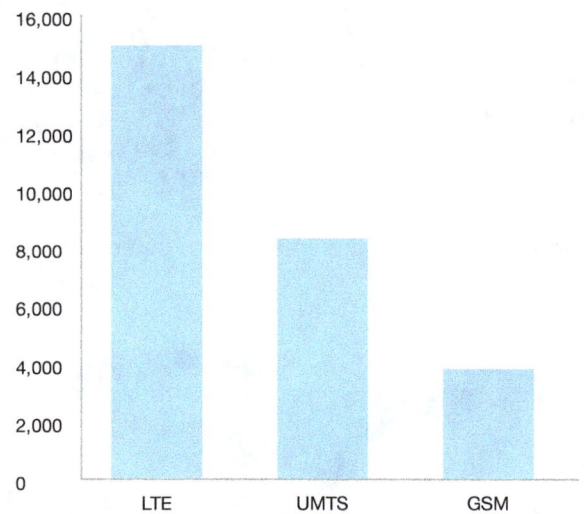

Note: A patent family is a set of interrelated patent applications filed in one or more countries or jurisdictions to protect the same invention. See the glossary in WIPO (2016).

Source: WIPO based on IPlytics database, downloaded in June 2017.

Figure 4.9 shows the breakdown for the GSM (top) and the more recent, fourth-generation, LTE standard (bottom). Over time, European and U.S. telecommunication companies' share of SEPs has declined whereas new entrants in the U.S. (mostly Internet firms such as Google) and new smartphone brands in the Republic of Korea (Samsung) and China (ZTE, Huawei) have seen their share grow – in part to utilize cross-licensing, reduce payments and fend off litigation. In addition to highlighting the fact that Asian players have become very active in contributing to the development of standards, these figures also demonstrate that firms such as Apple contribute less to their development.

Figure 4.9

The Republic of Korea, China and Internet-based firms are claiming a growing share of SEPs

Applicant company shares of worldwide SEPs for the GSM standard based on patent family count

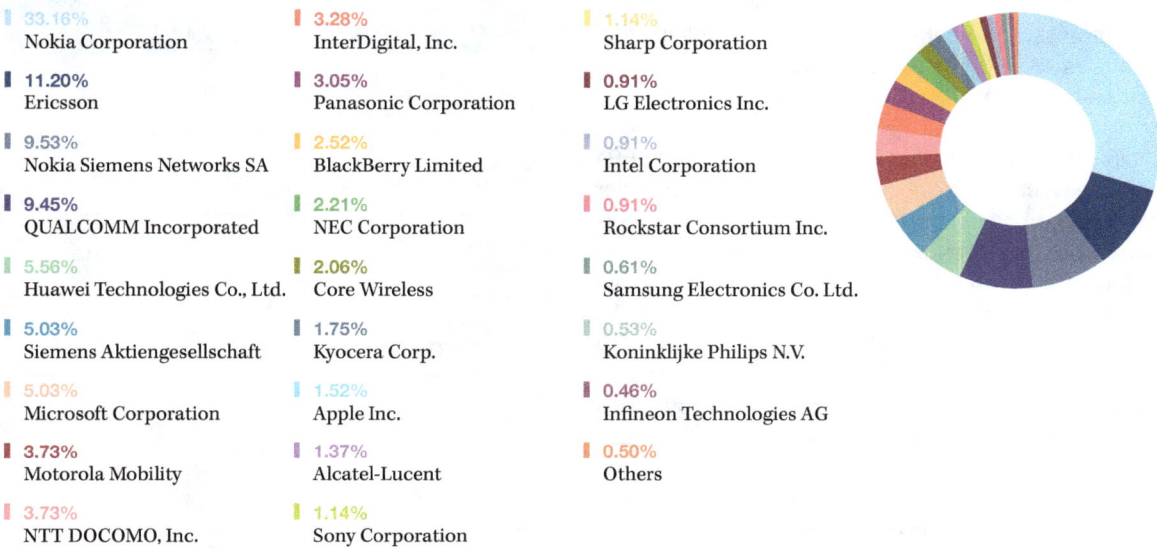

33.16% Nokia Corporation	**3.28%** InterDigital, Inc.	**1.14%** Sharp Corporation
11.20% Ericsson	**3.05%** Panasonic Corporation	**0.91%** LG Electronics Inc.
9.53% Nokia Siemens Networks SA	**2.52%** BlackBerry Limited	**0.91%** Intel Corporation
9.45% QUALCOMM Incorporated	**2.21%** NEC Corporation	**0.91%** Rockstar Consortium Inc.
5.56% Huawei Technologies Co., Ltd.	**2.06%** Core Wireless	**0.61%** Samsung Electronics Co. Ltd.
5.03% Siemens Aktiengesellschaft	**1.75%** Kyocera Corp.	**0.53%** Koninklijke Philips N.V.
5.03% Microsoft Corporation	**1.52%** Apple Inc.	**0.46%** Infineon Technologies AG
3.73% Motorola Mobility	**1.37%** Alcatel-Lucent	**0.50%** Others
3.73% NTT DOCOMO, Inc.	**1.14%** Sony Corporation	

Latest assignee company shares of worldwide SEPs for the LTE standard based on patent family count

13.49% Samsung Electronics Co. Ltd.	**2.08%** Panasonic Corporation	**1.20%** Siemens Aktiengesellschaft
9.88% Huawei Technologies Co., Ltd.	**2.05%** BlackBerry Limited	**1.20%** Electronics and Telecommunication Research Institute
9.41% QUALCOMM Incorporated	**1.74%** Apple Inc.	
8.74% Nokia Corporation	**1.61%** Institute of Telecommunication Science And Technology	**1.12%** Sony Corporation
6.58% Ericsson		**1.12%** Alcatel-Lucent
6.13% LG Electronics Inc.	**1.56%** NEC Corporation	**0.91%** Nokia Siemens Networks SA
4.79% Google Inc.	**1.47%** China Academy of Telecommunications Technology	**0.88%** Kyocera Corp.
4.52% InterDigital, Inc.		**0.70%** Microsoft Corporation
4.28% NTT DOCOMO, Inc.	**1.40%** ZTE Corp.	**8.15%** Others
2.14% Sharp Corporation	**1.26%** Texas Instruments Inc.	

Source: WiPO based on IPlytics database.

Note: SEP declarations exceed the number of patents which are actually standard essential. See Audenrode et al. (2017) for details.

Some of these SEPs were developed internally whereas others were acquired as part of patent portfolios, with, for example, Apple, Microsoft and others buying the Nortel patent portfolio, Google buying the Motorola portfolio and Lenovo buying an SEP portfolio from Unwired Planet that Unwired Planet had originally acquired from Ericsson. Lenovo also later acquired parts of the Motorola portfolio from Google.[47] Moreover, patent assertion entities (PAEs) such as Intellectual Ventures and Rockstar have been increasing their ownership share.[48]

While the share of litigated SEPs in total declared SEPs has been increasing over time up to 2015, the broader ownership of patent portfolios seems to have encouraged cross-licensing deals and patent pools, potentially reducing litigation in years to come. A drop in related litigation has been observable since 2012.[49]

Looking forward, firms are currently working on obtaining a stake in fifth-generation mobile technology, with a lead role for Huawei, Samsung and selected Japanese firms, but also for European and U.S. companies such as Nokia, Qualcomm, Ericsson and Orange. Other Internet firms are also claiming their stake; Google, for example, has made related acquisitions.[50]

For the purposes of this study, sensible estimates for the value of SEP-related licensing payments are required so as to better approximate total returns to intangible assets.

Unfortunately, most suppliers do not report licensing data, and for those who do, it is challenging to single out the income which is indeed driven by smartphone SEPs. Fortunately, a number of reports exist in the field, with some – often from the camp of licensees – suggesting that so-called "royalty stacks" are excessive while others – often from licensors – argue that they are reasonable.[51] Based on these studies, it is assumed here that SEP licensing costs range from 3 to 5 percent of the retail price of a phone (see box 4.1 and table 4.7).[52]

At the level of individual firms the related incomes are significant. Annual reports show that Nokia, for example, generated about USD 1 billion in licensing revenues in 2016 (and a predicted EUR 800 million in 2017), while Ericsson earned around USD 1.2 billion in 2016.[53] Two-thirds of Qualcomm's revenues in 2016 came from chip sales (USD 15.4 billion), and one-third from licensing its technology (USD 7.6 billion).

Table 4.7

Mobile SEP licensing fee revenues and royalty yields in the global handset market, 2014

	Revenues (USD bn)	Yield*
Major SEP owners with licensing programs: Alcatel-Lucent, Ericsson, Nokia, InterDigital, Qualcomm	10.6	2.6
Patent pools: SIPRO (WCDMA), Via Licensing and Sisvel (LTE)	< 4	<1
Others: including Apple, Huawei, RIM, Samsung, LG	< 6	<1.5
Cumulative maximum: fees and yield for mobile SEPs	~ 20	~5

Note: Yields are total licensing fee revenues including lump sums and running royalties as a percentage of USD 410 billion in total global handset revenues.

Source: Dedrick and Kraemer (2017) based on Mallinson (2014) and Galetovic et al. (2016).

The percentages used here – and also to derive value capture in section 4.2 – are conservative estimates. Moreover, they exclude IP revenues generated via technologies covered by implementation patents.

Implementation patents

Implementation patents involve technologies that can provide differentiation for specific products for individual manufacturers. Both lead firms and component suppliers patent and license such technology. The former, for example, might acquire a license to use a microprocessor from companies such as ARM.[54] For some firms, including Microsoft and BlackBerry, licensing their patents to third parties is at the core of their operations, whereas firms such as Apple do not license their patents.

Figure 4.10 illustrates the technology areas with the majority of implementation patents beyond the SEPs discussed earlier.[55] In terms of technology fields, the most important ones are in the areas of image display and screen (and more recently organic light-emitting diode screens), battery, antenna and more software-related ones like mapping, calendar management, voice recognition and other features in the field of artificial intelligence.[56]

Figure 4.10

Smartphones draw on an increasing number of technology fields

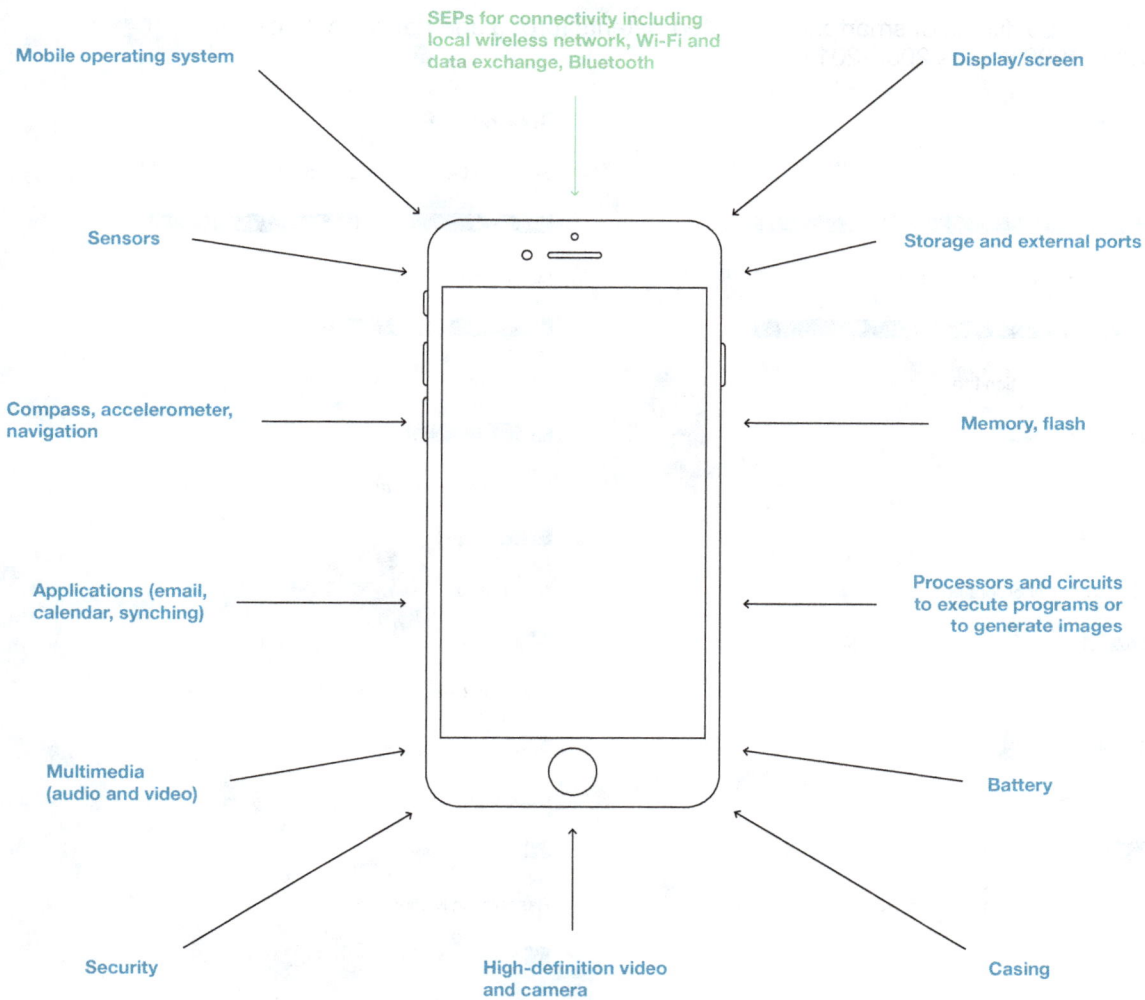

Mobile operating system

SEPs for connectivity including local wireless network, Wi-Fi and data exchange, Bluetooth

Display/screen

Sensors

Storage and external ports

Compass, accelerometer, navigation

Memory, flash

Applications (email, calendar, synching)

Processors and circuits to execute programs or to generate images

Multimedia (audio and video)

Battery

Security

High-definition video and camera

Casing

Smartphone patents worldwide are led by Samsung Electronics, LG Electronics, NEC Corporation – a Japanese IT services and product firm – and Qualcomm in the broad category, and LG Electronics, Samsung Electronics, Research in Motion and Nokia in the narrow category. Over time, NEC and Motorola have become less important players while others such as Apple, Microsoft and Google have joined the fray (see figure 4.11). As expected – see also table 4.8 – Apple's share of patent filings is more significant in the narrow smartphone category than if one considers broad fields of related technologies in which other firms excel.

Smartphone patents at the USTPO during the period 2000-15 were led by Samsung Electronics and Apple when the narrow definition is applied, and by IBM and Samsung under the broad definition (table 4.8). Thanks to its recent strong wave of patent filings, Huawei now ranks among the top 40 smartphone patent filers at the USPTO. In the broad category, however, Honghai Precision files more USPTO patents than Huawei, echoing a trend signaled earlier in this chapter. Table 4.8 also features some non-practicing entities such as ELWHA, a holding company of Intellectual Ventures, as well as universities such as the University of California.

Figure 4.11

Samsung Electronics, LG Electronics, NEC and Qualcomm are the global leaders in smartphone-related patents (broadly defined)

First global filings of smartphone-related patents (broad and narrow definitions), 1990-1999 versus 2005-2014

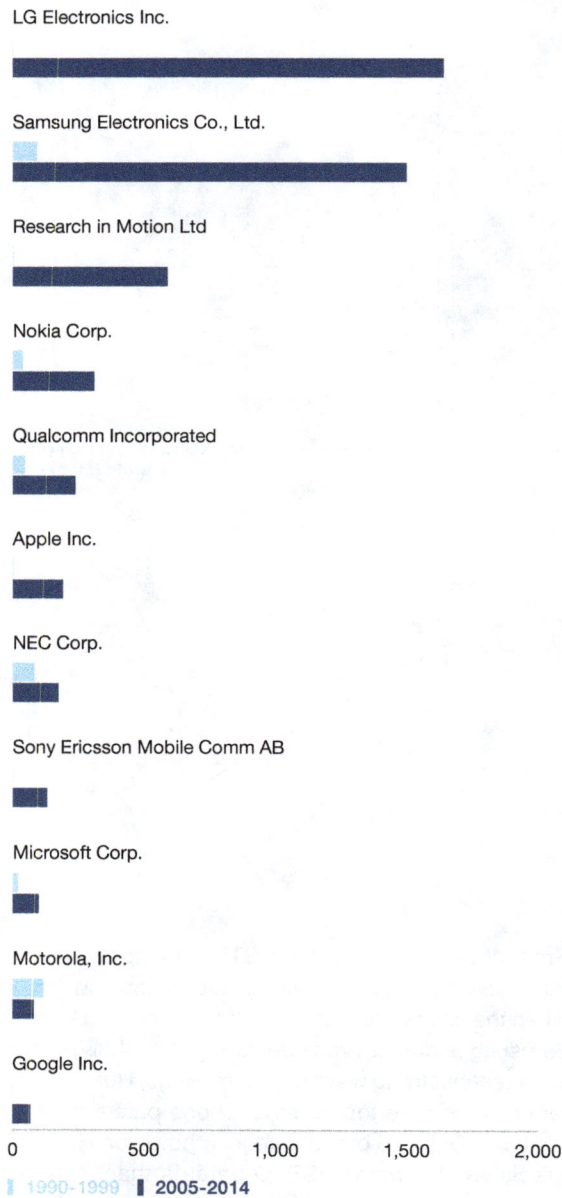

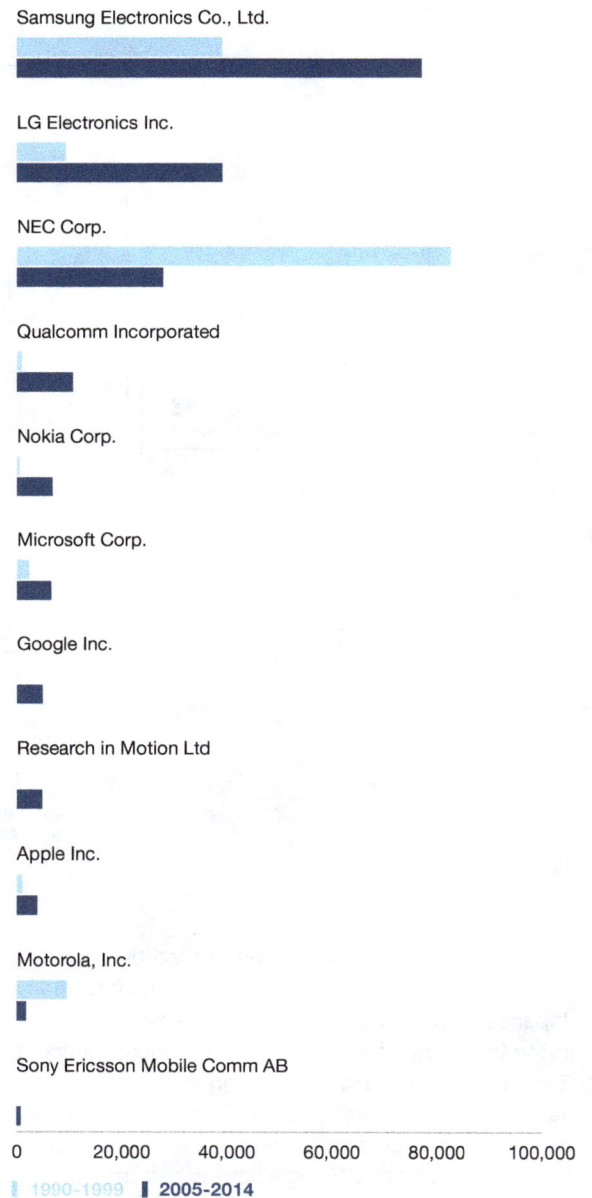

Note: For the narrow and broad approaches to mapping smartphone patents, see box 4.2.

Source: WIPO based on PATSTAT database.

Table 4.8

Smartphone-related patents at the USPTO are led by Samsung and Apple (narrow definition) and IBM and Samsung (broad definition)

First filings of smartphone-related patents (narrow and broad definitions) at the USPTO, 2000-2015

Narrow

Company name	USPTO patents	Percentage of USPTO smartphone patents
Samsung Electronics	1,239	3.2
Apple	810	2.1
Qualcomm	522	1.4
LG Electronics	502	1.3
Motorola	663	1.3
Intel	832	1.2
Digimarc	450	1.2
Nokia	443	1.1
Microsoft	556	1.1
Silverbrook Research, Australia	393	1.0
Sony Ericsson Mobile	303	0.8
NEC	293	0.8
Google	262	0.7
Research in Motion	256	0.7
Sony	230	0.6
IBM	201	0.5
Panasonic	163	0.4
BlackBerry	158	0.4
Broadcom	140	0.4
Fitbit	140	0.4
Fujitsu	137	0.4
Palm	134	0.3
Headwater Partners, U.S.	134	0.3
AT&T IP	133	0.3
Kyocera	131	0.3
Flextronics	113	0.3
Energous	107	0.3
Citrix Systems	103	0.3
Nokia Mobile Phones	100	0.3
FLIR Systems	90	0.2
Ericsson	85	0.2
Honda Motor	84	0.2
AT&T Mobility	83	0.2
Tencent Technology	82	0.2
Nant Holdings IP	72	0.2
Hewlett Packard	68	0.2
Huawei	65	0.2
Sharp	63	0.2
Elwha LLC	63	0.2
NTT DoCoMo	62	0.2

Broad

Company name	USPTO patents	Percentage of USPTO smartphone patents
IBM	57,414	1.8
Samsung Electronics	41,421	1.3
Qualcomm	29,572	0.9
Intel	26,150	0.8
Microsoft	22,844	0.7
Canon	18,983	0.6
Fujitsu	18,038	0.6
Sony	18,036	0.6
Panasonic	17,515	0.5
Hewlett Packard	16,881	0.5
Honda Motor	14,859	0.5
Hitachi	11,985	0.4
Google	11,243	0.3
Philips Electronics	10,818	0.3
Seiko Epson	10,645	0.3
Apple	10,598	0.3
Motorola	10,489	0.3
LG Electronics	10,369	0.3
Texas Instruments	10,213	0.3
Taiwan Semiconductor Mfg	9,399	0.3
NEC	9,093	0.3
Infineon Technologies	8,221	0.3
Cisco Tech	8,033	0.2
General Electric	7,764	0.2
Honghai Precision	7,613	0.2
3M	7,391	0.2
Honeywell	7,284	0.2
Samsung Display	7,212	0.2
Mitsubishi Electric	6,956	0.2
Toshiba	6,693	0.2
Nokia	6,567	0.2
Sharp	6,526	0.2
Ericsson	6,469	0.2
Broadcom	6,254	0.2
Advanced Micro Devices	6,027	0.2
Siemens	5,892	0.2
Huawei	5,845	0.2
Semiconductor Energy Lab	5,810	0.2
University of California	5,477	0.2
Sun Microsystems	5,341	0.2

Note: For the narrow and broad approaches to mapping smartphone patents, see box 4.2. Source: WIPO based on USPTO database.

The patents and other rights related to software and applications are important intangible assets, possibly determining a large share of future value capture. By using its own mobile operating system, Apple gains greater control of the downstream market for applications and content, such as on the App Store, typically asking 30 percent of in-app purchases from application developers, dropping to 15 percent under special conditions later.[57] According to information produced in IP-related litigation and unconfirmed reports in the press, firms such as Google paid Apple USD 1 billion in 2013 and possibly three times that amount in 2017 to be the default search engine in mobile Safari, the pre-installed web browser on iPhones and other iOS devices.[58]

Android is monetized in a different way, not through charging a direct usage fee. If phone makers want to run Android on their phones, they need to install the Google ecosystem (Search, Play Store, Maps) on their phone. Google makes money from Android in two ways: it takes a proportion of the sales of apps and media on the Google Play Store, and it shows display advertising to Android users. Google excludes phone makers from any revenue from the Play Store, reducing their ability to generate revenues from downstream content and services markets.

Firms such as Samsung using the Android system have also decided to pay significant patent royalties to Microsoft to settle claims by Microsoft that Google's Android violates Microsoft patents. Samsung made a royalty payment of over USD 1 billion to Microsoft in 2013, according to court filings and news articles.[59]

4.3.2 – Smartphone design is critical to consumers

The literature, consumer surveys and court decisions find that smartphone design – both physical and software-related – is one of the most critical factors driving consumer purchase decisions, technology acceptance and later brand loyalty.[60] This is particularly the case when technical features are the same across phones.

Understandably, then, all three handset lead firms in question invest considerable sums in new designs and related partnerships, and in recruiting a large number of designers.

Industrial designs are held mostly by large lead firms rather than component suppliers and smaller entities.[61] An econometric study suggests that in the case of Apple, filing industrial designs – referred to as design patents in the U.S. – is actually more important to the evolution of the firm's stock market value than patents.[62] In the well-known Apple-Samsung case, industrial design infringement and the copying of the look of Apple's smartphones – including elements of GUIs, especially icons – were the subject of legal dispute in U.S. and other courts.[63] Since the Apple-Samsung jury award in 2012 in the U.S., industrial design filings have also been increasing at the USPTO – potentially in part due to the high damages initially awarded to Apple (see also figure 4.12).[64] At time of writing, this case is not fully closed in the U.S.: the Supreme Court reversed the first trial decision in December 2016. Furthermore, related litigation is still pending or has produced different outcomes in other jurisdictions. All of this illustrates the inherent legal uncertainty associated with enforcing industrial designs. Still, the court cases and ensuing design filing activity reflect a broader movement toward using industrial designs as a tool for appropriating innovation rents in conjunction with other IP forms.

A look at the leading industrial design filers illustrates the point: Samsung, Sony, Microsoft, LG, Hon Hai Precision/Foxconn and Apple were among the top holders of design patents at the USPTO in 2015.[65] Identifying industrial designs which relate to the specific smartphones used in section 4.2, or to smartphones in general, is complicated by various factors.[66] For a start, there is no specific classification for smartphones in the International Classification for Industrial Designs under the Locarno Agreement, or in the United States Patent Classification System (USPC). Industrial designs for smartphones do not just concern the device itself, but also GUIs, icons, display screens, and so on. Moreover, some of the GUIs and icons are used across different product groups. For example, an industrial design for an Apple icon or GUI is likely to be used across all Apple family products (iPhone, iPad, iPod, etc.), and is thus not exclusively a smartphone design. Some Samsung GUIs may apply to washing machines, fridges, photo cameras or video cameras.

Figures 4.11 and 4.12 present the industrial designs protected by Apple, Samsung Electronics and Huawei using data from the USPTO and the European Union Intellectual Property Office (EUIPO). In the case of the USPTO, USPC class D14 (Recording, Communication, or Information Retrieval Equipment) was used as a starting point to then filter further using patent titles. The same approach was used for the EUIPO, with the difference that the initial dataset included all applications for classes 14-03 (Communications Equipment, Wireless Remote Controls and Radio Amplifiers) and 14-04 (Screen Displays and Icons) of the International Locarno classification for Industrial Designs.

The design portfolios of Apple and Samsung at the USPTO and the EUIPO are large and have been growing, with a particularly big spike in 2012 or 2013 (see figure 4.12). As noted above, Apple's initial success in enforcing a GUI design against Samsung in the U.S. courts may have contributed to this GUI filing growth. The number of registrations by Samsung Electronics far outstrips those of Apple, but this most likely also reflects potential measurement issues as Samsung is a more diversified electronics conglomerate than Apple. While Huawei has started registering industrial designs in recent years, Apple and Samsung still own considerably more extensive design portfolios.

The portfolios of designs protected by the three companies are also distinct. A large proportion of Huawei designs protected at the USPTO (41.9 percent, or 18) in the period 2007-2015 were designs of phones themselves. In contrast, most of Apple's designs in the same period were for GUIs (75.2 percent). Samsung Electronics designs were also mainly GUIs (43.7 percent of total), but followed in absolute number of registrations by designs for phones themselves (30.9 percent). Apple's design registrations at the EUIPO were largely for GUIs (70.1 percent of total), while all of Huawei's were for phones. There was a major peak in design registrations around 2012-2013, following the Apple-Samsung legal dispute. Industrial designs in these two years alone represent 42.4 percent of all Apple's designs at the USPTO in the period 2007-2015, and 22.2 percent at the EUIPO. For Samsung they represent 44.1 percent of total designs in the period 2007-2015 at the USPTO and 44.3 percent at the EUIPO.

Figure 4.12

Industrial designs by smartphone firms increased in 2012 and 2013

Number of industrial designs registered at the USPTO, 2009-2014

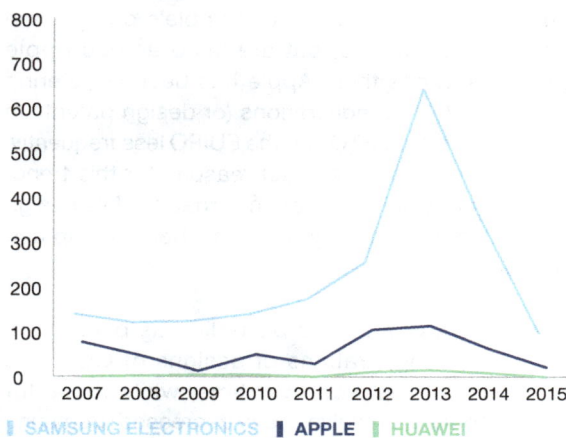

SAMSUNG ELECTRONICS   APPLE   HUAWEI

Number of industrial designs registered at the EUIPO, 2009-2014

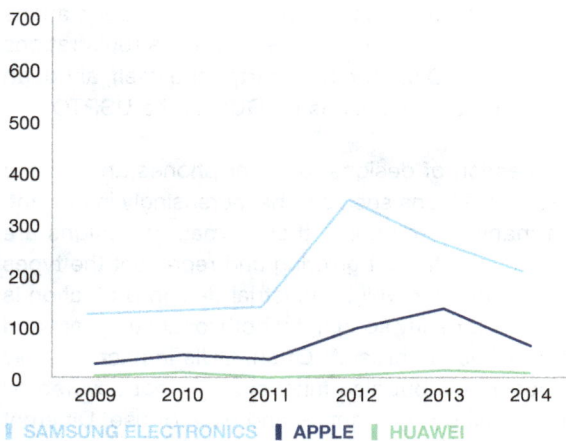

SAMSUNG ELECTRONICS   APPLE   HUAWEI

Notes: Data correspond to industrial designs that are registered and published. EUIPO data show the total number of individual designs published and registered in all applications filed. Only data for Samsung Electronics are presented. However, it is common practice that designs can be filed through subsidiaries. For example, Samsung Display Co. Ltd., a Samsung subsidiary, registered 22 industrial designs at the EUIPO in the period 2013-2015.

Sources: WIPO based on the USPTO and EUIPO databases.

Over time, the design portfolios of the three companies have also changed. Apple was an early mover in the industry. It filed a total of 370 designs at the EUIPO in 2007 and 2008 – 35.7 percent of its total in the period 2007-2015 – coinciding with the release of the first iPhone. None of these registrations related to the smartphone design itself, but rather to GUIs (69.2 percent) and icons (30.8 percent). This is not surprising given that most of Apple's designs are not iPhone specific, but are used across Apple products. Since then, Apple has been registering industrial design registrations (or design patents in the U.S.) at the USPTO and the EUIPO less frequently. It is hard to know the exact reasons for this trend, but one possible explanation is that Apple's design ecosystem and identity have now been set up and are relatively mature.

In contrast, Samsung's portfolio has been more volatile. Its registrations of designs of GUIs and icons have increased over time, while those for smartphones themselves have decreased. Samsung could be following Apple's strategy and adapting to the market, particularly after 2012 and the GUI legal dispute.

Finally, Huawei is an emerging player in the industry, with a low absolute number of design registrations relative to Apple and Samsung. All its registrations at the EUIPO are for the smartphone itself, although it has patented designs for GUIs at the USPTO.

Protection of designs for smartphones and related GUIs and icons seems to be increasingly important. In many jurisdictions, these types of designs are among the fastest growing and represent the types of designs for which industrial design protection is most frequently sought, by both local designers and those based abroad.[67] Often, GUIs impact not only appearance but also functionality – not covered by industrial design rights – and ease of use. Different IP rights offer different protection and have different eligibility requirements, and there may be significant variations in both protection and eligibility criteria across jurisdictions. Patent, design and copyright protection are the most likely options for legal protection.[68] In the U.S. a special form of trademark, trade dress, which covers the appearance of a product, its box, shape or otherwise, may also be relevant, for example to protect the distinctive design of Apple's iPhone boxes.

Figure 4.13 sets out filings (or registrations) by Apple and Samsung with respect to GUIs and icons. The number of GUI industrial designs filed by Apple and Samsung Electronics has grown considerably since 2012 at both the USPTO and the EUIPO. At the EUIPO, Apple filed 222 designs on GUIs between 2009 and 2014, while Samsung filed 379. In 2007, the same year the first iPhone was released, half (38) the industrial designs filed by Apple at the USPTO were for GUIs, and the other half were icon designs. In 2008, GUI industrial designs accounted for 89 percent (41) of Apple's filings at the USPTO. About 66 percent (189) of Apple's filings at the EUIPO in 2008 were for GUIs, and 34 percent (98) were icon designs. Icon designs have also grown, particularly for Samsung, which more than tripled its number of icon design applications at the USPTO between 2012 and 2013. Remarkably, Huawei filed only 17 designs for display screens with GUIs between 2012 and 2015 at the USPTO, and has so far filed no GUI designs at all at the EUIPO.

Comparing the absolute number of industrial designs filed by these firms is challenging, however. First, the methodology used to identify smartphone industrial designs is not exact. Second, Samsung Electronics is a conglomerate filing for a large product range of smartphones and other electronics products, whereas Apple has released 15 iPhone models onto the market since 2007.[69] Finally, Apple's designs for GUIs and icons are used across all Apple products and in many cases across iPhone models, which can result in even fewer absolute filings.

Lastly, in some cases an overlap between trademark and design protection arises, if and when firms later trademark a design, claiming distinctiveness. An industrial design and a trademark may be obtained covering the same subject matter:[70] the former grants a limited period of protection for a design, while the latter may in effect provide perpetual protection for the same design as a mark.

Figure 4.13

GUIs and icons represent the largest share of smartphone industrial designs

Number of industrial designs registered at the USPTO by company and type

Apple

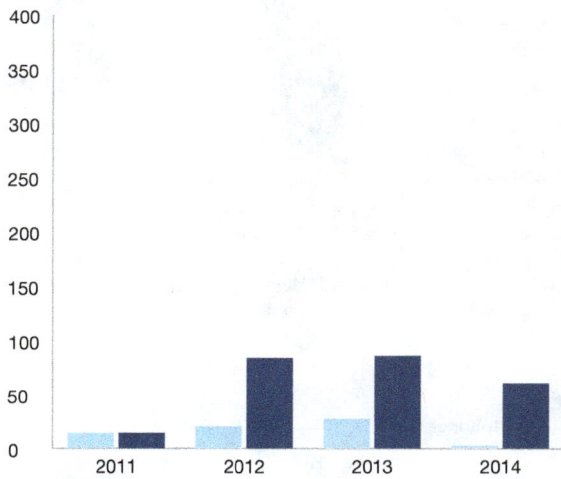

ICONS GUI

Samsung Electronics

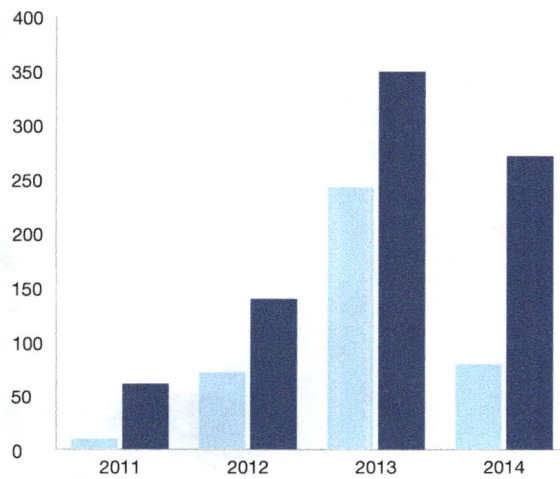

ICONS GUI

Number of industrial designs registered at the EUIPO by company and type

Apple

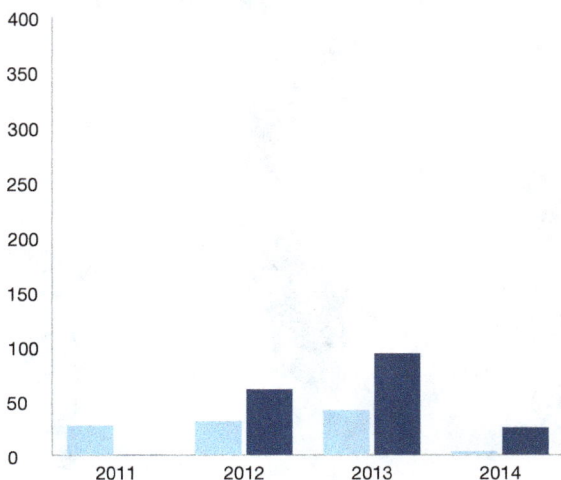

ICONS GUI

Samsung Electronics

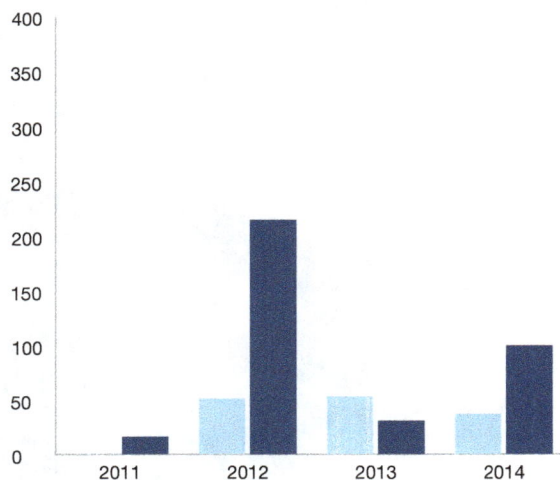

ICONS GUI

Source: WIPO based on USPTO and EUIPO databases; see technical notes.

Figure 4.13 (cont.)

Share of industrial designs ("design patents") registered at the USPTO by selected companies for different smartphone elements, 2007-2015

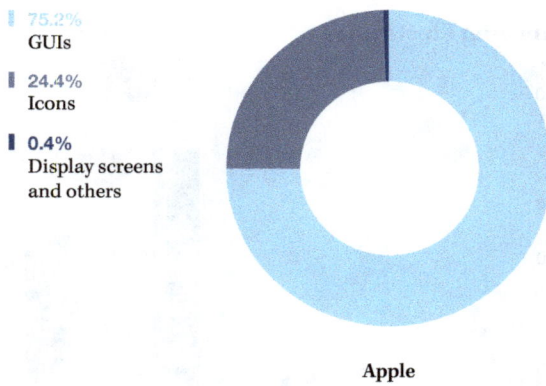

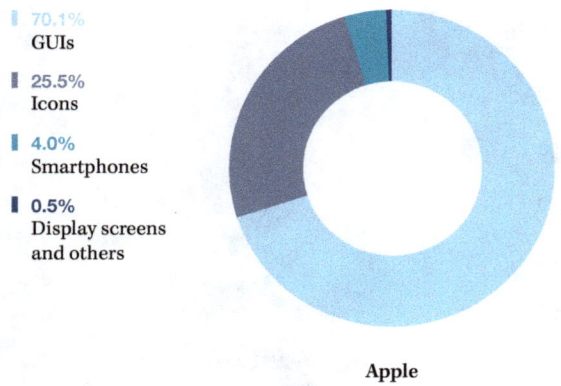

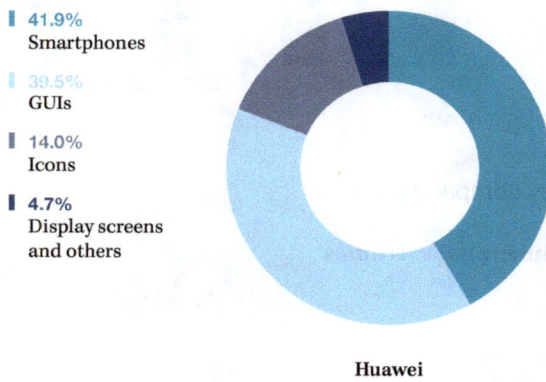

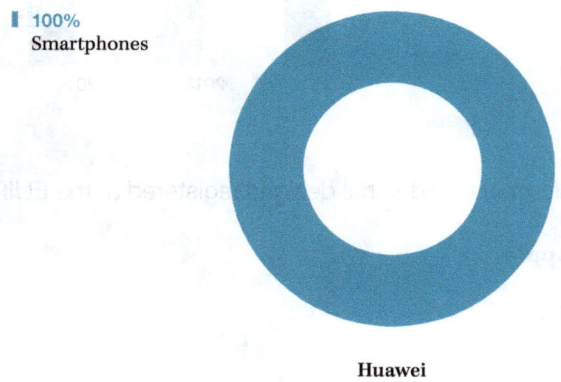

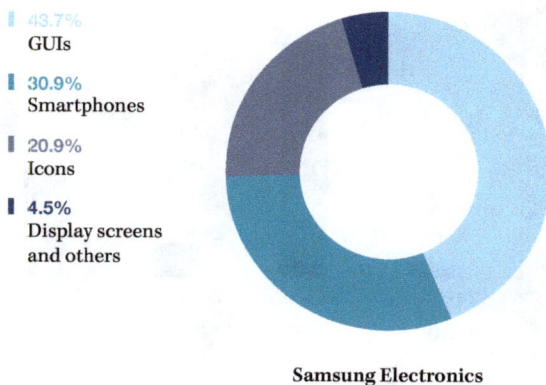

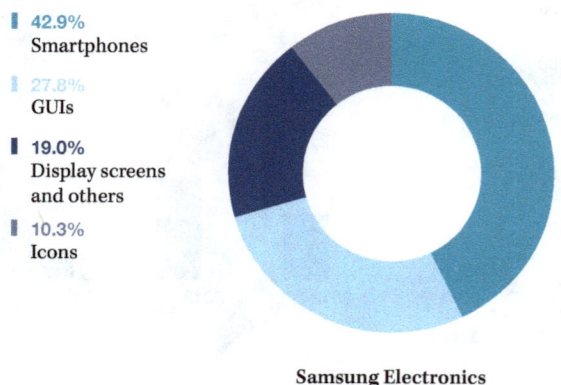

Share of industrial designs registered at the EUIPO by selected companies for different smartphone elements, 2007-2015

75.2% GUIs
24.4% Icons
0.4% Display screens and others

Apple

70.1% GUIs
25.5% Icons
4.0% Smartphones
0.5% Display screens and others

Apple

41.9% Smartphones
39.5% GUIs
14.0% Icons
4.7% Display screens and others

Huawei

100% Smartphones

Huawei

43.7% GUIs
30.9% Smartphones
20.9% Icons
4.5% Display screens and others

Samsung Electronics

42.9% Smartphones
27.8% GUIs
19.0% Display screens and others
10.3% Icons

Samsung Electronics

Source: WIPO based on USPTO and EUIPO databases; see technical notes.

4.3.3 – The high value of the brands behind the leading smartphones

The *World Intellectual Property Report 2013* outlined the importance of brands – and trademarks – as intangible assets, and as a driver of the ability to command higher prices, including in the smartphone sector.[71] Brands were also shown to play an important role in explaining why lead firms capture a majority of profits along the way.

Apple, Samsung and more recently Huawei spend heavily on advertising (see figure 4.14). Echoing the interrelationship between branding and innovation, all three firms put marketing on par with R&D for the development of innovative products. Apple increased spending to USD 1.8 billion in 2015 (with 2016 figures unavailable), while Samsung spent USD 3.8 billion in 2016 – rivalling companies with the largest advertising budgets worldwide such as Coca-Cola, after a sustained decision as of 2012 to vastly increase its yearly advertising spend, mainly to promote its Galaxy brand.[72] Official advertising data for Huawei are not available, but the ever-more global marketing campaigns around the company and its P-series smartphones demonstrate its intent to move out of the low-margin segment by building a premium brand.[73]

Identifying the value of brands for the smartphone business in general, or for specific smartphone models in particular, is challenging. Much of a brand's value rests with the reputation and image of the lead firm, such as Apple, Samsung or Huawei, and this brand value is particularly high, with Apple and Samsung at the top of brand rankings, and Apple in the number one spot for two out of the three rankings (see table 4.9 of this report plus table 1.1 and box 1.6 in WIPO, 2013 for a technical critique of these brand values). Huawei is worth less as a brand, but is catching up. Newer Chinese smartphone firms are still distant.

The three companies follow similar branding and trademark strategies. According to estimates produced for this report, Apple started registering trademarks related to its iPhone at the USPTO in 2006, including a trademark for the name "iPhone."[74] Sustaining its lead-time advantage, the company then registered a total of 15 trademarks in 2007, the year it introduced the iPhone. Samsung and Huawei started registering smartphone-related trademarks only in 2009 and 2011, with Samsung seemingly filing a relatively high number of trademarks without necessarily using them in the marketplace subsequently.

While Huawei registered few trademarks – just 10 in all over the entire period – Samsung immediately began to register a large number of trademarks; it has registered a total of 300 over this period. Samsung's spike in trademark registrations in 2012 coincided with the previously mentioned increased advertising that year (see figure 4.15).

Figure 4.14

Samsung and other smartphone makers are among the world's top advertisers

Global advertising expenditure (USD bn)

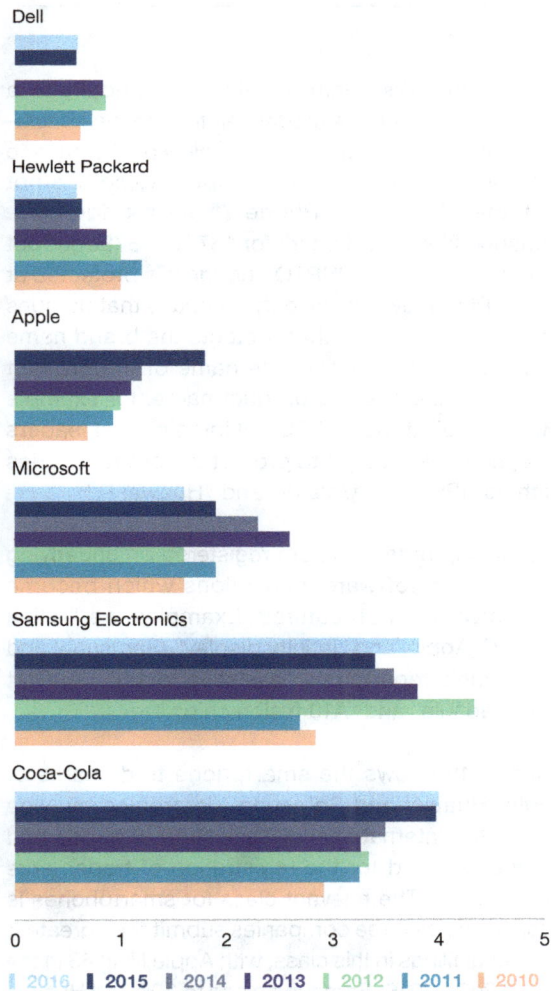

Notes: Data for Dell not available for 2014. Data for Apple not available for 2016. Data for Microsoft and Apple correspond to fiscal years.

Source: WIPO based on company annual reports.

Table 4.9

Brand values of leading smartphone makers, 2016

Company	Interbrand Rank and value	As a percentage of market cap	BrandZ Rank and value	As a percentage of market cap	Forbes Rank and value	As a percentage of market cap
Apple	Rank 1 USD 178 bn	23	Rank 2 USD 22 bn	30	Rank 1 USD 154 bn	20
Samsung	Rank 7 USD 52 bn	20	Rank 48 USD 19 bn	7.2	Rank 11 USD 36 bn	13
Huawei	Rank 72 USD 6 bn	0.4	Rank 50 USD 19 bn	1.3	–	n.a.

Sources: Dedrick and Kraemer (2017) based on WIPO (2013) and data from Interbrand (2016), Millward Brown (2016) and Forbes (2016).

Few trademarks seem to relate specifically to a particular smartphone model, reinforcing the conclusion that the brand value draws mainly on the generic company trademark. For example, Apple has not protected the term "iPhone 7" via a trademark. Samsung filed a trademark for "S7" or "S7Edge" but abandoned it at the USPTO, though it is protected at the EUIPO. Huawei is the only company that pursues a trademark strategy that protects the brand name displayed on the device, the name of the product series and the specific product name, for example "Huawei P9" at the USPTO. All three market leaders have, however, sought to protect the product series such as "iPhone", "Galaxy" and "Huawei P."

In addition, trademarks are registered on underlying hardware or software innovations which become distinctive product features. Examples are "retina display" (Apple) and "Infinity display" (Samsung) and – in Apple's repertoire – "assistive touch", "AirPort Time Capsule" and "A10 fusion chips."

Figure 4.16 shows the smartphone trademarks of Apple, Huawei and Samsung Electronics by Nice class – the international classification of goods and services applied for the registration of trademarks – over time.[75] The relevant class for smartphones is class 9, and all three companies submit their greatest number of filings in this class, with Apple filing 68 in the period 2007-2016, Samsung close to 300 and Huawei around 10. The most interesting aspect of this graph is the distribution across classes, precisely because the companies do not file only in class 9, but spread their trademarks across classes, especially services.

This is important for two reasons: (i) it helps them to build brand value and use their brand for a larger range of product and service categories than just "traditional" electronic products and (ii) occupying as much space across classes as reasonably possible means they are better placed to avoid the appropriation of brand value by competitors and other firms (and squatters), but bearing in mind that a mark must be used for the relevant class in order to be protected. The graph also shows that Huawei is starting to change its approach by filing in more classes.

Figure 4.15

Apple was the first to file smartphone trademarks

Number of smartphone-related trademarks registered annually at the USPTO by Apple, Huawei and Samsung, 2007-2015

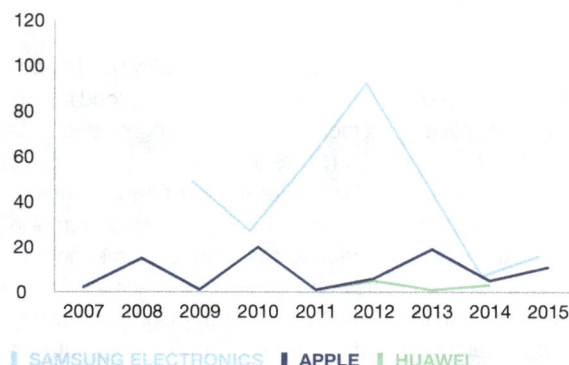

Source: WIPO based on USPTO database; see technical notes.

Figure 4.16

Smartphone trademarks are increasingly filed in service-related classes

Smartphone-related trademark registrations filed annually at the USPTO by Apple, Huawei and Samsung, by Nice class, 2006-2016

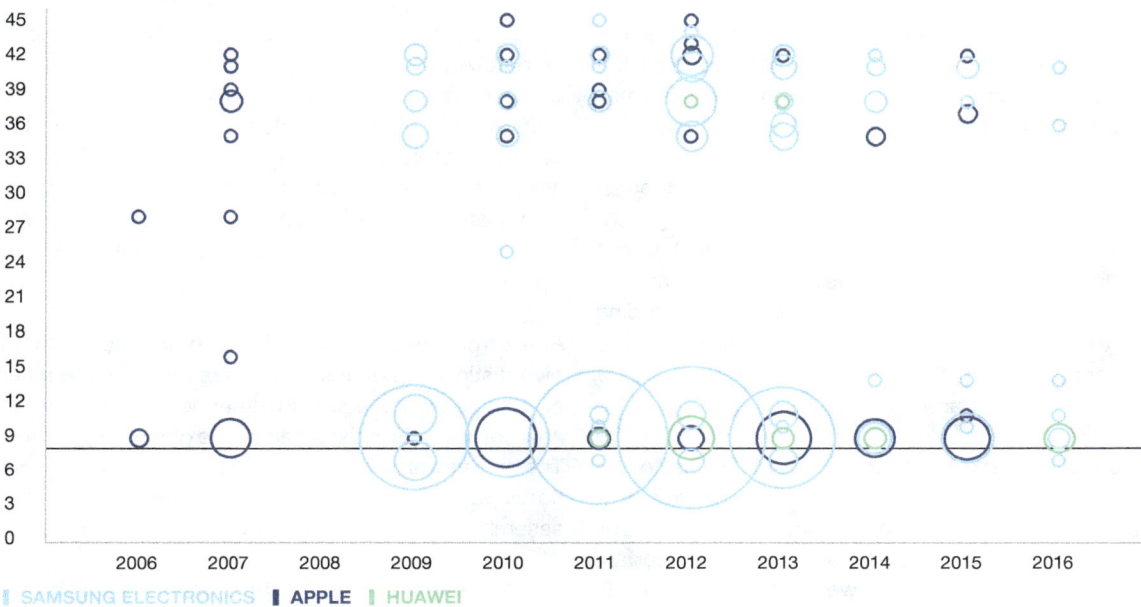

SAMSUNG ELECTRONICS | APPLE | HUAWEI

Note: The size of the bubble indicates the number of trademark filings for the relevant Nice class.

Source: WIPO based on USPTO database; see technical notes.

Huawei filed exclusively in class 9, but Apple and Samsung also filed smartphone-related trademarks in a number of other classes, including those related to services. For example, the first iPhone trademark in 2006 was also filed in class 28, which comprises games and toys, as a "hand-held unit for playing electronic games." The most common service class is class 38, which covers telecommunication services, but there are also a number of filings in class 42, which covers design and development of computer software, among other things.

As suggested earlier, Apple holds three trademarks on the design (trade dress) of its iPhone. Samsung also attempted to get such IP protection at both the USPTO and the EUIPO but failed. Rights in relation to packaging are interesting too. Apple has a trademark as well as a design right on the shape of the iPhone box.

In addition, some component suppliers also own trademarks which handset brands use when marketing their phones, such as Corning's Gorilla Glass trademark or Huawei's use of the Leica trademark to market its new smartphone camera.

Handset makers and component suppliers also refer to and license trademarks on standards and third-party technologies essential to the networking capacity of the phone, such as "LTE", "Wi-Fi" and "Bluetooth." Such marks are usually owned by standard-setting organizations or industry alliances, not individual component suppliers.[76]

Finally, elements which relate to smartphone software, content and services such as "Siri" for Apple and "Bixby" for Samsung, "iTunes" or "Apple Pay" are also protected by trademarks.[77] Some are owned by third-party providers such as "Android."

Trademarks are also filed on GUIs and icons related to smartphone applications and accessories. Apple and Samsung are particularly keen on filing for trademark and industrial design protection on GUIs, underling the notion that GUIs distinctively identify products.

4.4 – Perspectives on technological learning and intangibles

How has technological learning occurred in the smartphone global value chain? Is value capture shifting? And what role might IP play in this process?

Once more, a simple answer is impossible; the factors at work are too manifold. But it is useful to recall the timetable for smartphone innovation, and the small number of firms and locations involved.

In terms of the inventions required for smartphones, the development of mobile phones and underlying technologies dates back several decades. The first handset was launched by Motorola in 1973.[78] Cell phones also depend on a vast set of other technologies, including processors, which have their own long history.[79] The first critical patent for wireless communication, for example, can be traced back to 1974.

In terms of market penetration, NTT DoCoMo – a Japanese firm – reached relatively high penetration in Japan with its first smartphones, introduced in 1999. Still, it was in 2007 that Apple's iPhone made an important breakthrough. Apple was followed by Samsung in 2009, and only somewhat later by Huawei.[80] Apple defined the dominant design for a smartphone. In the innovation literature, establishment of dominant design is an important milestone, as the ensuing competition happens within these design parameters.

To this day, also, technological learning remains relatively concentrated among a few core firms and countries. There has been a shift in capacity, from Europe, Japan and the United States initially to selected firms in the Republic of Korea (Samsung and LG), Taiwan (Province of China) and China (Huawei and ZTE). As with other advanced technologies, participation in these technologies does not reflect a divide between developed and developing countries; Europe, for example, is no longer a serious contender, whereas China has become an important one.

There are important differences between the newcomer countries. The Republic of Korea built its capacity largely internally, supported by government policies and the strength of its domestic conglomerate enterprises. China's technological learning was shaped by extensive involvement with foreign entities, in particular through providing assembly services for foreign entities and foreign direct investment in China.

There were really two or three learning pathways in China. One involved companies from Taiwan (Province of China) setting up production facilities for multinationals in China (e.g., Foxconn assembling products for Apple and others). Another involved Chinese companies such as Huawei, ZTE and Lenovo that had established product lines (networking equipment and personal computers) subsequently moving into the smartphone market. A potential third pathway is the set of new Chinese firms selling cheap phones for China's home market without initially relying on strong internally generated technological inventions. As a result, China has a major role in the smartphone industry, but without necessarily having a large presence of mainland China firms in the global value chains of multinationals like Apple and Samsung.

Apart from these firms and countries, each with its own distinctive features, there has been little transfer of intangibles or creation of either new competitors or new participants in the smartphone global value chain. The only newer geographic shifts in global value chain participation can be seen in some limited transfer of assembly activities to countries outside East Asia.

Among the leaders, what do Apple, Samsung and Huawei have in common in terms of the development of their innovation capacity and the role of intangible assets?

First, before entering the smartphone market all three firms had backgrounds and innovative capacity in related fields of technology.

- Apple's history is well known. It started in the late 1970s with a focus on computer technology, and also developed core know-how in the field of drives, printers, input devices, displays and networking technologies over the course of the following four decades. It took some time for Apple to move from its audio player, the iPod, introduced in 2001, via software-related innovation such as iTunes to the simultaneous introduction of the iPhone and the iPad. Its capacity in internal component development is weaker than Huawei's or Samsung's – with the exception of the most expensive and strategic components such as processors and, more recently, graphics processing units.[81] In addition, Apple has substantial capacity in product design, integration and software.

- Samsung Electronics was always part of a larger conglomerate, entering initially as a supplier of components (specifically telecommunications hardware and phones) to other firms, beginning in the 1980s. Samsung Electronics initially manufactured inexpensive, imitative electronics for other companies. Samsung also produced a lot of its own-brand products for the Republic of Korea. Already back then, many of its plants were set up abroad, arguably benefiting from access to foreign-trained skills and labor. However, in 1996 it made a major shift towards developing internal design capabilities and building its own brand.[82] Today, Samsung remains unique in its reliance on internal transfer of technology, and production and product design capacities.

- Huawei started much later and with fewer integral capabilities, but had become the global leader in telecommunications networks by 2012.[83] Unlike other firms in China or Taiwan (Province of China), Huawei did not act as a contract manufacturer for Western entities. Instead, it focused consistently on telecom-related innovation and building its extensive relationships with operators worldwide. In 2003, Huawei started producing phones, mostly low-end types for Chinese telecom carriers. Since 2011, however, it has developed high-end devices. Rather than relying on joint ventures to secure technology transfer from foreign companies, Huawei focused on local R&D and on learning by reverse-engineering of foreign technologies (Chong, 2013). Today, Huawei is actually more R&D-intensive than Apple or Samsung (see table 4.3) and is maintaining this high R&D investment despite falling revenues and margins.[84] Academic studies show that this rapid catch-up by Huawei was due to its technological capabilities rather than cost advantages alone – by creating its own technological path rather than remaining a technological follower. Huawei grew rapidly by developing technologies that are different from those of Ericsson, a main competitor, with Huawei relying on recent scientific knowledge in its innovation strategies.[85] More recently, Huawei has looked to upgrade, setting up a number of partnerships or joint ventures with firms such as IBM, Siemens, 3Com and Symantec plus R&D partnerships with Motorola and other telecommunication operators, and it has also learned management practices from Western firms.

While each company has followed a different development path, all three have been heavily involved in the creation of innovation capacity and related intangibles, including brands. All three are highly R&D-intensive with an express goal of increasing their in-house production of technologically sophisticated, high-margin components such as chips. All three have also learned to use IP intensively, and now operate large IP portfolios and have significant IP litigation experience. Moreover, Samsung and Huawei are involved in related standard-setting technologies and IP.

Second, all three firms operate in extensive value networks and with component suppliers (sections 4.1 and 4.2). Learning and upgrading does not occur just within these smartphone lead firms, but also in related technology fields. These interactions lead to two-way flows of knowledge in the process of co-designing and manufacturing. At the component level, the "fabless" chip model adopted by major chip makers such as Qualcomm, Broadcom and Apple involves close collaboration with foundries such as Taiwan Semiconductor Manufacturing Corporation (TSMC) to design chips to meet specific manufacturing processes.[86] Partnerships between Qualcomm and Huawei to create next-generation mobile chipsets also involve significant knowledge exchange.

Involvement in the smartphone global value chain entails learning and upgrading right down to the level of contracted manufacturing. When Apple works with Foxconn on processes such as plastic molding, machine tooling and quality control, learning is involved. Firms such as Foxconn started by making simpler contributions but nowadays add value to the iPhone through their own intangible assets (machine tooling, rapid prototyping, high volume ramp-up, supply chain management), some of which may soon take place at Foxconn's plant in the United States.[87]

When Huawei assembles outside Asia, for example in Brazil, knowledge transfer ensues.[88] In the same vein, knowledge transfer also occurs within multinational corporations. Samsung, for example, manufactures half its mobile phones in its own plants in Viet Nam. Apple has software developed in various countries. These activities lead to knowledge spillovers to domestic research institutes, suppliers and competitors, including business understanding as well as technological knowledge. In general, a great deal of the knowledge in these set-ups is tacit – never codified but flowing within and across organizations – whereas other knowledge gets codified to facilitate collaborations.

Third, acquisitions have helped these companies to progress. For example, Samsung purchased firms in areas as diverse as mobile music services, speech recognition technologies and nanotechnology firms delivering display solutions in 2016 and 2017 alone. This is also true of upcoming firms such as Foxconn, which bought Sharp in 2016 and is bidding for Toshiba's chip business.[89]

Fourth, labor mobility plays a large role. Firms such as Samsung benefited from labor mobility by learning from Japanese engineers in the 1990s, and by having access to Korean engineers trained in the United States. Huawei is known to have hired Western professionals in the area of marketing and public affairs, and key design experts from Apple or Samsung, and has set up design centers in London.[90] Apple also regularly hires from top U.S. firms such as Qualcomm or from U.S. universities.

Fifth, insourcing of technology and IP-based exchanges have been an important source of knowledge exchange and of firms' ability to operate. All three firms are engaged with SEPs, including through cross-licensing or licensing (e.g., licensing deals with Nokia).

Finally, another important factor in this story is the role of government policy and the broader environment for doing business and innovation. All three companies operate in countries with a pronounced emphasis on innovation-driven growth, a strong private and public commitment to science and R&D, excellent (or rapidly improving) research infrastructures, an abundance of engineering and science skills and a recognition of the value of technological and non-technological innovation. All three countries had a strong commitment to the borderless operation of global value chains, and their participation within them. They also had frameworks and policies in place to encourage IP filings and foster telecom standards; historically, China jumped on this bandwagon last, but it has made considerable progress in a short time.

From the perspective of international trade, all three firms benefited from very open international markets in the field of information technology products – markets secured through the Information Technology Agreement concluded in 1996 at the World Trade Organization, among others.[91]

All in all, government policy – and sometimes also the absence of explicit policy intervention – has played a role in fostering the smartphone industry.

Notes

1. This chapter draws on Dedrick and Kraemer (2017) and Stitzing (2017).

2. IDC (2017).

3. Credit Suisse (2017).

4. IDC (2017).

5. Credit Suisse (2016, 2017).

6. IDC (2017).

7. iri.jrc.ec.europa.eu/scoreboard.html.

8. Credit Suisse (2017).

9. BCG (2017).

10. Koski and Kretschmer (2007).

11. "Qualcomm calls for iPhone ban as Apple patent case intensifies," *Financial Times* (FT), July 6, 2017.

12. "China smartphone maker Xiaomi designs its first chip," FT, February 28, 2017; "China's Xiaomi to take on top tier with smartphone chip of its own," *Wall Street Journal* (WSJ), February 9, 2017; "Apple's building its own graphics processor for the iPhone, dropping Imagination GPUs," *PC World*, April 3, 2017.

13. See Dedrick et al. (2010) and Dedrick and Kraemer (2017) for more details.

14. IHS Markit (2016).

15. IHS Markit (2016), Samsung Galaxy S7.

16. It is not always the lead firm that pays the bill; sometimes component suppliers may pay. This is the case for Apple, which does not hold a license for Qualcomm's IP but instead relies on agreements between its contract manufacturers and Qualcomm.

17. See Neubig and Wunsch-Vincent (2017), a study produced for this report, which notes how taxation issues lead to distortions in the measurement of IP transactions.

18. Dedrick et al. (2011) found that the carriers capture most value, ahead of handset makers.

19. See Neubig and Wunsch (2017), which also discusses how companies shift their R&D and IP portfolios, including for tax reasons (e.g., Apple and other high-technology companies in Ireland).

20. See Ali-Yrkkö et al. (2011) for similar findings in this sector.

21. For the 90 percent estimate, which is widely echoed in other business stories, see S. Ovide and D. Wakabayashi, "Apple's share of smartphone industry's profits soars to 92%," WSJ, July 12, 2015: www.wsj.com/articles/apples-share-of-smartphone-industrys-profits-soars-to-92-1436727458.

22. Shapiro and Varian (1998), OECD (2005), Garcia-Swartz and Garcia-Vicente (2015). Korkeamäki and Takalo (2013) similarly demonstrate that – relative to its competitors – Apple captures most value from smartphone sales in terms of its positive stock price evolution.

23. Apple Annual Report, 2016.

24. See Dedrick and Kramer (2017).

25. Dedrick and Kramer (2017) based on FT Markets Data: markets.ft.com/data.

26. OECD (2011), Blind et al. (2014), and Cecere et al. (2015).

27. Korkeamäki and Takalo (2013).

28. Teece (1986).

29. Sharma (2016) and WIPO (2011, 2013 and 2015).

30. "Apple-Samsung case shows smartphone as legal magnet," *New York Times*, August 25, 2012: www.nytimes.com/2012/08/26/technology/apple-samsung-case-shows-smartphone-as-lawsuit-magnet.html; "There are 250,000 active patents that impact smartphones; representing one in six active patents today," *Techdirt*, October 18, 2012: www.techdirt.com/articles/20121017/10480520734/there-are-250000-active-patents-that-impact-smartphones-representing-one-six-active-patents-today.shtml. The original source for the 250,000 patent figure stems from an SEC filing by RPX Corporation, a "defensive patent aggregator", www.sec.gov/Archives/edgar/data/1509432/000119312511240287/ds1.htm, and is largely unverified.

31. WIPO (2017).

32. WIPO (2016).

33. The CPC is available at: www.cooperativepatentclassification.org. Experts at Clarivate, previously Thomson Reuters, provided advice on this choice, also based on Derwent World Patents Index's manual code for smartphones.

34. The IPC is available at: www.wipo.int/classifications/ipc.

35. worldwide.espacenet.com and Datenbankrecherche, Deutsche Patent- und Markenamt (DPMA), www.dpma.de/patent/recherche/index.html.

36. A patent family is a set of interrelated patent applications filed in one or more countries or jurisdictions to protect the same invention. See the glossary in WIPO (2016).

37. See OECD (2008) for a discussion of the role of IP in the ICT industry.

38. See WIPO (2011) on the economics of patents, and Blind et al. (2014) for an application to the ICT industry.

39. Engstrom (2017).

40. Reidenberg et al. (2012, 2014).

41. Gurry (2013).

42. PwC (2017).

43. Gurry (2013).

44. PwC (2017).

45. Reidenberg et al. (2012) show that the majority of patents relate to communications technology, followed by hardware and software patents.

46. Audenrode et al. (2017) and Baron et al. (2016).

47. Kumar and Bhasin (2017).

48. See Fan (2006) on Huawei and ZTE; and see IPlytics (2016) and Thumm and Gabison (2016) on the increasing role of PAEs and the increased SEP-related litigation.

49. Pohlmann and Blind (2016) and Reidenberg et al. (2014).

50. For example, Google purchased Alpental Technologies in 2014.

51. Sullivan and Cromwell (2013), Armstrong et al. (2014) and Mallinson (2015).

52. Galetovic et al. (2016) identify royalties for smartphone SEPs of USD 14.3 billion, equivalent to 3.4 percent of the value of smartphones. Sidak (2016) estimates that SEP royalty payments were between 4 and 5 percent of revenues using 3G and 4G standards in 2013 and 2014.

53. Nokia 2016 annual report: www.nokia.com/en_int/investors; Nokia News release, February 2, 2017: www.nokia.com/en_int/news/releases/2017/02/02/nokia-corporation-report-for-q4-2016-and-full-year-2016; Ericsson 2016 annual report: www.ericsson.com/assets/local/investors/documents/2016/ericsson-annual-report-2016-en.pdf; Ericsson press release, January 26, 2017: www.ericsson.com/en/press-releases/2017/1/ericsson-reports-fourth-quarter-and-full-year-results-2016, and "Top licensors Ericsson, Microsoft and Nokia all see drop in year-on-year patent revenues," *IAM Market*, February 9 2017

54. Shimpi (2013).

55. See Engstrom (2017), Kumar and Bhasin (2017) and "Royalty fees could reach $120 on a $400 smartphone," ZDNet, May 31, 2014: www.zdnet.com/article/patent-insanity-royalty-fees-could-reach-120-on-a-400-smartphone/for similar exercises.

56. Thomson Reuters (2012).

57. "iOS versus Android. Apple App Store versus Google Play," ZDNet, January 16, 2015; "App Store 2.0," *The Verge*, June 8, 2016; and see Campbell-Kelly et al. (2015) for a review of Google's and Apple's mobile platforms and the related business models at play.

58. "Google is paying Apple billions per year to remain on the iPhone, Bernstein says," CNBC, August 14, 2017. Estimate based on court documents and Apple's financial conference call in the first half of 2017 demonstrating that Apple's services revenues will equal USD 7.3 billion in the first quarter of 2017, with 22 percent growth on the previous year.

59. See unsealed filing on October 3, 2014 in the *Microsoft v. Samsung* U.S. District Court patent-royalty case filed in early August 2014. "Document sheds light on Samsung's payments to Microsoft over Android," CNET, October 4, 2014; "Samsung paid Microsoft $1 billion last year for Android royalty, filing says," WJS, October 3, 2014; and "Microsoft and Samsung end Android royalties dispute," *The Verge*, February 9, 2015.

60. See Liu and Yu (2017), Liu and Liang (2014) and related surveys by agencies and firms such as KISA (2014) and Samsung, "The most important feature in a mobile device", September 29, 2015: www.samsung.com/ae/discover/your-feed/the-most-important-feature-in-a-mobile-device; and *Apple v. Samsung*, C-11-01846-LHK (N.D. Cal. 2012).

61. Reidenberg et al. (2012).

62. Johnson and Scowcroft (2016).

63. *Apple v. Samsung*, C-11-01846-LHK (N.D. Cal. 2012).

64. See also Golinveaux and Hughes (2015) and PwC (2017) for a reference to this trend and/or effect.

65. USPTO Design Patent Report, January 1, 1991-December 31, 2015, published in March 2016: www.uspto.gov/web/offices/ac/ido/oeip/taf/design.pdf; and Reidenberg et al. (2014).

66. The discussion here draws on a collaboration between the WIPO Economics and Statistics Division and contributions by Christian Helmers, notably "Smartphone Trademark and Design Mapping", unpublished background report to the *World Intellectual Property Report 2017*, June 16, 2017.

67. WIPO Standing Committee on the Law of Trademarks, Industrial Designs and Geographical Indications (SCT), Proposal by the Delegations of Israel, Japan and the United States of America, "Industrial Design and Emerging Technologies: Similarities and Differences in the Protection of New Technological Designs", September 12, 2016, SCT/35/6 Rev. 2.

68. WIPO SCT, "Compilation of the Replies to the Questionnaire on Graphical User Interface (GUI), Icon and Typeface/Type Font Designs," October 17-19. 2016, SCT/36/2 Rev. 2; and WIPO SCT, "Analysis of the Returns to the Questionnaire on Graphical User Interface (GUI), Icon and Typeface/Type Font Designs," March 27-30, 2017, SCT/37/2 Rev.

69. iPhone (2007), iPhone 3G (2008), iPhone 3GS (2009), iPhone 4 (2010), iPhone 4S (2011), iPhone 5 (2012), iPhone 5C (2013), iPhone 5S (2013), iPhone 6 (2014), iPhone 6 Plus (2014), iPhone 6S (2015), iPhone SE (2016), iPhone 7 (2016), iPhone 7S (2017), iPhone 8 (2017).

70. See www.uspto.gov/web/offices/pac/mpep/s1512.html.

71. WIPO (2013).

72. Note, however, that the Samsung Electronics portfolio is vastly larger than that of Apple. These figures are thus not directly related to smartphone advertising alone and are not easily comparable. On the 2012-2015 estimates, see "The cost of selling Galaxies," *Asymco*, November 29, 2012; Adbrands Global Advertising Expenditure Ranking, December 2015: www.adbrands.net/top_global_advertisers.htm.

73. Huawei 2016 Annual Report: www.huawei.com/en/about-huawei/annual-report/2016.

74. See note 66 and technical notes.

75. See www.wipo.int/classifications/nice.

76. See, by way of example, www.wi-fi.org/who-we-are/our-brands, www.3gpp.org/about-3gpp/19-lte-logo-use and www.bluetooth.com/membership-working-groups/membership-types-levels.

77. www.apple.com/legal/intellectual-property/trademark/appletmlist.html.

78. Theodore Paraskevakos, U.S. Patent #3,812,296/5-21-1974.

79. See WIPO (2015) for the historical case of semiconductors and the underlying work of Professor Thomas Hoeren.

80. Samsung had experimented with earlier smartphone models, such as the SPH-I300 as early as October 2001 and the SGH-i607 in 2006.

81. "Apple looks long term with development of GPUs," FT, April 4, 2017; "Apple's building its own graphics processor for the iPhone, dropping Imagination GPUs," PC World, April 3, 2017.

82. Yoo and Kim (2015) and Song et al. (2016).

83. Boutellier et al. (2000), Zhang and Zhou (2015) and Kang (2015).

84. Huawei 2016 annual report. "Huawei 2016 numbers reveal the extent of Ericsson, Nokia and ZTE's challenge," Telecoms.com, March 31, 2017.

85. Joo et al. (2016).

86. Brown and Linden (2009). Fabless chip manufacturing is the design and sale of semiconductor chips while outsourcing the production of the chips to a specialized semiconductor foundry.

87. See Wunsch-Vincent et al. (2015) for a correspondingly growing patent portfolio of the Foxconn holding company.

88. Huawei and Xiaomi already have assembly facilities in places such as China, Viet Nam, India, Brazil and Indonesia in response to such forces. Apple's recent decision to set up production in India was in response to market demand and government incentives (Phadnis, 2016).

89. "Fight at Toshiba: Some board members want deal with Foxconn," WSJ, September 6, 2017.

90. "Huawei hires a former Apple creative director as a design chief," WSJ, October 29, 2015.

91. For more details, see www.wto.org/english/tratop_e/inftec_e/inftec_e.htm.

References

Ali-Yrkkö, J., P. Rouvinen, T. Seppälä and P. Ylä-Anttila (2011). Who captures value in global supply chains? Case Nokia N95 smartphone. *Journal of Industry, Competition and Trade*, 11(3), 263-278.

Armstrong, A.K., J.J. Mueller and T. Syrett (2014). The Smartphone Royalty Stack: Surveying Royalty Demands for the Components Within Modern Smartphones. SSRN, May 29, 2014: ssrn. com/abstract=2443848.

Audenrode, M.V., J. Royer, R. Stitzing and P. Sääskilahti (2017). Over-Declaration of Standard-Essential Patents and Determinants of Essentiality. SSRN, April 12, 2017. papers.ssrn.com/sol3/papers. cfm?abstract_id=2951617.

Baron, J., K. Gupta and B. Roberts (2016). Unpacking 3GPP Standards. Unpublished working paper, available at: pdfs.semanticscholar.org/bb7a/902cded bc5fb97b039372d0c7541c696e539.pdf.

Blind, K., T. Pohlmann, F. Ramel and S. Wunsch-Vincent (2014). The Egyptian IT Sector and the Role of IP. *WIPO Economic Research Working Paper No. 18*. Geneva: WIPO.

Boston Consulting Group (BCG) (2017). *The Most Innovative Companies 2016*. Boston, MA: Boston Consulting Group.

Boutellier, R., O. Gassmann and M. von Zedtwitz (2000). Huawei: Globalizing through innovation – case study, Part IV.7. In *Managing Global Innovation – Uncovering the Secrets of Future Competitiveness*. Berlin: Springer Verlag, 507-523.

Brown, C. and G. Linden (2009). *Chips and Change: How Crisis Reshapes the Semiconductor Industry*. Cambridge, MA: MIT Press.

Campbell-Kelly, M., D. Garcia-Swartz, R. Lam and Y. Yang (2015). Economic and business perspectives on smartphones as multi-sided platforms. *Telecommunications Policy*, 39(8), 717-734.

Cecere, G., N. Corrocher and R.D. Battaglia (2015). Innovation and competition in the smartphone industry: is there a dominant design? *Telecommunications Policy*, 39(3), 162-175.

Chen, W., R. Gouma, B. Los and M. Timmer (2017). Measuring the Income to Intangibles in Goods Production: A Global Value Chain Approach. *WIPO Economic Research Working Paper No. 36*. Geneva: WIPO.

Chong, G. (2013). *Chinese Telecommunications Giant Huawei: Strategies to Success*. Singapore: Nanyang Technopreneurship Center, Nanyang Technological University.

Credit Suisse (2016). *The Wireless View 2016: Smartphones – The Wireless Slowdown*. Global (Americas, Europe and Taiwan) Equity Research.

Credit Suisse (2017). *The Wireless View 2017: Smartphones – A Slight Pickup in Growth Ahead*. Global (Americas & Europe) Equity Research.

Dedrick, J. and K.L. Kraemer (2008). Globalization of innovation: the personal computing industry. In Macher, J.T. and D.C. Mowrey (eds), *Running Faster to Stay Ahead? Globalization of Innovation in High-Technology Industries*. Washington DC: National Academies Press, 21-57.

Dedrick, J. and K.L. Kraemer (2017). Intangible Assets and Value Capture in Global Value Chains: The Smartphone Industry. *WIPO Economic Research Working Paper No. 41*. Geneva: WIPO.

Dedrick, J., K.L. Kraemer and G. Linden (2010). Who profits from innovation in global value chains? A study of the iPod and notebook PCs. *Industrial and Corporate Change*, 19(1), 81-116.

Dedrick, J., K.L. Kraemer and G. Linden (2011). The distribution of value in the mobile phone supply chain. *Telecommunications Policy*, 35(6), 505-521.

Engstrom, E. (2017). So how many patents are in a smartphone? Blog, January 19, 2017. San Francisco: Engine. www.engine.is/news/category/so-how-many-patents-are-in-a-smartphone.

Fan, P. (2006). Catching up through developing innovation capability: evidence from China's telecom-equipment industry. *Technovation*, 26(3), 359-368.

Forbes (2016). The World's Most Valuable Brands. www.forbes.com/powerful-brands/list/3/#tab:rank.

Galetovic. A., S.H. Haber and L. Zaretzki (2016). A New Dataset on Mobile Phone Patent License Royalties. *Working Paper Series No. 16011*. Stanford, CA: Hoover Institution, Stanford University.

Garcia-Swartz, D.D. and F. Garcia-Vicente (2015). Network effects on the iPhone platform: an empirical examination. *Telecommunications Policy*, 39(10), 877-895.

Golinveaux, J.A. and D.L. Hughes (2015). Developing trends in design patent enforcement. *World Trademark Review*, issue 54.

Graham, S.J.H., G. Hancock, A.C. Marco and A.F. Myers (2013). The USPTO trademark case files dataset: descriptions, lessons, and insights. *Journal of Economics & Management Strategy*, 22, 669–705.

Graham, S.J.H., G. Hancock, A.C. Marco and A.F. Myers (2015) Monetizing Marks: Insights from the USPTO Trademark Assignment Dataset. SSRN, April 1, 2015: ssrn.com/abstract=2430962 or dx.doi. org/10.2139/ssrn.2430962.

Gurry, F. (2013). Rethinking the role of intellectual property: a speech at Melbourne Law School: law.unimelb. edu.au/alumni/mls-news/issue-10-december-2013/rethinking-the-role-of-intellectual-property.

IHS Markit (2016). Teardown reports and spreadsheets for the Apple iPhone 7. Samsung Galaxy S7 and Huawei P9. Englewood, U.S.A.: technology.ihs.com/Categories/450461/teardowns-cost-benchmarking.

Interbrand (2016). Best Global Brands 2016 Rankings. interbrand.com/best-brands/best-global-brands/2016/ranking/#?sortBy=rank&sortAscending=desc.

International Data Corporation (IDC) (2017). Data Tracker Database on the Smartphone Industry, 2005-2017. Boston. MA: International Data Corporation.

Johnson, D.K.N. and S. Scowcroft (2016). The Importance of Being Steve: an econometric analysis of the contribution of Steve Jobs's patents to Apple's market valuation. *International Journal of Financial Research*, 7(2), 2016.

Joo, S.H., C. Oh and K. Lee (2016). Catch-up strategy of an emerging firm in an emerging country: analysing the case of Huawei vs. Ericsson with patent data. *International Journal of Technology Management*, 72(1-3), 19-42.

Kang, B. (2015). The innovation process of Huawei and ZTE: patent data analysis. *China Economic Review*, 36, 378-393.

Korea Internet and Security Agency (KISA) (2014). Final Report of Research on Actual Status of Mobile Internet Usage. 24 February, 2014.

Korkeamäki, T. and T. Takalo (2013). Valuation of innovation and intellectual property: the case of iPhone. *European Management Review*, 10(4), 197-210.

Koski, H. and T. Kretschmer (2007). Innovation and dominant design in mobile telephony. *Industry and Innovation*, 14(3), 305-324.

Kumar. A. and B.S. Bhasin (2017). Innovation and survival: lessons from the smartphone wars. In *Intellectual Asset Management Yearbook 2017*.

Liu, C.-J. and H.-Y. Liang (2014). The deep impression of smartphone brand on the customers' decision making. *Procedia – Social and Behavioral Sciences*, 109, 338-343.

Liu, N. and R. Yu (2017). Identifying design feature factors critical to acceptance and usage behavior of smartphones. *Computers in Human Behavior*, 70, 131-142.

Mallinson, K. (2014). Smartphone royalty stack. *IP Finance*, September 19, 2014: www.wiseharbor.com/pdfs/Mallinson%20on%20Intel's%20Smartphone%20Royalty%20Stack%2019Sept2014.pdf.

Mallinson, K. (2015). Busting smartphone patent licensing myths. Policy Brief, September 2015. Arlington, VA: Center for the Protection of Intellectual Property, George Mason School of Law. sls.gmu.edu/cpip/wp-content/uploads/sites/31/2015/10/Mallinson-Busting-Smartphone-Patent-Licensing-Myths.pdf.

Millward Brown (2016). *BrandZ Top 100 Global Brands*: www.millwardbrown.com/brandz/top-global-brands/2016.

Neubig. T.S. and S. Wunsch-Vincent (2017). A Missing Link in the Analysis of Global Value Chains: Cross-Border Flows of Intangible Assets, Taxation and Related Measurement Implications. *WIPO Economic Research Working Paper No. 37*. Geneva: WIPO.

Organisation for Economic Co-Operation and Development (OECD) (2005). Digital Broadband Content: Music. DSTI/ICCP/IE(2004)12/FINAL: www.oecd.org/internet/ieconomy/34995041.pdf.

OECD (2008). ICT research and development and innovation. In *OECD Information Technology Outlook 2008*. Paris: OECD, Chapter 4.
OECD (2011). Global Value Chains: Preliminary Evidence and Policy Issues. DSTI/IND(2011)3. Paris: OECD.

Phadnis, S. (2016). Apple plans to make iPhones in Bengaluru from April. *The Times of India*, December 30, 2016.

Pohlmann, T. and K. Blind (2016). Landscaping Study on Standard-Essential Patents (SEPs). Berlin: IPlytics GmbH. Commissioned by the European Commission.

PricewaterhouseCoopers (PwC) (2017). *2017 Patent Litigation Study – Change on the Horizon?* and earlier editions: www.pwc.com/us/en/forensic-services/publications/assets/2017-patent-litigation-study.pdf.

Reidenberg, J.R., D. Stanley, N. Waxberg, J. Debelak, D. Gross and E. Mindrup (2012). The Impact of the Acquisition and Use of Patents on the Smartphone Industry. *WIPO Working Paper. IP and Competition Division*. Geneva: WIPO: www.wipo.int/export/sites/www/ip-competition/en/studies/clip_study.pdf.

Reidenberg, J.R., N.C. Russell, M. Price and A. Mohan (2014). Patents and Small Participants in the Smartphone Industry. *WIPO Working Paper, IP and Competition Division*. Geneva: WIPO. ssrn.com/abstract=2674467.

Shapiro, C. and H.R. Varian (1998). *Information Rules: A Strategic Guide to the Network Economy*. Boston, MA: Harvard Business School Press.

Sharma, C. (2016). Mobile Patents Landscape 2016: An In-Depth Quantitative Analysis, and previous editions of this report. Chetan Sharma Consulting: www.chetansharma.com/publications/mobile-patents-landscape-2016.

Shimpi, A.L. (2013). The ARM diaries, part 1: How ARM's business model works. *AnandTech*, June 28, 2013: www.anandtech.com/show/7112/the-arm-diaries-part-1-how-arms-business-model-works.

Sidak, J.G. (2016). What aggregate royalty do manufacturers of mobile phones pay to license standard-essential patents? *Criterion*, 1, 701-719.

Song, J., K. Lee and T. Khanna (2016). Dynamic capabilities at Samsung: optimizing internal co-opetition. *California Management Review*, 58(4), 118-140.

Stitzing, R. (2017). World IP Report – Smartphone Case Study – Presentation at the workshop for the World Intellectual Property Report. Geneva, March 16 and 17, 2017.

Sullivan & Cromwell (2013). Royalty rates for standard-essential patents. April 30. New York: Sullivan & Cromwell LLP: www.sullcrom.com/siteFiles/Publications/SC_Publication_Royalty_Rates_for_Standard_Essential_Patents_414F.pdf.

Teece, D.J. (1986). Profiting from technological innovation: implications for integration, collaboration, licensing and public policy. *Research Policy*, 15, 285-305.

Thomson Reuters (2012). Inside the iPhone Patent Portfolio. Thomson Reuters IP Market Reports.

Thumm. N. and G. Gabison (2016). *Patent Assertion Entities in Europe*. European Economics for the Joint Research Centre. European Commission.

World Intellectual Property Organization (WIPO) (2011). The economics of IP – Old insights and new evidence. In *World Intellectual Property Report: The Changing Face of Innovation*. Geneva: WIPO, Chapter 2, 75-107.

WIPO (2013). Branding in the global economy. In *World Intellectual Property Report: Reputation and Image in the Global Marketplace*. Geneva: WIPO, Chapter 1, 21-79.

WIPO (2015). Historical breakthrough innovations. In *World Intellectual Property Report: Breakthrough Innovation and Economic Growth*. Geneva: WIPO, Chapter 2, 49-93.

WIPO (2016). *World Intellectual Property Indicators 2016*. Geneva: WIPO.

WIPO (2017). *PCT Yearly Review 2017*. Geneva: WIPO.

Wunsch-Vincent, S., M. Kashcheeva and H. Zhou (2015). International patenting by Chinese residents: constructing a database of Chinese foreign-oriented patent families. *China Economic Review*, 36, 198-219.

Yoo, Y. and K. Kim (2015). How Samsung became a design powerhouse. *Harvard Business Review*, September, 72-78.

Zhang, Y. and Y. Zhou (2015). *The Source of Innovation in China: Highly Innovative Systems*. London: Palgrave, Appendix 2.2.

Acronyms

ASP	average selling price
bn	billion
BNEF	Bloomberg New Energy Finance
COE	Cup of Excellence
COGS	cost of goods sold
CPC	Cooperative Patent Classification
EIPO	Ethiopian Intellectual Property Office
EPO	European Patent Office
EUIPO	European Union Intellectual Property Office
EUR	euro
FAO	Food and Agriculture Organization of the United Nations
FBR	fluidized bed reactor
FDI	foreign direct investment
FITs	feed-in tariffs
FNC	Colombian Coffee Growers Federation
FOB	free on board
FT	*Financial Times*
GDP	gross domestic product
GI	geographical indication
GPU	graphics processing units
GSM	Global System for Mobile Communications
GUI	graphical user interface
GVC	global value chain
ICA	International Coffee Agreement
ICO	International Coffee Organization
ICT	information and communication technology
IDC	International Data Corporation
IEA	International Energy Agency
IP	intellectual property
IPC	International Patent Classification
JPO	Japan Patent Office
JV	joint venture
KIPO	Korean Intellectual Property Office
KISA	Korea Internet & Security Agency
LTE	Long-Term Evolution
MNC	multinational company
NCAUSA	National Coffee Association U.S.A.
NGO	non-governmental organization
NREL	National Renewable Energy Laboratory
NYT	*New York Times*
OECD	Organisation for Economic Co-operation and Development
PAE	patent assertion entity
PATSTAT	Worldwide Patent Statistical Database
PBR	plant breeders' right
PCT	Patent Cooperation Treaty
PPA	power purchase agreement
PQC	Premium Quality Consulting
PV	photovoltaic
R&D	research and development
SCA	Specialty Coffee Association
SEP	standard-essential patent
SG&A	selling, general and administrative expenses
SIPO	State Intellectual Property Office of the People's Republic of China
TSMC	Taiwan Semiconductor Manufacturing Company
U.K.	United Kingdom
UMTS	Universal Mobile Telecommunications System
UPOV	International Union for the Protection of New Varieties of Plants
U.S.	United States
USD	United States dollar
USPC	United States Patent Classification
USPTO	United States Patent and Trademark Office
VSS	voluntary sustainability standards
WIOT	world input-output table
WIPO	World Intellectual Property Organization
WSJ	*Wall Street Journal*

Technical notes

Country income groups

This report uses the World Bank income classification to refer to particular country groups. The classification is based on gross national income per capita in 2016 and establishes the following four groups: low-income economies (USD 1,005 or less); lower middle-income economies (USD 1,006 to USD 3,955); upper middle-income economies (USD 3,956 to USD 12,235); and high-income economies (USD 12,236 or more).

More information on this classification is available at http://data.worldbank.org/about/country-classifications.

IP mappings

The case studies in chapters 2, 3 and 4 rely on mappings of patents and trademarks developed for this report. The patent data for these mappings come mainly from the WIPO Statistics Database, the EPO Worldwide Patent Statistical Database (PATSTAT, April 2017) and the USPTO Trademark Case Files and Assignment Datasets (2016). Key methodological elements underlying the mapping exercise include the following.

Unit of analysis

The main unit of analysis in patent data is the first filing of a given invention. Mappings include data on utility models whenever available. The date of reference for patent counts is the date of first filing. The origin of the invention is attributed to the first applicant in the first filing; whenever this information was missing an imputation strategy has been applied, as described further below.

The only departure from this approach occurs when analyzing the share of patent families requesting protection in each patent office (e.g., see figures 2.8 or 3.12). In this case, an extended patent family definition – known as the INPADOC patent family – has been used instead of the one relying on first filings. In addition, only patent families with at least one granted application have been considered for this analysis, and the date of reference is the earliest filing within the same extended family. The main rationale for using the extended patent family definition and imposing at least one granted patent within the family is to mitigate any underestimation arising from complex subsequent filing structures, such as continuations and divisionals, and from small patent families of lower quality such as those filed in only one country and either rejected after or withdrawn before examination.

The unit of analysis in trademark data is any filing for trademark protection at any of the sources employed – namely the USPTO, the Madrid System and the national offices included in WIPO's Global Brands Database. This definition includes trademarks for both products and services. It also includes renewals of existing trademarks and trademarks claiming a priority based on existing trademarks.

Imputing country of origin

When information about the first listed applicant's country of residence in the first patent filing was missing, the following sequence was adopted: (i) extract country information from the applicant's address; (ii) extract country information from the applicant's name; (iii) make use of the information from matched corporations (as described further below); (iv) rely on the most frequent first applicant country of residence within the same patent family (using the extended patent family definition); (v) rely on the most frequent first inventor's country of residence within the same patent family (again, using the extended patent family definition); and (vi) for some remaining historical records, consider the IP office of first filing as a proxy for origin.

Mapping strategies

The patent mapping strategy for each of the three sectors is based on existing evidence and experts' suggestions. Each strategy was tested against existing alternative sources whenever possible.

The coffee patent mapping is based on the following combination of CPC and IPC symbols and keywords sought in titles and abstracts.

IPC/CPC symbols: A01D46/06, A23C11/00, A23F5*, A23L27/00, A23L27/10, A23L27/28, A23N12/06, A23N12/08, A47G19/14, A47G19/145, A47G19/20, A47J42*, A47J31* and C07D473/12.

Including keywords: *coffe*; caffe*; espresso; cappuccino; robusta; arabica; fertilizer* AND coffe*; fertilizer* AND robusta; fertilizer* AND arabica; coffe* AND (arabica OR robusta)*.

Excluding keywords: *coffee table; cleaning system for a coffee machine; coffee cream; coffee pot holder; coffee stirrer; coffee maker pod holder; coffee latte printer; coffer*; method and structure for increasing work flow; not a product selected* from coffee; cosmetic*; cleaning agent; washing agent; smart home; dietary fiber; repellent; residues; grevillea; food; malus; eucalyptus; hypsipyla robusta moore; health; wine; leaf; cannot place coffee cup; coffee stain; coffee car*; coffee by-products; coffee shop 510; extract; coffee owner board.

These patents are classified in five segments of the coffee supply chain as follows:

Coffee farming: A01B; A01C1/00; A01C11/00; A01C13/00; A01C14/00; A01C15/00; A01C17/00; A01C19/00; A01C21/00; A01C5/00; A01C7/00; A01G11/00; A01G7/00; A01G9/00; A01H1/00; A01H3/00; A01H4/00; A01H5/00; A01M1/14; A01N25/00; A01N27/00; A01N29/00; A01N31/00; A01N33/00; A01N35/00; A01N37/00; A01N39/00; A01N41/00; A01N43/00; A01N45/00; A01N47/00; A01N49/00; A01N51/00; A01N53/00; A01N55/00; A01N57/00; A01N59/00; A01N61/00; A01N63/00; A01N65/00; C12N15/00.

Harvesting and post-harvesting: A01D46/06; A01D46/30; A47J42/00; B02B1/02; B02B1/04; C02F1/00; C02F3/00; C02F5/00; C02F7/00; C02F9/00; F26B11/04; F26B21/10; F26B23/10; F26B9/08; G01N7/22; G06K9/46; G06T7/40.

Raw material storage and transportation: A01F25/00; A23F5/00; A23N12/02; B03B5/66; B65B1/00; B65B3/00; B65B35/00; B65B7/00; B65G65/00; C02F1/00; C02F3/00; C02F5/00; C02F7/00; C02F9/00; E04H7/00; G01G1/00; G01G11/00; G01G13/00; G01G15/00; G01G19/00; G01G21/00; G01G23/00; G01G3/00; G01G5/00; G01G7/00; G01G9/00; G01N.

Bean processing: A01D46/06; A01D46/30; A23F3/36; A23F5/00; A23F5/02; A23F5/04; A23F5/08; A23F5/10; A23F5/12; A23F5/14; A23F5/18; A23F5/20; A23F5/22; A23F5/24; A23F5/26; A23F5/28; A23F5/30; A23F5/32; A23F5/36; A23F5/46; A23F5/48; A23L3/44; A23N12/10; A23N12/12; A47J31/42; A47J37/06; A47J42/00; A47J42/20; A47J42/52; B07B4/02; B07C7/00; B07C7/04; G01N27/62; G01N30/06; G01N33/14; G06K9/46; G06T7/40.

Final distribution: A23F3/00; A23L1/234; A23L2/38; A23P10/28; A47J27/21; A47J31/00; A47J31/02; A47J31/047; A47J31/06; A47J31/10; A47J31/18; A47J31/20; A47J31/26; A47J31/34; A47J31/36; A47J31/38; A47J31/40; A47J31/42; A47J31/44; A47J31/46; A47J31/54; B01D29/35; B01D29/56; B65B1/00; B65B3/00; B65B31/02; B65B31/04; B65B35/00; B65B7/00; B65D33/01; B65D33/16; B65D85/804; B67D1/00; G06Q10/00; G06Q50/00.

The trademark mapping strategy for the coffee industry in chapter 2 is based on the following keywords sought in trademark statement descriptions: coffe*; caffe*; kaffe*; cafe*; kopi; espresso; cappuccino; robusta; arabica.

The photovoltaic mapping is based on the following combination of CPC and IPC symbols relating to specific segments of the photovoltaic supply chain.

Silicon: C01B33/02*; C01B33/03*.

Ingots/wafers: C30B29/06.

Crystalline cells: H01L31/036*; H01L31/037*; H01L31/038*; H01L31/039*; Y02E10/541; Y02E10/545; Y02E10/546; Y02E10/547; Y02E10/548.

New material cells: H01L31/0687*; H01L31/073*; H01G9/20*; Y02E10/542; Y02E10/543; Y02E10/544; Y02E10/549; H01G9/200*; H01G9/201*; H01G9/202*; H01G9/203*; H01G9/204*; H01G9/205*; H01G9/2063; H01G9/209*.

Other cells: H01L31/052*; H01L31/053*; H01L31/054*; H01L31/055*; H01L31/056*; H01L31/058*; H01L31/06* (excl.H01L31/0687*); H01L31/07; H01L31/072*; H01L31/074*; H01L31/075*; H01L31/076*; H01L31/077*; H01L31/078*; H02N6/*.

Modules (concentrators): Y02E10/52*.

Modules (conversion): Y02E10/56*; Y02E10/58.

Modules (others): H02S*; H01L31/042*; H01L31/043*; H01L31/044*; H01L31/045*; H01L31/046*; H01L31/047*; H01L31/048*; H01L31/049*; H01L31/05; H01L31/050*; H01L31/051*; H01G9/2068; H01G9/207*; H01G9/208*.

Production equipment: (H01L31/1876*; H01L31/188*; H01L31/206*) OR ((C23C14*; C23C16*; C23C22*; C23C24*; B32B17*; B32B27*; B32B37*; B32B38*; H01L21/67*) AND (H02S*; H01L31*; C01B33/02*; C01B33/03*; C30B29/06; H01G9/20*; H02N6/*; Y02E10/5*)).

The trademark mapping strategy for the photovoltaic industry in chapter 3 is based on the following keywords sought in trademark statement descriptions: *solar panel*; *photovoltaic*; **polysilicon*; *fotovoltaic*; *solar module; solarmodul**.

The patent mapping strategy for the smartphone industry in chapter 4 follows a narrow and a broad definition which are based on the following combinations of CPC and IPC symbols, respectively:

Narrow IPC/CPC symbols: H04M1/247; H04M1/2471; H04M1/2477; H04M1/72519; H04M1/72522; H04M1/72525; H04M1/72527; H04M1/7253; H04M1/72533; H04M1/72536; H04M1/72538; H04M1/72541; H04M1/72544; H04M1/72547; H04M1/7255; H04M1/72552; H04M1/72555; H04M1/72558; H04M1/72561; H04M1/72563; H04M1/72566; H04M1/72569; H04M1/72572; H04M1/72575; H04M1/72577; H04M1/7258; H04M1/72583; H04M1/72586; H04M1/72588; H04M1/72591; H04M1/72594; H04M1/72597.

Broad IPC/CPC symbols: F01L1*; F02P17*; F03G5*; F04C25*; F04D27*; F16C17*; F16H61*; F16K7*; F16M11*,13*; F21S2*; F21V23*,33*; F24B1*; F24F11*; F25B21*-23*; F28D15*; G01B7*; G01B11*; G01C1*,5*,17*-22*; G01D18*; G01G19*,23*; G01J1*,3*,5*; G01K1*,7*; G01L1*,7*,17*; G01M11*,15*-17*; G01N15*, 21*,27*,29*,33*; G01P15*&21*; G01R19*-22*,27*,31*-33*; G01S1*-5*,11*-15*&19*; G01T7*; G01V3*; G01W1*; G02B1*-9*,13*,15*,21*,26*-27*; G02C7*; G02F1*; G03B5*,13*-17*,21*,35*; G03F7*; G03H1*; G04B19*,47*;G04F3*; G05B1*,11*-15*,19*-21*,24*; G05D1*-3*,7*,23*; G05F1*,5*;G06F*; G06K5*-9*,15*-19*; G06N5*,99*; G06Q10*-50*,99*; G06T*; G07B15*; G07C1*,5*,9*,13*; G07F1*,7*,17*,19*; G08B1*-6*,13*,17*,21*-25*,29*; G08C17*,19*; G08G1*; G09B5*-9*,19*,21*,29*; G09C*; G09F3*,9*,15*,19*,27*; G09G3*,5*; G10G1*,7*; G10H1*,7*; G10K11*,15*; G10L13*-25*; G11B19*,20*,27*; G11C7*-13*,16*,29*; G21C17*; H01B1*,5*,7*,11*; H01C10*; H01F17*,27*,38*; H01G4*,5*; H01H11*,13*,25*; H01L21*-33*,43*,45*,49*,51*; H01M2*,4*,10*,12*; H01P3*; H01Q1*,5*-9*,19*,21*; H01R12*,13*,24*,31*,33*,43*; H01S5*; H02B1*,7*; H02H3*,7*; H02J1*,5*,7*,17*,50*; H02M1*,3*,7*; H02N2*; H03B5*; H03C7*; H03F1*,3*; H03G3*,7*; H03H9*,11*,21*; H03J7*; H03K3*,5*,17*; H03L7*; H03M1*,3*,11*,13*; H04B1*-13*,15*,17*; H04H20*,60*; H04J1*,3*,11*,13*; H04K1*,3*; H04L1*-12*,23*-29*; H04M1*,3*,7*-11*,15*-19*; H04N1*,5*-9*,13*,17*-21*; H04Q1*-9*; H04R1*-5*,9*,17*,25*,29*; H04S7*; H04W4*-92*; H05B33*,37*; H05K.

The trademark and industrial design mapping strategy for the smartphone chapter draws on an unpublished background report by Christian Helmers, June 16, 2017. Apple, Samsung Electronics and Huawei's industrial designs and trademarks were mapped using USPTO and EUIPO data. USPC class D14 was the starting point in USPTO industrial design data, and Locarno classes 14-03 and 14-04 in the EUIPO one. The resulting data were filtered into four categories – mobile phones, GUIs, display screens and icons – using the industrial design titles. A manual check was then performed for each design patent where it was unclear whether it was a smartphone design. Industrial designs used not only for smartphones were kept.

The trademark mapping strategy for the smartphones in chapter 4 is based on keywords sought in trademark statement descriptions, such as: *smartphone* and *handheld mobile digital electronic device*. Additional filtering was applied by manually checking individual filings to verify whether they were indeed related to smartphones. Trademarks were limited to those assigned to Apple, Samsung Electronics or Huawei.

Brands

The brand mapping strategy for the coffee industry in chapter 2 is based on Premium Quality Consulting™ data (www.pqc.coffee). These data identify the most valuable brands in the U.S. coffee industry and the wave they pertain to. Brands were associated with USPTO trademark data based on the name of applicants or the mark text.

Stakeholders

The stakeholder mapping strategy for the coffee industry in chapter 2 is based on the *UKERS Tea & Coffee Global Directory & Buyers Guide* (www.teaandcoffee.net/ukers-directory). These data identify the main companies and other stakeholders in the coffee industry. The directory's categories are recategorized to match the five segments of the coffee supply chain: coffee farming, harvesting and post-harvesting, raw material storage and transportation, bean processing, and final distribution.